LIMITED EDITION OF 750 COPIES

SOME RECORDS OF SMETHWICK

by

FREDK. WM. HACKWOOD, F.R. Hist. Soc.,

EDITED BY ALAN A. VERNON

Brewin Books

First published in a Limited Edition of 80 copies by
The Smethwick Telephone 1896

This edition of 750 numbered copies published by
Brewin Books Ltd., Studley, Warwickshire B80 7LG, 2001

© Introduction – Alan A. Vernon 2001
All rights reserved

The editor's rights have been asserted

British Library Cataloguing in Publication Data
A catalogue record for this book is available from
The British Library

ISBN 1 85858 183 4

Made and printed in Great Britain by
Warwick Printing Company Ltd.
Theatre Street, Warwick CV34 4DR

Dedicated to the memory of Frederick William Hackwood
and to members of the Hackwood family.

Published in a limited edition

of 750 copies

No. 661

FREDERICK WILLIAM HACKWOOD

F. W. Hackwood was born to Enoch and Sarah Hackwood on the 18th April 1851 at 69 High Street East, Wednesbury. His father, Enoch was a tailor, the family had settled in Wednesbury in the middle of the 18th century, the Hackwoods originally came from Stoke-on-Trent.

In 1868 he was admitted to St. Peter's Teachers Training College, Saltley and in 1871 he was appointed headmaster of St. Bartholomew's Church Schools at Wednesbury. In 1878 he was Headmaster of Dudley Road Board School, Birmingham and in 1888 he became Headmaster of Soho Road Board School also in Birmingham where he stayed until 1916 when he retired.

In 1874 he married Sarah Phoebe Simkin and they had two children, a son, Harold and a daughter, Louisa. He lived with his family at Comberford Lodge, Bridge Street, Wednesbury, until a subterranean fire at a neighbouring colliery forced them to leave the house and move to Handsworth. During the course of his life Frederick Hackwood wrote 28 books about Staffordshire and the Black Country, 'Some Records of Smethwick' being one of them, published in 1896. Apart from writing on local history, he wrote books on a variety of other subjects including Natural History, Education, Church Lessons, Biography, Marriage, Sport and Food.

In addition to being a teacher and an author he was also a magistrate, a town councillor, a footballer, and the founder of several clubs and societies and was involved in creating open spaces like parks, allotments and re-afforestation of reclaimed colliery waste areas.

The last years of his life were spent at 2 Veronica Road, Balham near to his son, where he died on the 4th December 1926 aged 75 years.

PREFACE

This first attempt at compiling a History of the rising and important Town of Smethwick is a reprint from the columns of the *Smethwick Telephone*, in which it appeared by weekly instalments between February 1st and November 14th, 1986. Such method of publication has been found by the writer to be the only one practicable, so far as covering the cost of production is concerned; for topographical works dealing with a circumscribed area are always of limited interest, and are, consequently, in but small demand.

The compilation is by no means what it ought to be, or might have been; it is felt to be somewhat fragmentary, and to have some of its parts occasionally but ill-balanced. The fault of having some of its chapters out of perspective with the general view of the work is due to those well-known contrarieties common to human nature wheresoever it is found, either in Smethwick or elsewhere. In this world there are, according to the topographer, but two classes of people. There are found one set of persons in possession of special local information who are anxious and eager to thrust it upon the snapper-up of such historical trifles; and there are others possessing even more valuable and exclusive information who decline to part with it upon any terms.

Smethwick is an exceptional gathering-ground for the local historian for two reasons, and neither of them add to the interest or effectiveness of his work. First, Smethwick is a place which can boast of none of that ancient parochial history which is so characteristic of all English mediæval life, and which is to be found connected, almost without exception, with the social communities of the whole of its ten thousand parishes. And secondly, among the large and ever-increasing population of modern Smethwick, so very few comparatively are native-born, or bear any strong attachment to the soil. This little book is, therefore, likely to become more valued as the rising generation grow to maturity, and duly develop the sentiment of local patriotism.

Wednesbury,
*   1st December, 1896.*   F.W.H.

ACKNOWLEDGEMENTS

I wish to thank the following for their help and assistance in republishing this volume. Firstly, to Alan Brewin, in agreeing to my suggestion to make this book available once more to a wider public. Sandwell Community History and Archives Service and in particular to Maureen Waldron, Community History Education Officer, at Smethwick Library, Mrs. Betty Hackwood for supplying the details of F. W. Hackwood's life and career, to my son Jeremy who is still trying to teach me how to use a word processor and finally Smethwick Local History Society and its members for the inspiration in the first place to produce this book.

BOOKS BY F. W. HACKWOOD.

Notes on Lessons on Moral Subjects. 1883.
Darlaston. 1887.
Tipton, 1891.
West Bromwich. 1895.
Records of Smethwick. 1896
Sedgley Researches. 1898
Handsworth Old and New. 1908
Annals of Willenhall. 1908
Oldbury and Round About. 1915
Story of the Black Country. 1892
Chronicles of Cannock Chase. 1903
Staffordshire Curiosities and Antiquities. 1905
Staffordshire Stories. 1906
The Birmingham Midlands. 1906
Staffordshire Worthies. 1911
Staffordshire Sketches. 1916
Staffordshire Customs. 1924
Staffordshire Glimpes. 1925
Staffordshire Miscellany. 1927. [posthumously]
Through the Midlands. 1905
Westward of the Wash. 1906
Story of the Shire. 1921
Olden Warwickshire. 1921
Notes of Lessons on Kindness to Animals. 1892
The Practical Method of Class Management. 1896
Natural History Reference Notes. 1897
Notes of Lessons on the Church Service. 1897
New Object Lessons [Animal Life] 1898
Chatty Object Lessons in Nature Knowledge. 1900
The Good Old Times. 1910
Old English Sports. 1907
Inns, Ales and Drinking Customs. 1909
Good Cheer, The Romance of Food and Feasting. 1911
William Hone, His Life and Times. 1912
Life of Lord Kitchener. 1913
Dragons and Dragon Slayers. 1923
The Bridal Book. The Lore, History and Philosphy of Love, Courtship and
    Marriage 1923
Wednesbury Papers 1884
Wednesbury Workshops 1889
Olden Wednesbury 1899
Religious Wednesbury 1900
Odd Chapters in the History of Wednesbury 1920
Wednesbury Notes & Queries. 3 Vols. 1902.
Wednesbury Ancient & Modern. 1902.
Pocket Guide to Wednesbury. 1908.

INTRODUCTION

It was after I became a member of Smethwick Local History Society in 1985 that I discovered a book had been published in 1896 called 'Some Records of Smethwick' by Frederick William Hackwood, F. R. Hist. Soc., It was some years before I saw a copy of this book, even though I had been a bookseller for some time. Eventually I was offered an Ex-Library copy by another bookseller which I bought without hesitation.

Since then I have seen only two other copies of this volume, which is not surprising since there were only 80 copies of the first edition published. Local historians and collectors have asked me to find copies of this sought after publication, but I have had little success. I wondered if it would be possible to make this book available to a wider public by publishing a reprint.

After discussing my idea with Alan Brewin to republish this book, it has become possible to provide those interested in Smethwick with an opportunity to read about the history of their town.

Alan Vernon January 2001
A & B Books ©

CONTENTS

CHAPTER		PAGE
I.	Introductory: A Rapid Survey of the Whole Historical Ground to be Covered:	1
	At no time a Parish	2
	A Manufacturing Suburb–	3
	A Busy Borough of Smoky Smethwick.	4
II.	Geologic and Prehistoric: Probable Anteriority of Harborne:	
	Boulder Stones	5
	Etymology of "Harborne."	6
III.	Romano – British Period: Smethwick Unoccupied, but near to a British Settlement and a Roman Camp: A Roman Well	
	A Roman Camp	7
	The Icknield Street	8
IV.	The Saxon Settlement of Smethwick: Mercia, A.D. 600–	9
	"Smith-wick"	10
	Heaths and Heights–	11
V.	Cartographical: A Search for "Smethwick" on the maps:	
	Surrounding Woodlands	12
	Smethwick in 1675	13
	Soho	14
VI.	The Domesday Manor of Smethwick [1086]:	
	Staffordshire Customs	15
	"Wasted" Lands	16
	Condition of Lichfield	17
	"Kings Rowley."	18
VII.	Manorial Lords from 1086 to 1216: Hales Owen Abbey Lands in Smethwick [1229–1261]: The Family of Gerold	19
	Smethwick as a Bribe	20
	The Holders of Smethwick Manor	21
VIII.	Church Lands in Smethwick [1230–1277]: The Mother Church	22
	Ecclesiastical Foundations.	23
IX.	Some Mediaeval Taxings of Smethwick [1291–1340]:	
	Smethwick Taxed for the Crusades	24
	Smethwick Taxed for the Scotch Wars	25
	The Landed Families of Smethwick	26
	Lone Lands and Ridding Lands–	27
X.	Territorial Records: Manor Lands [1221–1263]; The Abbey Lands [1229–1230]. The Abbot Holds under The Erdingtons	28
	A Mesne Tenant Between Bishop and Abbot	29
XI.	Rise of the Yeoman and the Landed Gentry [1519–1537]:	
	Birch of Birchfields	30
	Soho Boundary Brook	31
XII.	Smethwick Lands Parted Between the Paget Family and the Barons of Dudley [1536–1593]: The Pagets of Wednesbury	32
	The Manor Records	33
	In the Barony of Dudley	34

XIII.	The Cornwallis Family [1616–1648]: The Manor of Oldbury: Blakeley Hall	35
	Descent of Oldbury Manor	36
	Curates of Oldbury	37
XIV.	The Period of the Civil War: The Foley Family: War-Footing of Smethwick, 1640	38
	Local War Incidents, [1643–5]	39
	Rise of the Foley family	40
XV.	Stuart Period: Descent of the Manor to the Hinckley and the Reynolds Families: The Jennings Family: Shireland Hall: Taxation in 1663	41
	The Jennings Estates	42
	The Last of Shireland Hall	43
XVI.	The Hinckleys: and Mr. John Baddeley: Rents in Smethwick, 1769:	44
	Smethwick, A Pleasant Suburb	45
XVII.	The Chapelry of Smethwick–What is its Status as a Parish? A Chapel of Ease	46
	The Chapelry district of Smethwick	47
	Smethwick Acts of Parliament	48
XVIII.	The Founding of Smethwick Chapel, 1719. Dorothy Parkes	49
	Mary Halfpenny's Annuity	50
	The Chapel Furniture	51
	The Curacy	52
	"Jennings of Gopsall"	53
	A Parish Library	54
	The Election of a Minister	55
	An "Exhibited" Copy 1741	56
XIX.	The Fabric of the Old Chapel: The Register, &c. A Georgian Chapel	57
	Old Family Memorials	58
	Parish Registers	59
XX.	The Holders of the Benefice: The Parsonage House	60
XXI.	Parochial Benefactions [Harborne and Smethwick]: "An Ancient Book of Charities"	61
	"The Bailiff of Smethwick"	62
	A Charity Timely Recovered	63
	The Free School Re-built, 1852	64
XXII.	The Growth of Anglicanism: An Uneducated Church	65
	Rev. J. H. Crump, R. D.	66
	Mitchell Memorials	67
	An Iron Church	68
	A Utilitarian Church	69
XXIII.	The Re-Planting of Romanism: A Penny a Week for Eleven Years	70
XXIV.	The Spread of Nonconformity: Under two Presbyteries	71
	Windmill Lane Chapel [1873]	72
	Despised Dissenters	73
	High Street Chapel [1853]	74
	West Smethwick Mission [1872]	75
	Cross Street Chapel [1842]	76

	Regent Street Chapel	–	–	–	–	–	–	–	77
	Hugh Stowell Brown	–	–	–	–	–	–	–	78
	Bapist Offshoots	–	–	–	–	–	–	–	79
	The Cinder Chapel	–	–	–	–	–	–	–	80
	A Select Sect –	–	–	–	–	–	–	–	81
	Local Swedenborgians	–	–	–	–	–	–	–	82
XXV.	A Smethwickian Shakespeare Relic: A Precious Autograph –	83
	Exhibited in Smethwick in 1780. – – – – –	84
XXVI.	The Era of Canals: Planning of Canals – – –	85
	The Wednesbury Coal Supply [1733] – – – –	86
	The Summit Cutting [1789] – – – – –	87
	The Galton Bridge [1829]– – – – – –	88
XXVII.	The Soho Influence: Soho, from Handsworth to Smethwick –	89
	Rearing Feast, Soho Foundry [1796] – – – –	90
	The Records of Soho – – – – – –	91
	Classic Ground – – – – – – –	92
XXVIII.	A Few Industrial Epochs: Glass-Making a Monopoly [1643]	93
	Foreign Workmen [1838] – – – – –	94
	Building the Crystal Palace [1851] – – – –	95
	The Saturday Half-Holiday [1853] – – – –	96
	The Nailer Superseded – – – – – –	97
XXIX.	Mineral Resources: A Collier's "Saying" – – –	98
	Piercing the Permians for Coal – – – –	99
	A Ballad [1874] – – – – – – –	100
XXX.	Local Government: A Gas Lighting Act [1876] – – –	101
	Sanitary Work – – – – – – –	102
	Public Parks – – – – – – – –	103
	Constitutional Changes – – – – – –	104
XXXI.	Incorporation: A Town's Meeting [1893] – – –	105
	Birmingham Opposition – – – – – –	106
	A Draft Charter – – – – – – –	107
XXXII.	Work of the School Board: Educational Deficiency in 1873	108
	Chance's Schools, Spon Lane – – – – –	109
	How Smethwick and Harborne Parted, 1891 – – –	110
	"Extra-Municipal" Smethwick – – – – –	111
	"Voluntary" Schools– – – – – – –	112
XXXIII.	Sports and Pastimes: Prize Fights on the Commons – –	113
	Bull-Baiting at Nineveh – – – – – –	114
XXXIV.	Topographical: Place-Names, Roads, and Railways:
	Old Roads and Lanes – – – – – –	115
	Heaths, Holloways, Undulations– – – – –	116
	A Road Itinerary of 1810 – – – – –	117
	Local Railway Making, 1846–1886 – – – –	118
XXXV.	Topographical: Old Residences and Family Seats:
	The Yellow Yew – – – – – – –	119
	Mock Beggar Hall – – – – – – –	120
XXXVI.	Bibliographical: Eminent Persons, Families, and Names of
	Note: A Poet and a Painter – – – – –	121
	Sir Charles Fox – – – – – – –	122
	Galton and Withering of the Lunar Society – – –	123
	Dramatic records – – – – – – –	124

SOME RECORDS OF SMETHWICK,

BY

FREDK. WM. HACKWOOD, F.R.H.S.,

AUTHOR OF

"A History of West Bromwich," "Wednesbury Workshops," "Notes of Lessons on Moral Subjects," "Notes of Lessons in Kindness to Animals," &c., &c.

I. – INTRODUCTORY: A RAPID SURVEY OF THE WHOLE HISTORICAL GROUND TO BE COVERED

In tracing the history of Smethwick, the first peculiarity which will arrest the mental consciousness of the observant reader will be the long continuance of the place in a state of quasi-oblivion.

In status never anything more than an insignificant Hamlet, whose very existence was almost always unrecognised, its individuality was for more than a thousand years practically disregarded in all its external relationships. This was probably because its population was not only inconsiderable, but was also so sparsely scattered over its area, that its inhabitants scarcely troubled themselves to remember or to preserve the name of the place in which it was their mundane lot to dwell. Possibly, too, it was because it never acquired the civic status of the one, nor attained to the official dignity of the other, that it all but became lost amongst the other Villages and Parishes by which it was surrounded. No village seems to have been properly constituted by its inhabitants simply because they never became concentrated on any particular spot. Solitary cottages and out-lying farms were separated by fields, orchards, and gardens; homesteads and yeomen's houses by broad fields intervening, and rolling pastures coming in between; no Manor House indicated the presence of authority, the absence of a public being thus reflected by a non-existent officialism. Not even the church itself was here established by the outward evidence of any material fabric. No church; no parish. In fact, there were no tangible and immediate governors simply because there were too few to be governed. During all this period, therefore, it can scarcely be said that as a distinct entity Smethwick had any existence at all; but such as it had was involved in the civic life of another place—the parish of Harborne.

Before attempting to bring into line—for the first time as an ordered story—the many recorded facts and the few popular traditions connected with Smethwick, it may be well at the outset to cast one rapid and comprehensive glance over the whole area of time, across which our retrospection will have to range in its proposed chronological survey.

Of unwritten history, as gleaned from geology or pre-historic remains, there will be available scarcely matter enough to weave as a mere fringe into the story. And then, secondly, the story itself, as it unrolls before the eye of the reader, will give a sense of the overwhelming disproportion between the meagreness of its ancient records as compared with the fulness and the numbers of those contained in the modern chapters.

A mild interest in the life-story of the locality may be excited at that moment when Harborne is found occupied by a settlement of Ancient Britons; Smethwick as yet remaining a wilderness in all its pristine solitude. The interest of the local reader increases, however, when a few centuries later Smethwick itself becomes the centre of human life and interest for the first time, some tribal offshoot of the Anglo-Saxons being induced by economic reasons—which were then sound enough, no doubt, but which now cannot be explained—to take up a residence there, and to name the place after the manner of their own tongue.

The second advent of Christianity advances the story another step. When the conversion of the land had been duly completed, the mission priests gave way to a settled and resident clergy with specific areas of ministerial duty assigned and allocated to them. In the constitution of these ecclesiastical areas, Smethwick appears to have been almost a neglectable quantity; and when considered at all, it was only as an appendage to the "parish" (or that newly-constituted area placed within the ecclesiastical jurisdiction) of Harborne.

A little later, and local self-government was everywhere in England lost for the time-being. For now Feudalism had reared its aggressive head and the land was carved out into manors, and held in the grasp of proud lords and great estate owners. But whether at this time Harborne and Smethwick became respectively the two moieties of one manor (as they had already become the halves of one parish) or whether Smethwick became an independent manor, it is not now quite clear after this lapse of time.

During the Middle Ages, when local independence was again being gradually won back under the "parochial system," the individuality of Smethwick was then in greater danger than ever of being lost through the prominence given to Harborne under that system, and the domination which it acquired thereby over Smethwick.

Either this subordinate position as an out-lying hamlet, or, if not that, it can only have been the sparsity of its population, which will account for the almost entire absence of the name of Smethwick from the various parochial and diocesan records of the next few centuries. While in the parish registers of Aston, Handsworth, Rowley, and all the other surrounding villages the names of each other may be found mutually recorded, recurring over and over again, the name of Smethwick scarcely occurs in any of them, if at all; and in the list of wills proved, and administrations granted, at the Lichfield registry during the same long period a similar strange absence of the name Smethwick may be noted.

A MANUFACTURING SUBURB

The eventual emancipation of Smethwick may be said to date from the beginning of the eighteenth century when a pious benefactress erected a chapel-of-ease there. But even then Smethwick scarcely became relieved from the irksome control of Harborne, inasmuch as the benefice and charities of the new "chapelry of Smethwick," as it was called, were linked to and bound up in those of Harborne to a degree which was almost vexatious. Perhaps this again was because the population still remained so insignificant. The rural simplicity of the place was certainly long retained after this; for what life and activity it then possessed were most effectively cut off from the outside world by a wide and barren heath which hemmed it in on three sides; while on the fourth the uplands rolled away to the foot of hills that were lonelier still.

When at last Smethwick does begin to shine forth before an admiring world, it is even then by a reflected greatness, and by the light of what were then manufacturing industries of a very novel character. But perhaps the first indirect step in this belated development of the place, may be set down as the cutting through its borders of a wonderful artificial waterway, or canal, which was intended to connect the busy artificers of Birmingham at one end with the coal, iron and other mineral resourses of Wednesbury and Bilston at the other. It was, however, the planting of Watt's Soho Foundry in the midst of its verdant fields and by the margin of its pleasant streamlet, which gave the first visible impetus to the growth and development of modern Smethwick,

Other industries followed in due course, but at considerable intervals; it was thus the green freshness of a rural Smethwick gradually faded away until at last almost all its verdant features became obscured in the overhanging smoke which was belched forth from its countless chimney-stacks. But, again, one is struck by the fact that when the first factory made its appearance—that under the auspices of James Watt—it was said to be in Soho, not in Smethwick; the latter name indeed seems always to have been so vaguely known or so little used, that long afterwards, when Muntz's Metal Works were established in the same vicinity, these, too, were described as being located at French Walls—the place-name Smethwick being persistently ignored.

Yet, after all, the situation of Smethwick has proved by no means an unhappy one. It may rightfully claim to be, as indeed the Directories make it, a suburb of Birmingham, when such a pretension may suit its purpose in gaining some coveted commercial prestige. Or it may with equal justification repudiate this domination of Birmingham, and declare itself part and parcel of that Staffordshire which is so renowned throughout the world for its great coal and iron industries. And while its dingy streets are characteristically typical of the Black Country, Smethwick remains exceptionally happy in the possession of at least one pleasant quarter—that side which is closely contiguous to the adjoining and fair County of Worcester. This one green borderland serves Smethwick as its residential quarter, where its prosperous manufacturers and well-to-do citizens may remain seated within its boundaries, and so take their fair and proper share in all the social life and local concerns of the place.

The enquiring stranger, set down in the midst of Smethwick, is at once made cognisant of the all-pervading bustle and noise of a great manufacturing activity; this is self-evident in the sordid thoroughfares and grimy purlieus of the place; in the arterial waterways, whose long lines of wharfage pour in raw material for its heavy manufactures, supplemented by a network of railways which are equally eager to nourish the prosperity of the place by offering every additional facility for all its other external trafficings. Here are to be found manufactures, processes, and productions, all in that endless variety which alone can fortify a productive locality against the reverses of a trade depression. Not only is its mercature far from dependent upon any single staple, but every one of its varied industries is carried on with an enterprise and a thoroughness which is unrivalled, even by the great hardware centres of the busy north. Smethwick, by that fortuitous but fortunate juxta-position to Birmingham on the one side, and to the Black Country on the other, has been enabled to manipulate all the resources of the latter, guided in its operations by the superior commercial skill, and backed up by the great financial capacities of the former. Already, under this happy combination of circumstances, has the weekly wages-sheet of this once insignificant hamlet to be calculated in tens of thousands of pounds; and ere long it promises to total up to a yet higher figure than that.

Thus by industrial art, to which a fortunateness of location contributed natural resources on the one hand, and a vast financial power on the other, Smethwick has raised itself in a remarkably short period of time to some individual eminence, even among a contending throng of rival neighbours.

After a few decades of very rapid growth Smethwick sought and obtained the right of local self-government. Having enjoyed this privilege for some years, and having always acquitted itself most worthily in the administration of its own internal affairs, local patriotism has now soared towards the very highest form of civic autonomy. To give effect to this expression of a laudable ambition on the part of the community, there has been presented to Her Majesty's Privy Council a petition for a Charter of Incorporation, which shall constitute Smethwick a Municipal Borough. In any case, whether this dignity be achieved or not, the commercial future of Smethwick is fully assured; and in very many respects it may be said to be a model of what a Black Country town ought to be, by virtue of its own mercantile energy and public-spirited enterprise.

II.—GEOLOGIC AND PREHISTORIC: PROBABLE ANTERIORITY OF HARBORNE.

Of the Cave Men who in far-away ages inhabited the land, at a period in the world's history which was so cold that a great field of ice stretched over the uplands of Smethwick (and indeed the same was the condition of all the higher valleys and plains of England) not one single human trace has been found here. In the gravel pits of some localities, however, relics of this ancient race have been plentifully discovered; they take the shape of flint arrow-heads, pointed bones, shaped antlers, and other rude tools or implements of war. The extensive gravel pits of Smethwick, so far as is known, have yielded no single trace of these people, who eked out a bare subsistence along the river banks, perhaps not near here, but more generally along the eastern and southern coasts of the country. Yet there is one natural object still remaining in the place, which looked out on the bleak and desolate prospect of Smethwick during the remote Ice Age; it was carried here then, and has remained *in situ* ever since. It was when these wretched Cave Men struggled and fought for their very existence with the musk ox and the arctic fox; it was when the great elk roamed the plains, the mammoth haunted the river-mouths, and wild horses herded in the meads and marshes; and when all of them fell equally a prey to the cave lion, the cave hyena, and the cave bear; it was then that the Boulder Stone which yet, after an unknown number of centuries, looks out upon the Smethwick of to-day, first found its long resting-place in the field near the Old Chapel.

But on this point the cautious reader would perhaps prefer the testimony of an expert. Mr. W. Jerome Harrison, F.G.S., of Birmingham, has been good enough to supply, specially for this work, the following opinion:—

Within the confines of its legal boundaries Smethwick does not possess any geological features of importance. The "solid" geology consists of red and grey sandstones, sands, and gravels, of Triassic Age. Resting upon these Triassic deposits are patches of gravel and boulder clay, laid down during the Glacial Epoch. Thus the large gravel-pit beyond the Bear Inn consists of "drift," which was probably deposited by the waters from the melting and retreating of the glaciers during the last Great Ice Age. The large boulder of felsite which may be seen on the site of the old reservoir between the Old Chapel and Thimble Mill pool is an old '. Welshman " from the Arenig Hill, and was brought down on the back of a glacier, and left in its present position on the melting of the ice. This boulder is similar in composition and origin to those of Cannon Hill Park, Birmingham. Tradition says that this Smethwick boulder turns round once every time the bell of the Old Chapel is rung. In the days of my youth I and my fellow school-mates have frequently visited the spot to see if this were so. Alas, however for tradition!

Another popular tradition of this same stone is "that two horses brought it thither in the night, and that twenty could not remove it." A second large Boulder Stone near the Summit Bridge, at the corner of Holly Lane, is mentioned on p.2 of that admirable work "HARBORNE AND ITS SURROUNDINGS *(Birmingham, Cornish Brothers, 1885),* written by Mr. James Kenward, F.S.A.

Nor of the next race of men, who long afterwards appeared upon the scene, when the Ice Age had at last given way to more genial conditions, can any trace be discovered of their occupation of Smethwick. No barrow or burial-mound has revealed the presence here of Man during the second epoch; no dug-up weapon or ornament of this locality serves to remind us of the men who gave the name of Albion to England, and of Erin to Ireland, as the Boulder Stone reminds us of that earlier race.

It was not till the Celts landed in England, some five-and-twenty centuries ago that any part of this immediate vicinity became permanently occupied by members of the human family. And then it was not Smethwick, but Harborne which was settled. Some Celtish families in search of a fixed home discovered this place, adopted it, and gave it the Celtish name "Harborne," by which it has been known ever since. In a dialect allied to Welsh may be traced two words akin to the two syllables of this name—*Har* or *Hardd,* signifying "fair" or "pleasant," and *bryn,* "a hill."

This is Mr. Kenward's etymology, and is certainly as feasible as any other which could be suggested; as he says (p. 4)—"Did I say that no sign of Celtic nationality survives among us? I am wrong. The name of Harborne itself survives, a trustworthy witness to its own antiquity." So that the name Harborne signified " the pleasant hill "; because no doubt it presented a more genial and inviting appearance than the bleak and inhospitable heaths of Smethwick, flanked, as they were, by those of Birmingham and Handsworth (the latter extended in a further dreariness of prospect by Bromwich Heath), and all of them swept by the same searching north-east winds which had already crossed the equally exposed "Coldfield" of Sutton.

III.—ROMANO-BRITISH PERIOD: SMETHWICK UNOCCUPIED, BUT NEAR TO A BRITISH SETTLEMENT AND A ROMAN CAMP.

Assuming Harborne to be of Celtic origin, it will be of interest to identify other places in its vicinity which were in existence with it at that early period of our country's history.

On p. 2 of A HISTORY OF WEST BROMWICH some account is given of the British occupation of Barr Beacon and other neighbouring heights. Mr. Kenward in his HARBORNE (p. 4) also observes—"Perhaps the Archdruid's high-seat was Barr Beacon. Perhaps the May-fires flashed from Warley Tor." On pp. 7 and 8 the same writer enters more fully into the subject. He holds "that a village was already in existence here (Harborne), and called by its present familiar name, when perchance the light-armed troops of the Latin Emperors first ventured cautiously but confidently along its slopes."

This introduces us to the period of the Roman occupation of Britain; and on p. 10 Mr. Kenward gives a description of what he claims to be a Roman well, which was recently discovered in Harborne. It was found lined with blocks of sandstone from Warley quarry, and was situated in Park Road, which is a portion of the ancient and direct road from Smethwick to King's Norton, and lies three-quarters of a mile west of Icknield Street, where it skirted Harborne.

This old road (namely, Park Road) was possibly a British trackway, utilised by the Romans to connect their great military Icknield Street with Metchley Camp, a defensive earthwork which they are said to have also usurped from the conquered Britons. This is quite feasible, as it would have been impolitic to have left unoccupied by their own forces a military station so calculated to threaten their communications along the Icknield Street; a military highway which had been specially constructed for the very purpose of maintaining such communications.

As this assumption of an earlier occupation by the Britons is evidence in favour of the theory previously advanced that Harborne is of Celtic origin a brief reference to this Metchley Camp may be appropriate here.

Metchley Camp is in the very heart of England, indisputably a tactical point near the very centre of one of the great military highways. A survey made in the year 1822 shows the Camp to have covered an area of $15\frac{1}{2}$ acres. (Hutton, the historian of Birmingham, calls it a Danish Camp, describes a third embankment, and gives it an area of 30 acres.) The outer vellum was measured as 330 yards long by 228 wide, and the interior Camp was found to be 187 yards by 165. Both fosse and vellum have suffered by lapse of time, not only by the succession of its occupiers, but by the cutting through it of the Worcester and Birmingham Canal, to make the banks of which the southern extremity of the Camp was totally destroyed. It is said that although ancient weapons have been dug up there, none of them were of a type either distinctively Roman or Danish. But were they Celtic in their character, like those discovered at Sutton and Aldridge? (See HISTORY OF WEST BROMWICH, p.2.)

The Midland districts of this country were traversed by quite a number of roads which had been either originated or improved by the Roman conquerors. Of their great military road joining the eastern country of the

Iceni—whence its name, Icknield Street—with the western (or southern) colonies of the Romans, something has already been said. It was found to approach the very confines of Smethwick, passing through Harborne, Edgbaston, Hockley, Handsworth, along Hunter's Lane, and on through Sutton.

Another road of equal importance led from London and St. Alban's through Mancetter in Warwickshire, and then on to Wall near Lichfield, crossing the Penk (Pennocrucium) and passing between Shifnal and Oakengates to reach Wroxeter.

Beyond these, "the central districts of Roman Britain appear to have been traversed in every direction by cross roads," says the eminent authority, Thomas Wright, F.S.A. Droitwich (Salinae) was approached by various roads on account of its extensive salt trade. These were often known as Salt-ways; one passed through Saltley. Then there were Port-ways, or market roads; one of these passed through Oldbury, West Bromwich, and Wednesbury. These latter were little better than old British trackways, following along those ridges of the land which were naturally self-drained.

Confusion has arisen, as may well be imagined, after the lapse of so many centuries since their first construction, as to the actual lines taken by these ancient roads. While in many parts they may be traced with marked ease owing to their unmistakable distinctiveness, in other places they have become quite obliterated. Another route which has been claimed for Icknield Street—that particular road which has the more closely affected Smethwick—is as follows: Commencing at Southampton, it passed through Winchester, Wallingford, and over the Isis at Newbridge; thence to Burford, crossing the Foss Way at Stour-in-the-Wolds, near Bitford Bridge in the county of Warwick; to Alcester by Studley, Ipsley, Beely, Wetherick Hill, Stuteley Streets, it then crosses the Birmingham and Bromsgrove Road at Selly Oak, leaving Harborne a mile to the left; it next crosses the Halesowen Road a mile west of Birmingham; thence by the Observatory it enters the parish of Birmingham, crosses the Smethwick and Dudley road, takes the line of Warstone Lane, and quits the parish again at Hockley brook; across Handsworth, and then over the Tame at Oldford; in Sutton it passes Ridgeway 126 yards east of King's Standing (an artificial mound where Charles I. addressed the local levies of his troops in 1642) through the park and over Radley moor to Wall, where it joins the Watling street. The writer who gives this line of route, adds as a piece of local colouring—"The Romans properly termed their ways *streets*; one of the smaller roads issuing from London passes through Stratford-on-Avon (*Streetford*) Monkspath *Street*, and Shirley *Street*, to Birmingham; all of which serves to prove that Birmingham was a place of note in the time of Cæsar." He might, with equal accuracy, have substituted the name of Smethwick for that of Birmingham in his far-fetched surmise.

From the foregoing, dome faint idea may be formed of the environment of Smethwick at the Romano-British period of this country's history; it may be pictured as a wild open and unoccupied heathland, lying to the north of the great Forest of Arden, with habitations of a Celtic population no nearer than at Harborne; with possibly a small Roman camp stationed at certain seasons of the year at Metchley; end with the aforementioned roads and trackways serving as a more than sufficient means of communication between this immediate vicinity and all the outer world of Britain.

IV.—THE SAXON SETTLEMENT OF SMETHWICK

The argument that Metchley Camp was of Roman origin is very much favoured by the fact that it is found to be rectangular in its shape. Even if the Britons had utilised the site before the Romans, and had, after their custom, thrown up earthworks of no particular or regular shape, their more systematic successors would inevitably have gone to the trouble of reducing this irregularity of outline to something approaching a four-sided figure. The Saxons, on the other hand, generally raised their earthworks in a circle or double circle—these various characteristics of outline aid very much in the identification of origination, when examining ancient camps. And while it is not contended that Metchley camp was a permanent Roman encampment *(castra stativa)* it is almost beyond doubt that it was used as a temporary camp *(castra exploratoria)*.

Mr. W. Salt Brassington is of opinion that "Metchley was the chief Roman station on the military road between Alcester and Wall. Two lines of earthwork may even now be clearly traced. Its situation near the juncture of one of the Salt-ways with the Icknield Street may account for its importance. There is an old well in the outer part of the Camp, near the Bristol Road."

After the withdrawal of the Roman troops (A.D. 418) the Britons began to fall an easy prey to the invading Saxons. The history of the next two centuries is mainly concerned with the conquest of the land by these new-comers.

In the founding of the Heptarchy the last kingdom to be established was that which embraced the whole of the midland district. It was known as Mercia, and its boundaries coincided to a very near degree with those of the ancient diocese of Lichfield. In this latest of all the Saxon Kingdoms, the point nearest to Smethwick which attained to any eminence was Wednesbury.

It was in the year 600 that Mercia was founded by a chieftain named Crida. Shortly after, and certainly during the Pagan period,* Wednesbury was built; its name discloses this fact; the signification of which is, plainly, Woden's Fort—Woden being the Saxon god of war, from whom all the great chieftains claimed descent. By about 660 Christianity had secured a footing. Wolfere, King of Mercia—the name Wolverhampton signifies "Wolfere's high town"—dominated the whole of England, and tried to force Christianity upon the King of Sussex.

In the meantime Smethwick, Handsworth, Birmingham, and other places innumerable, had become the sites of Saxon settlements. By 715 (Ceolred, King of Mercia, was forced to contend for the supremacy with the rising Kingdom of Wessex; in this year was fought the battle of Wednesbury. The result of this battle was the repulse of Ceolred; and shortly afterwards he went mad while feasting with his Thanes. In course of time the Heptarchy gave way to one united England. Then the Danes began to ravage the land, the whole strength of which was scarcely sufficient to repulse their incursions. Under Edward the Elder, eldest son of Alfred the Great, and successor to the throne of all England, Mercia still ranked as a sub-kingdom. It was ruled by one Ethelred, who had married the warlike princess Ethelfleda, a daughter of Alfred the Great, and therefore a sister to the King, Edward

---

* Green's History, under date 685, says—"Heathenism indeed still held its own in the Western Woodlands; we may perhaps see Woden-worshipping miners at Alcester in the demons of the legend of Bishop Ecgwine, of Worcester, *who* drowned the preacher's voice with the din of their hammers."

the Elder. In 910 Edward defeated the East Anglians with great slaughter, at Tettenhall. In 912 the sub-king Ethelred died, but his widow, Ethelfleda, known as the Lady of the Mercians, remained as a tower of strength to her brother in his unceasing conflicts with the Danes.

It was the military genius of Ethelfleda which called into existence a fortified quadrilateral, against which the Danes could only dash themselves to pieces. This was formed by the castles of Bridgnorth, Tamworth, Stafford, and Warwick, with Wednesbury Castle in their centre as an inner defence. Wednesbury thus became a royal *burh* in the year 916.

Reverting to the minor Saxon settlements, the origin of them may be traced through the purport of their names. Thus Birmingham was the *home* of the tribe of *Berm*, and Handsworth was the appropriated *farm* or *manor* of the chieftain *Hondes;* the former name indicative of an early tribal settlement, and the latter of a much later occupation, when feudalism had cankered the free institutions of these Gothic settlers.

Smethwick was so-called because it was the *wic* or village on the *smooth* heathland That is, it was smooth by comparison.

In support of this derivation, which was given by the present writer on p. 6 of A HISTORY OF WEST BROMWICH, the opinion of Mr. W. H. Duignan was invited as soon as this work on Smethwick was projected. Mr. Duignan unhesitatingly says that the name Smethwick "is clearly from the Anglo-Saxon *smethe,* in modern English equivalent to 'smooth.' and one meaning of which is 'a level field or plain.' The situation of Smethwick corresponds to this, as it lies on a plain at the foot of Rowley Hills; and of course locally all things are comparative; so that the interpretation of the name is 'the village on the plain.'" Mr. Duignan adds—"There is a Smethwick in Cheshire, a Smeeth in Kent, a Smethcoc in Salop, and a Markham Smeeth near Swaffham in Norfolk." According to Mr. Kenward—HARBORNE AND ITS SURROUNDINGS, p. 21—the nucleus of the old village which afterwards grew into Falmouth was in 1653 known as Smithick, because of the numerous smithies it contained.

As to the economic reasons which induced the settlement of Smethwick, they are to be found amongst the political and social influences rather than in any motive which can be designated as industrial.

There were no "exposed" mineral resources to attract the Saxon settlers to Smethwick, for it lies just outside the prolific mining area of South Staffordshire. The ironworking era of Smethwick is quite modern, and of this fact there is not a shadow of a doubt. And as the place is known to have borne its present name right away from that Saxon period, it is illogical to contend that it could ever have been *Smith-Wick,* to indicate "a village of smiths"; whenever the place has been so miscalled, it has been owing entirely to the literal inaccuracy of some ancient scribe. What traces of ancient ironworking have ever been discovered in Smethwick, in the shape of cinders or scoriae, such as are met with in the Forest of Dean? And as to ancient iron-getting, such as is evidenced by the "Dane-shafts" or old ironstone openworks on The Delves, that would be a physical impossibility anywhere within the confines of Smethwick. The name "Smith-wick" is only a piece of slip-shod orthsography, which a fanciful conceit of the modern Iron Age has endeavoured to foist on the credulous Smethwickian.

Smethwick, however, as a wild open upland, presented no physical features which were likely to prevent its settlement by the Anglian invaders, inhospitable (or, rather, incapable of defence) as it may have been in the eyes of the Celtic Britons. Its open spaciousness would be positively a recommendation for its occupation by these Teutonic new-comers.

The average elevation of Smethwick, as measured from the mean water-level at Liverpool, is 520 feet. The average altitude of Malvern above sea-level is only 500 feet—not the Malvern Hills, of course, which reach about 1,400 feet. The highest point in Smethwick is in the Hagley Road, near the boundary of Warley, and is 623 feet, while the lowest point, which is in Foundry Lane near Vittoria Street, is not less than 425 feet above mean water-mark. Barr Beacon on one side of Smethwick is about 750 feet high, and Rowley Hill on the other, about 900 feet.

Among these Gothic forefathers of ours the free-man was strictly the freeholder; and the landless man ceased for all practical purposes to be free, though he was no man's slave. They all had a deep hatred of cities and of town life, and were essentially land-tillers. Perhaps this deep-seated feeling explains why they did not occupy Celtic Harborne. They preferred to live apart, "each by himself, as woodside, plain, or fresh spring attracts him." Here is the real actuating motive, as we have quoted it from Tacitus, which accounts quite satisfactorily for the settlement of Smethwick. Each dweller in any given settlement was jealous of his own isolation and complete independence. This same feeling is accountable for the wide belt of waste land which once encircled Smethwick, and cut it off from all the surrounding settlements—the remnants of this waste lasting almost to the present century, and known to us variously as Bromwich Heath, Handsworth Heath, Gib Heath, and Birmingham Heath. No man might appropriate the land of this free belt; but respecting the inviolable neutrality of such a "mark," the Saxons dwelt side by side, uniting freely together in war time to fight side by side against the common enemy. Berming abode by Berming in the liberty of their "ham" or home; and Willing by Willing on their "worth" or farm; the blood-bond of kinsmen who were descended from one Berm or from one Willa thus constituting a tie which was religiously respected by every tribe of this liberty-loving people. To the Saxon character, isolated freedom on the spaciousness of Smethwick heathland was infinitely preferable to the occupation of a usurped British village like Harborne, or even to the defensive advantages of a Roman camp like Metchley.

V.—CARTOGRAPHICAL: A SEARCH FOR "SMETHWICK" ON THE MAPS

A good criterion of the relative importance of any place is offered by the frequency with which its name appears on the maps. It would be idle to expect to find on maps illustrative of ancient or mediaeval England any indication of our insignificant hamlet of Smethwick.

In that admirable standard work, Mr. C. H. Pearson's HISTORICAL MAPS OF ENGLAND, even the name of ancient Wednesbury fails to appear in the map of "Anglia Anglo-Saxonica." Yet in Collins' STUDENTS' ATLAS *(Glasgow, 1890)* on the map "Britain under the Saxons," we may find prominently marked "Weadesbyrig (Wednesbury)."

Renewing our search through Mr. Pearson's exhaustive atlas we find in his next historical map, which is that of "Norman England," that the whole region for miles around Smethwick is left quite blank, no names appearing nearer thereto than at the three points named by him respectively "Lichfeld," "Coventre," and "Dudlei." In his letter-press, however, the author observes that at the period of Domesday, all Staffordshire was very heavily wooded. He mentions the dense forest tracts which then surrounded all this locality in which we are at present interested; they were Kinver, Pancet (Pensnet), and Cannock, all in Staffordshire; and Arden, in Warwickshire. In Worcestershire the writer gives a long list of forests; but a number of them might very properly be comprehended under the one appellation of the great "Wire-wood" which gave its came to Wire-ceaster or Worcester.

Consulting the last of this series of historical maps, which is "Anglia Monastica," it may be noted that in the vicinity surrounding where Smethwick now stands there are marked Halesowen, Dudley, and Sandwell. No reference whatever is made to St. Thomas' Priory in Birmingham, an establishment of which there seems to be very little known. Bordsley Abbey in Worcestershire is marked, as well as the canonical foundations at Wolverhampton and Tettenhall.

Acknowledging this Mr. C. H. Pearson as an undoubted authority, we may safely accept from the explanatory letter-press of his valuable work, the interpretation which he places on the terminal of the word Smethwick; namely—

WIC—"an enclosure of any kind, from a dwelling-place *(vicus)* to a salt-pan."

Also the terminal of the name Wednesbury, which he gives thus—

BURH or BYRIG—a fortress [and, gradually, the township which grew up around the fortress.]

Smethwick being an ordinary free settlement, having no defence save the mark or belt of common waste-land, and no industry beyond the tillage of the common fields, was, in all this, characteristically Saxon, and in no way different to many thousands of other settlements.

Mr. Kenward says of Harborne also (p.17) " The only industry which our Saxon ancestors pursued in Harborne, though they worked elsewhere for iron and salt," was agriculture. This was no doubt true of the later Saxon period, when the population had so increased that even most of the older Celtic villages had to be occupied by the Teutonic immigrants. This later settlement would also have its surrounding mark or belt of free common land; and quoting from the same writer (p. 41) we read—"In the Elizabethan times Harborne Heath was really an open heath between the east and west brows of the hill."

Wednesbury, it has been said, boasted a castle. The Saxons were not clever masons, and this fortification would be merely a timbered fort, strengthened by strong stockades, a circle of walls, and deep ditches. The only remains ever discovered of this castle were in the foundation of the church; and the Moat-field is a place-name undoubtedly derived from the situation of that ancient ditch or *motæ*. (See SALT COLLECTIONS, VIII. pt. 2, p. 138.)

Resuming our cartographical researches, perhaps the earliest map on which our subject is marked is SAXTON'S "Warwic" of 1576, where may be found both "Horborn" and "Smethwik."

A little later, namely, in 1603, OVERTON'S Warwickshire gives "Smethwik," and also "Wartley Hall."

To Dr. Plot's NATURAL HISTORY OF STAFFORDSHIRE, published in 1686, there is an excellent map. On this we find Smethwick duly appearing with New Inn and Handsworth lying to the N.E. of it, and Aston-juxta-Birmingham still further outlying in that direction; to the East is Hockley; to the S.W. Worley Wigorn; and to the S.E. Shire Lanes, with Edgbaston outlying beyond; to the S. is Harbourn, outflanked by Selley and Weeley Park on its two farther sides; and right away to the N.W. are marked The Oake and Bromwich Heath, with Wednesbury in the farther distance. The latter town is shown with the somewhat unusual number of three windmills (important institutions in those days) with a fourth on its Darlaston boundary. Around the borders of this interesting old map appear the arms of the various county families; among them (with reference numbers to their seats, the mansions as well as the windmills and churches being all carefully marked on the map) are the heraldic coats of the Turtons of The Oak, Ward of Willingsworth, Hopkins of Oakeswell (Wednesbury), Gough of Pury Hall, Wyrley of Hamstead, and Jennens (? of Shireland Hall, Smethwick).

But better than ordinary maps for such a topographical purpose as this, is the Road Map of the old travelling days before the era of modern railways. The finest specimen is Ogilby's BRITANNIA DEPICTA, published in 1675, before roads were even really fit for coaching or for scarcely any kind of vehicular traffic; and when pack-horses, pillions, panniers, and horse-blocks were in constant use. This work is folio size, and the plates are beautifully engraved, depicting the "principal roads of England" in ribbon-fashion, up and down the page; and as the scale is a mile to the inch, a very graphic idea of the country, as it was in 1675, may be gathered from it. Reference to this book will show on plate 50 the Road from London to Shrewsbury by way of Dudley and Bridgnorth. Pictorially represented on it are all the points described for the adventurous traveller in the accompanying letterpress, page 99; as thus (taking, of course, only the few miles of road in which these Records are concerned):—

Birmingham *vulgo* Bromicham is marked on the map between the 109th and 110th mile from London, and near to a branch road leading to Lichfield. Says the letterpress, "Leaving Bermingham at 110 a direct Road brings you to the Entrance of Staffordshire at 112.. 3 furlongs, whence through a little wood [this remnant of the old forest land is drawn on the map, the trees being dense near the rise of what is now Cape Hill] and a discontinued [?scattered] Village call'd Smethwick you are conveyed at 115 Miles by Blakeley Hall a furlong to the Right; and 7 furlongs farther to Oldbury Chapel, a Village of about 3 furlongs Extent and some Accommodation" [*i.e.* stabling, post-horses, and an inn.] The map shows the road at Oldbury to make two angular turns, almost Z-shaped. Smethwick is shown to line the road with houses on both sides. A by-road is shown to cut across towards Hales Owen, then a few more houses, and then at the 114th mile a second by-road cuts across to Rood End.

In 1736 when carriages were coming more into vogue owing to improved roads, a small octavo edition of this Road Book was published by Eman. Bowen. It is chiefly interesting here because it calls attention to "a better way" from Birmingham to Shrewsbury than through Smethwick; namely, through "W. Bermingham" [West Bromwich], Wednesbury and Wolverhampton; in fact that which soon afterwards became the great coaching route known as the Holyhead Road. Probably the road through Smethwick had fallen into a very neglected condition; it is certain that its former level was in some parts ten or twelve feet lower than the present level.

The cross road just mentioned was a very ancient one, running from Walsall to the South, via West Bromwich Old Church. Roebuck Lane, Smethwick, Harborne, and Selly Oak, falling there on to the great road.

Coming to more modern maps, there is an excellent STREET MAP OF SMETHWICK (1890) drawn by Mr. J. Charles Stuart, C.E., the Public Surveyor of Smethwick.

* * * * * * * * * * *

On ARROWSMITH'S MAP OF BIRMINGHAM, published in 1834, is given an inset plan of Soho, which shows "The Soho Manufactory," "The Mint," with the adjoining house, stables, and the now effaced Soho Pool. This was about the period when the famous Soho was beginning to decline.

Now SOHO, whose name has so often displaced that of Smethwick, is not even the moiety of a parish, which at least Smethwick could always claim to be; it is a mere district, the boundaries of which are always vague and undefined. It is clear that Soho ranged indiscriminately across the legal boundary lines of no less than three contiguous parishes; at the present time there is a Soho Station on the Stour Valley Railway within the confines of Smethwick; there is Soho Road Station on the new Perry Barr branch of the London and North-Western Railway, situated within the legal borders of Handsworth parish; and there is Soho Station of the Great Western Railway, which is in the city of Birmingham.

As to the name of this locality, which has its duplicate in a part of London, it is said that the word "Soho" is of sporting origin—in fact a hunting term which has come down from the good old days when the nobles and gentles went forth with horse, and hound, and hawk. In corroboration of this, REEVES' HISTORY OF WEST BROMWICH, p. 117 says, "Mr. Boulton in 1762 purchased a lease of The Soho, at that time a barren heath, on the bleak summit of which stood a naked hut, the habitation of a Warrener." This was written in 1837. A contributor to the Notes and Queries of a Birmingham weekly newspaper, writing some twenty years ago, says that "the house (presumably the hut just referred to) before the Park was enclosed was a public-house, and had for its sign a representation of a hunt; there was a hare, hounds, horses, and men, and the huntsman represented with the word 'Soho!' proceeding from his mouth. The Park and Works were named after that sign. Eighty or ninety years ago it was a public-house on a wild common."

"Soho!" was the war-cry of the romantic Monmouth at the battle of Sedgemoor (1685), in his "hunt" for the English crown.

VI.—THE DOMESDAY MANOR OF SMETHWICK (1086)

Some time during the Saxon period—say within the four centuries between A.D. 600 and A.D. 1000—the free Saxon settlement of Smethwick, in common with most other similar settlements, became converted into a manor. On most of these feudal seats, when Christianity became fully established in the land, the mission priests settled down as resident clergy, and so a manor frequently became a parish, but it was not always so.

Manors originated in this way: A great lord obtained a piece of land from the King; part he disposed of to his tenants, who held of him in freehold (until, however, this process of sub-infeudation was stopped in 1290, by the *Statute of Quia Emptores*); and the rest of this land was called his domain, on part of which he built the manor house, while another part was cultivated by his villeins; the cottars, too, had portions of land to their dwellings; and then the residue was "waste," where all the folk of the manor pastured their cattle in common, gathered their fuel, and made their ways. At first these villeins were slaves, but each had a patch of soil for which he rendered some servile office to the lord, as ploughing his land, and garnering his crops.

Among these feudal retainers and tenants of a manor, living together almost as one family, certain customs often grew up. To some manors very peculiar customs attached themselves as acknowledged privileges, In this county of Stafford some of these ancient "customs of the manor" are as strange as in any part of England. For instance: A curious privilege attached to an, oak in Knoll Wood, in the manor of Tirley, near Drayton, as thus—"In case oath were made that the bastard was got within the umbrage or reach of its boughs," neither spiritual nor temporal power had aught to say, and the man got off scot free. Another strange Staffordshire custom prevailed at Essington, where the lord of the manor had to bring a goose every New Year's Day to the head manor at Hilton. Here he was to drive it about the fire, while "Jack of Hilton" at the same time blew the fire furiously, and (one regrets to say) very indecently. But as "Jack" is nothing but "an image of brass about 12 inches high" he may be forgiven, although some reservation may be made as against the originator of this mad prank. Again, and even locally it may not be generally known, at Wichnor there exists a similar custom to the more famous one at Dunmow, but the flitch of bacon in the Staffordshire case must be presented to the happy couple at Lent. And, as a fourth and last example, there formerly existed within the manor of Wednesbury the *jus primæ noctis,* whether or not that lewd historic jest was ever in England anything more than a sheer delusion. This fine (or money penalty to which in England, if not in Scotland, this "right" was commuted) was not to spare the blushes of the bride, but to compensate the lord of the manor for the loss of services, the new wife taking the domicile of her husband. In fact, the customs of a manor generally made for morality within its borders.

Apparently Smethwick was not within the domain, or home farm, of the lord of the manor, for no record exists of any manor house ever having stood within its boundaries. And although at the time of the Norman Conquest "Horeborne" and "Smedewich" are recorded, as separate manors, they ultimately became one parish, probably because of the wasted or valueless condition of Smethwick.

But very frequently manors of an early date were held under other manors, or as part of "honours," and sometimes on the strangest of tenures, too; as we have seen with regard to Essington and Hilton. Smethwick would seem to have been in some such subordinate position, as will be seen here presently, with regard to Longdon. All manors, large or small, were held of the Crown in return for certain feudal services. As to the services by which Smethwick was held, nothing definite is known; it seems to have been quite unimportant by itself, and is often found included with other territorial holdings under one lord. And as to the franchises, liberties, privileges, and other rights, such as Markets, Fairs, Courts, &c., no trace whatever of these can be found in the records of Smethwick. Similarly the quaint old customs, to which attention has been directed, are also missing from the traditions of this place.

The first time the name of Smethwick occurs in any historical document is the appearance thereof in DOMESDAY BOOK. This was an authorised return of nearly all the land in England about the year 1086, giving details as to the extent of each holding under the King, the name of the holder, the condition of the land, and other particulars which it was necessary to know under the system of Feudalism which then prevailed. Mainly it was a return of the full military strength and resources of the Kingdom, and got its strange name because men fondly imagined that it would prove so complete and final as to settle the ownership of all the soil of England till "Domesday"! In the year following the completion of this vast piece of clerical work, namely, in 1087, the instigator of it, William the Conqueror, incontinently lost all his interest in the land—he died !

In the Domesday Book the name of Smethwick is written "Smedewich"; the "d" in the middle of the word being nearly always so written by the Norman scribes in lieu of the Saxon character "th." But by the twelfth and thirteenth centuries the name appears more properly as "Smeythewick" and "Smethewyke."

The 1086 record of Smethwick sets forth that there was in "Smedewich" two carucates of arable land. This area at the utmost would be little more than 200 acres, a carucate being a variable measurement, generally estimated as equivalent to the tillage of one plough per annum. Mr. Eyton, in his admirable studies on the Domesday records of Staffordshire, inclines to the opinion that the Smethwick of these Norman times was equivalent to that which now covers an area of 1,886 acres. This ought to have left a large proportion of the soil under pasture, waste, and perhaps wood, at that period. And this was usually the case elsewhere. But at Smethwick the record leaves us to infer that there was neither wood nor pasture, and therefore that Smethwick was in a "wasted" condition; that is, practically unoccupied, and perhaps of little value.

The record also shows that Smethwick was not then held by the same tenant-in-fee or immediate holder as Harborne, who was named Robert; but was held by one William, who also held "5 carucates in Tibintone" (Tipton). It is not improbable that even these ploughlands were almost valueless at that time owing to the wasted condition of this part of the country, after the "fire and sword" of the Conqueror had swept through it. But Harborne, Smethwick, and Tipton were all included at that same period within the great manor of Longdon (near Lichfield), a holding of vast extent, and comprising some thirty other manors, townships, and villages, which all owed suit and service to it; the whole being among the territorial possessions of that feudal baron, the Bishop of Chester.

In this great national land-register it is further indicated that not only was Smethwick in the holding of the Bishop of Chester as tenant-in-capite, but that its Saxon possessor before the Conquest, namely in the reign of Edward the Confessor, had been the (Cathedral ?) Church of St. Chad, Lichfield.

This requires some little explanation; for apparently, on the face of it, the lands of the Bishop of Lichfield had thus passed into the hands of the Bishop of Chester. But really this was not so. It was simply that the bishop's seat had been moved from Lichfield to Chester—it was afterwards removed to Coventry.

The DIOCESAN HISTORY OF LICHFIELD *(London, S.P.C.K.)* p. 50, says of Lichfield at this time: "It was a poor little place, surrounded only by woods and some forty acres of meadow. The canons had dwindled down to five, noted as much for poverty as for piety. . . Wild havoc was made in the Bishop's woods by the Conqueror. . . . Besides, the manors round Lichfield were wasted. . . Yet Peter, the Norman Bishop whom William (the Conqueror) left here (1072-1085) seems to have had many ploughs at work as the land would bear, and to have owned no less than 93,740 acres of wood in Lichfield, 11,530 in Eccleshall, and 4,320 in Baswich and Brewood. His Canons had 49 ploughs. and would thus seem to be beginning those extensive farming operations by which capitular bodies subsisted. The Bishop was the largest forest-owner in Staffordshire, a county which, out of a total surveyed area of 468,004 acres, had 319,538 acres of wood.

"Population was scarce . . . ; and the rough character of the Trent Valley may be inferred from the fact that the Norman Earls of Chester endowed an hereditary guide who had to meet them on their journeys from London at Hopwasbridge, near Tamworth, to conduct them through the mazy swamps and tangled woods. . . Of Peter [the Bishop] we know little. . . He attended the Synod in London. It was then agreed that the seats of bishops should be fixed in large towns, as centres of influence. . . Peter therefore tranferred his episcopal chair to Chester, which contained 500 houses. And for many centuries afterwards his successors were commonly called Bishops of Chester, though none of them were ever enthroned there."

This, therefore, accounts for the substitutions in Domesday Book of the "Bishop of Chester's" name for that of the "Church of Lichfield." Peter died in 1084, and his successor in the Bishopric was Robert de Lymesey (1086-1117) who schemed very hard to get away from Chester, and the overshadowing power and influence of its great Earls. On the death of the Abbot of Coventry in 1095, the Bishop managed to secure the revenues of the Abbey; and in 1102, by papal licence, he removed the bishop's stool to Coventry and fixed it in the abbey church there. Hence the title, subsequently, of "Bishop of Coventry and Lichfield."

Having thus satisfactorily accounted for the change of title, the next point needing attention is the position of the spiritual lord of Smethwick as its feudal baron, a dual capacity which, in these modern days, would appear altogether anomalous and irreconcilable. There is certainly nothing now extant to show that this right reverend father in God ever called upon the men of Smethwick to follow him to battle. But the thing was quite possible, and supposing Smethwick had possessed any fighting men, it was highly probable. That Bishops have gone forth to battle, followed by their armed retainers, history furnishes many instances, not the least important being that of Archbishop Scope in the reign of Henry IV.

The military inclinations of the prelates were directly encouraged by the feudal system, and as a consequence fighting bishops were by no means uncommon. Sometimes, however, bishops appointed their feudal advocates to fulfil the terms of the military tenures by which they held their lands, such as those by which, in the present instance, the Bishop of Chester held the manor of Longdon, including Smethwick among its many appurtenances. The military advocates held their lands under the church; and their service in protecting the interests of the church estates, and in leading its vassals to war was deemed peculiarly honourable service. Yet, as before stated, the prorates themselves were not averse to take the field in person; and it is by no means improbable that one of these earlier bishops may have donned full armour, and have ridden forth amidst the lances of his men-at-arms, some few of whom would be drawn from the manor of Smethwick. In the mimic warfare of the hunt, it was very certain these bishops had ample opportunities in wooded Staffordshire; and they were all, without exception, keen lovers of the chase.

* * * * * * * * * * *

The Domesday status of ROWLEY REGIS may here be noted.

The Domesday Book does not give a record of quite every place, without any exception. For instance the royal cities of London and Winchester are conspicuous omissions from the record—probably an inquiry into their condition may have been impolitic in those critical times of conquest and innovation. Coming nearer home, no mention of Tamworth is made, either as part of Staffordshire, or of Warwickshire, between which two counties as a burgh, a chatellany, a manor, or a parish, it has always been divided. It had just previously been in the seigneury of the Mercian earls, but at the death of the last Earl, Edwin, it had escheated to the Conqueror. Burton-on-Trent, too, does not appear; perhaps its record of tempting "fatness" was cunningly suppressed by the powerful influence of its Abbott. Stoke, Stone, and nearer home, Walsall, are all missing, with places of minor importance. All of which may prepare us for the fact that Rowley Regis is not to be found in Domesday. Erdeswick, in his STAFFORDSHIRE, written in 1538, says that at the Conquest "Rowley Regis remained in King's demesne, and so remained till the 20th of his reign." Now on the maps Rowley Regis is but a peninsula of Staffordshire, attached to this county by a very narrow isthmus. At that time, on all sides both peninsula and isthmus were girt by manors reputed to be in Worcestershire, viz., Dudley, Cradley, and Hales Owen. Ecclesiastically, too, Rowley Regis was associated with Worcestershire rather than Staffordshire. All of which uncertainty may account for its absence from the Domesday rolls.

Its name clearly implies that it was the Rowley [or the *Rough-lea,* in immediate contrast to *Smooth-wick*] belonging to the King; for Rowley is not an uncommon place-name. Perhaps it was really what was at that time described as part of Vetus Dominicum Coronæ or ancient domain of the crown, like *King's* Swinford, and the royal Saxon burgh of Wednesbury. Or there were two other classes of Terræ Regis which came into the Norman King's possession at that time; for instance the escheated Earldom of Mercia gave him *King's* Bromley, Cannock, &c.; and lastly, and more probably as applying to Rowley, there were the numerous "wasted" estates of the evicted Thanes, whom William I. punished and harried for any display of Saxon patriotism.

Rowley-Somery is a name sometimes found, and seems to indicate that Rowley, or some portion of it, once belonged to :the Someri family who held the Barony of Dudley.

VII—MANORIAL LORDS FROM 1086 TO 1216: HALES OWEN ABBEY LANDS IN SMETHWICK (1229–1261).

The next great national record in which Smethwick is referred to is *Liber Niger Scacarii,* otherwise THE BLACK BOOK OF THE EXCHEQUER. This ancient register, amongst other things; contains a list of Knights' fees in Henry II.'s- time (A.D. 1166), and is certainly the earliest document of the kind, except the Domesday Book. It is generally thought to have been a return made for the purpose of levying an aid on the marriage of the King's eldest daughter—an "Aid" being one of those money taxes which the feudal system sometimes permitted in addition to the usual liability to military service; for it would seem that kings and governments have invariably been in need of payments in cash ever since civilisation invented this handy medium of exchange. Other authorities, however, have regarded *Liber Niger* as a return for general fiscal purposes connected with the levying of Scutage; "Scutage," or shield-money, being at that particular time a newly-invented feudal tax which the King was willing; to accept in lieu of personal military service in war-times.

Whatever its purport' this national record of the year 1166, a date not quite a century later than DOMESDAY, contains an entry relative to Smethwick. It is set down under the heading—

BARONY OF THE BISHOP OF COVENTRY.

The entry itself runs—

"Henricus filius Geroldi ½ f.m."

This being interpreted sign)fies that the holding in question (the same "fee" that appears in Domesday Book among the said Bishop's lands as Horeborne and Smedewic, the former held by Robert and the latter by the sub-tenant William, as stated in the previous chapter) constitutes "half a Knight's fee in the hands of one Henry fitz Gerold." A "Knight's fee," it may be further explained, consisted of so much land—variable in extent according to its nature as would suffice to maintain a knight, and enable him to present himself and his retainers fully equipped for the defence of the country.

As to the personality of this lord of Smethwick; it would appear that "Henry, son of Gerald," was royal chamberlain to the Queen of Henry II.; and to many of the charters granted by this monarch his name, as that of a handy courtier, may be found attached as a witness. His son, Warin fitz Henry, also called Warin fitz Gerold, became in his turn chamberlain to King John; and in the 18th year of that reign, the Smethwick lands, with much more territory, passed from him to Thomas de Erdinton.

All the local interest of this noble family, however, did not cease with that transaction.

The daughter and heiress of Warin was Margaret, who married Baldwin de Redvers, Earl of Devon. She had by this marriage a son, Baldwin, who was styled "de Insula," because he held the lordship of the Isle of Wight; and it was he who at a later period (45 Henry III., or 1261) acknowledged the advowson of the church of Horborne to be the right of the Abbot of Hales Owen.

Another similar record, of the time of Edward I., and known as KIRBY'S QUEST, states that the said Abbot held "¼ fee in Horburn and Smeythwik."

At this point it becomes particularly necessary to call attention to the distinction which must now be clearly made, and preserved throughout the whole of these records, between those Smethwick lands which were held as forming part of the great Manor of Longdon, and those newer holdings in Smethwick which were part of the lands belonging to Hales Owen Abbey. In both cases these Smethwick lands were held by a churchman of high rank —a Bishop and an Abbot; Longdon, as we have seen, being part of the episcopal barony.

With this explanation of the introduction of a newer territorial influence in Smethwick, a return may be made to resume the manorial history at the point to which it bad been brought.

A long note occurs in Vol. III., p. 182, of THE SALT COLLECTIONS, on one "Ralph de Harborne," in whose person is afforded a typical instance of the supersession of an English tenant by one of Norman blood. This was about 1150, or about a century after the Conquest. The favoured interloper obtained certain estates, including Harborne, his tenure giving him, somewhat exceptionally, the services of the Bishop's free tenants—the grant, seeming to distinguish them from the villeins of the manor, or customary tenants.

Another note (p. 184) also speaks of the aforementioned family of fitz Gerold, giving additional details.

Henry II., it would appear, had bestowed on Warine fitz Gerold the escheated barony of Eudo Dapifer—the word *dapifer* signifying literally "a feast bearer," but no doubt conveying the notion of "a high steward." This Warine seems to have died by the year 1166, and his brother Henry had by that date become enfeoffed [or placed in feudal possession] of the Bishop's manors of Harborne and Smethwick. Such a feoffment, made to the powerful favourite of a reigning sovereign, was invariably of the nature of a bribe to secure some favour. It may therefore be accepted that the manor of Smethwick played the part of a counter in some game of intrigue played by this great Lord Spiritual who then controlled the destinies of Smethwick. The effect of the transfer would be to reduce the former tenant to a subsidiary position; and as the name "de Harborne" disappears at this time from cotemporary records, the inference is that the issue of Ralph probably took up their abode at Bromhale, another manor with which they were connected, and the name of which they then adopted as their substituted territorial title, "de Bromhale."

Summarised, and put briefly, this chapter conveys the following main facts in the manorial and general territorial history of Smethwick:

Whereas the average extent of a Knight's fee in Staffordshire, as allotted and granted by the Conqueror, was 3,000 acres, Harborne and Smethwick together were reckoned only as half-a-fee; which does not speak much for their fertility or productiveness at that time.

While Smethwick continued as a small integral portion of the great Barony of the Bishop, who was tenant-in-capite, or chief-tenant holding direct from the king; its direct holders by sub-infeudation were various. As thus—

1086—Smethwick held by one *William* (Harborne being in other hands at that time).

1149(?)—Smethwick, with Harborne, held by an Englishman, probably resident in the latter as his demesne; he is styled *Ralph de Harborne*

1150—Ralph dispossessed, retires to his other manor, Brombale; Smethwick given to a Norman favourite, *Warine fitz Gerold.*

1166—*Henry, son of Gerold* (Chamberlain to Queen Eleanor) succeeds his brother Warine in the possession of Smethwick. Henry, who perhaps wielded considerable Court influence owing to his official position, and to the King's domestic weakness through his intrigues with the Fair Rosamund, seems to have been bribed by the Bishop with these Smethwick lands.

[Wednesbury manor changed hands very curiously through the same royal *liaison.*]

1216—*Warine, son of Henry,* and Chamberlain to King John, found in possession of Smethwick manor, which now passes into the hands of *Thomas of Erdington.*

1261—By this time (and also later by the Exchequer returns of Kirby, the business-like Treasurer to Edward I.) some portion of the land in Smethwick had passed into the hands of the Abbot of Hales Owen. probably granted by Warine or one of his descendants who had some interest in Tipton lands also. Earlier than this, however, about 1229, a law suit had been waged over these same Abbey lands.

VIII.—CHURCH LANDS IN SMETHWICK (1230–1277).

Referring to the chronicles contained in the preceding chapter a few comments may be useful. Reference was made to one Ralph de Harborne. He is in all probability the same individual to whom Mr. Kenway refers in his HISTORY OF HARBORNE (p. 22)—"About 1160 Ralph dapifer or sewer of Walter Durdent, Bishop of Lichfield, was lord of Harborne under the Bishop."

Reference was also made to a law suit of 1229–1230; here is the record of the case:—

In the SALT COLLECTIONS VI. are a number of Staffordshire Pleas of the time of Henry III. At the Michaelmas Term of the year 1230, " the Abbot of Halesowen sued Margaret Rivers [de Ripariis] to acquit him of the service which the capital lords exacted from him for the tenement which he held of Margaret in Horeburn and Smethewic; and he stated that Alexander, the Bishop of Coventry, destrained the said Margaret for the tenement which the Abbot holds of her for suit of court, and for scutage, by which the Abbot is damaged." [The suit has been abstracted from the original MS. word for word by the Editors of THE COLLECTIONS; but what is probably meant is that the Abbot was destrained for the service for which Margaret was responsible to the Bishop—Harborne and Smethwick forming the half Knight's-fee held under the Bishop of Coventry and Lichfield]. Margaret put in an appearance and denied any injury to the Abbot; she stated that she did not hold the fee of the Bishop of Coventry, but of William Lungespeie and Idonea, his wife. She then formally called them both to warranty, because it was to them she had done homage for the land. It was therefore ordered by the Court that William and Idonea should be summoned (in county Berks), and in the meantime the Sheriff of Staffordshire was to leave the Abbot unmolested, until the Court had ascertained who was really bound to acquit him of the service in dispute.

As to the advowson of Harborne Church, it would seem that from its earliest existence the patronage of the living had belonged to the Dean and Chapter of Lichfield; to whom it now belongs. But for a certain period it would also seem that Hales Owen Abbey had exercised the right of presentation, and that some friction existed in regard to this privilege.

Mr. Kenway, in his HARBORNE (p. 23), says that among certain capitular rights of the Dean and Chapter of Lichfield, set forth in a manuscript book supposed to have been written by one Henry Griswold, a Canon under Bishop Hackett (1661–1670), he finds accorded by Roger Weseham, Bishop, A.D. 1255, and confirmed at Lambeth by Archbishop Boniface, of Canterbury, 12 February, 1259, "Cum Ecclesiis de Prees, Berkswich, Thatchbrooke, *Gaya, Harbourn,*" &c., &c. It may be noted that Harbourne is always designated *ecclesia,* "a church," while similar records of the period describe Edgbaston as *capella,* or only "a chapel," of which Harborne was the mother church.

In the year 1277 a grant of lands in Smethwick was made by the Abbey of Hales Owen to the Church of Harborne. There are several other references to lands in Edgbaston and other places being held by the same church, which church in 1279 is claimed to pertain to the commonalty of the Dean and Chapter of Lichfield; and, in fact, in the same year (1279) Henry de Gamo, Prebendary of Gaia Minor, having previously claimed the said church as pertaining to his prebend, resigned it into the hands of the Bishop "for ever." (SALT COLLECTIONS VI., pt. 2, pp. 111 and 119).

As the territorial history of Smethwick during this period is so much involved in that of the church, it may not be out of place here to give a very brief chronology of local matters ecclesiastical:—

A.D. 1130, Sandwell Priory founded.

1155, Dudley Priory established.

Dudley Church built.

1210, King John appoints one of his royal chaplains to Wednesbury Church (Ethelfleda had *repaired* Wednesbury Chapel, A.D. 916).,

1215, Hales Owen Abbey founded.

1224, *(circa)* West Bromwich Church erected.

1240, *(circa)* Harborne Church built.

1280, St. Thomas' Priory, Birmingham, established.

In 1264 both Weoley Castle and Dudley Castle were being rebuilt by Roger de Somery, Baron of Dudley, by license of Henry III.

IX.—SOME MEDIÆVAL TAXINGS OF SMETHWICK (1291–1340)

A.D. 1291.—In Lichfield Chapter House is preserved an excellent copy of *Taxatio Ecclesiastica P. Nicholai IV*: which records the "tenths" due to the Papal Exchequer, but which the lofty spirit and burning zeal of Pope Nicholas IV. permitted to be diverted to the use of King Edward I. for six years to defray the cost of a Crusade in the Holy Land. Edward, to avail himself to the very fullest of this generous offer, ordered the preparation of this roll in 1288, and it was completed by 1291 under the direction of two bishops. So well was the work done that this *Valor Ecclesiasticus* remained in force as the basis of all Papal contributions till the Reformation (1536). In this roll of 1291 we have perhaps the first recorded taxing of "Horeborn" and "Synewyk," which was levied as a tenth of all rentals and other sources of revenue.

* * * * * * * * * * *

A.D. 1323.—In some curious way or other the collection of taxes has always been a fruitful field for the exercise of official corruption. Almost the first record which we have of any tax-paying whatever in Smethwick, is associated with fraud. The frivolity of the Court of the pleasure-loving Edward II. no doubt left a free hand to the various officers of State, and those in the treasury department evidently availed themselves of their opportunity. But before the reign closed retribution overtook the wrong-doers, and they were brought to justice by an awakened and discontented public.

This is set forth in certain *Assize Rolls* (SALT COLL. ix. pt. 1, p. 93). At Tutbury, on Wednesday, "the morrow of St. Nicholas, 17 Edward II." (otherwise December 7th, 1323) before John de Stonore and other of the King's judges, the juries of various Hundreds within this County of Stafford made certain presentments to the effect that Thomas de Pipe, Knight, and Philip de Lutteleye, who had lately acted within this said County as the principal Taxers and Collectors, had some seven and ten years previously (10th and 6th of the reign) taken great sums of money from various "vills" (or parishes) under colour of their office, appropriating the same to their own private uses. They appeared hereon a summons, and pleaded guilty, but prayed the Justices that they might be admitted to the payment of a fine for their transgressions. Thomas was fined the then goodly sum of £40, for the payment of which he produced six sureties of his own knightly order; and Philip was fined 50 marks (a mark being 13s. 4d.)

As to the identity of these knightly culprits, it would seem that "Thomas de Pype," a scion of the Pipe family of Ridware, was lord of Bradley Manor, near Bilston (see Lawley's HY. OF BILSTON, p. 144); and he had been to the Scotch Wars between the two nefarious acts of which he stood convicted. The other aristocratic oppressor of the poor, Philip de Litteley, was no doubt the same Sheriff of Staffordshire whose official acts in the following reign were regarded with great suspicion, as recorded in HY. OF WEST BROMWICH, p. 23.

Having caught and punished, perhaps very inadequately, the bigger sinners, the same Court of Justice proceeded with equal vigour against a great number of the lesser extortioners. Among those fined for maladministration we have the record—

"John de Clodeshale and John Gregori, subtaxers of Horbourne and Smethewick, 1 mark."

This kind of official oppression was evidently very common in those days. Who were really to blame, the higher officials or their underlings, cannot be decided. The Chief Taxers—and the same two, Pipe and Lutley, were presented for similar misconduct at three other taxings, namely of the 20th, 18th, and 16th of the reign—pleaded that they had assessed each vill at a certain sum, and had trusted to the tenants and Subtaxers to see that it was fairly apportioned on the true value of all chattels.

* * * * * * * * * * *

A.D.1327.—The next taxing of which we have any record is contained in the *Subsidy Roll* of 1327. This subsidy was granted by the first Parliament of Edward III. to meet the expenses of the Scotch war. The grant was that of one-twentieth of all moveable goods. The collectors proceeded by swearing an Assessment Committee of four or six of the most loyal men in each vill or parish. Yet an iniquitous distinction was made by the Commissioners appointed, and exemptions of certain goods, chattels, horses, armour, jewels, and robes among the upper classes were as numerous as they were unjust; while among the lower orders no difference was made between free men and the villein tenants of a manor; the principle of taxation being to include all classes indiscriminately, thus degenerating towards that poll-tax which produced the insurrection of the following reign.

The return of 1327, with which this history is most nearly concerned stands thus—

Horburne et Smethwik

	s.	d.	
De Adam de Watecroft	iij		
Madoke Wyr		xviij	
Will 'o Doggyng		xv	
Joh'e de Clodeshale	ij		
Rob'to de Breuera		....	
Will'o le spynnere		viij	
Henr' de Weleye		ix	ob
Will'mo de Birches	iiij		
Joh'e Gregory	v		
Will'o Burel		xviij	
Will'mo de Oumbresley	iij		
Rad'o Godman	ij	vj	
Will'o de Lynhurst	ij		
Rad'o Attegorstes	ij		
Will'o filio Hugonis	ij	vj	
Joh'o de Hasterleye	iij		
Rob'yo atte lee	ij		
Joh'e le fremon	ij		
Summa	xxxix s	vd	ob. pb.

A few words of explanation on the games and amounts appearing in this list of taxpayers will be useful to the average reader:—

(1) John de Clodeshale and John Gregory, the names of the former sub-taxers, re-appear on this list. A Walter de Clodeshale was assessed at 15s. in Birmingham.

(2) William the Spinner is interesting as indicative of the way surnames were derived from trades and callings; as a rule this kind of work was included in the women's labour, hence the feminine form of the word "spinster," used to denote all unmarried women.

(3) Among the surnames derived from places of birth or of residence we note the use of the well-known place.names Weoley (Weleye), Ombersley (Oumbresley), Wyre Piddle (Wyr), Haustley (Hasterleye), all proper names. Similarly constructed surnames from common nouns are those of "William in the birches," "William from the waterfall in the wood" (*Lyn*, waterfall, *hurst*, wood), "Randolph living at the gorse," and "Robert at the lee" (lee, a field or clearing in the wood).

(4) One Randolph is distinguished as the "goodman," or head of a household; and one "John the freeman" was probably but recently manumitted from velleinage on the manor.

(5) "William, son of Hugh." is a personal description, which shows that the fashion of surnames was not yet universal.

(6) The tax paid by "Robert of Breuera" must have been 9d, inasmuch as this is the amount missing to make the "summa" or total cast up to 39s 5½d.—"ob" being a contraction for *obolus* or "halfpenny"; and "pb." for *probata*, "proven" or "audited."

It is interesting to note that at this same taxation the list for the parish of Biddulph contains the name of one "Willmo de Smethe Wyk."

Touching this same taxing Mr. W. B. Bickley, has published through William Downing, Birmingham (1885), INHABITANTS OF BIRMINGHAM, EDGBASTON, AND ASTON, POSSESSING GOODS TO THE VALUE OF TEN SHILLINGS AND UPWARDS IN THE YEAR 1327 a work which was very favourably reviewed in THE MIDLAND ANTIQUARY, Vol. III., p. 153.

* * * * * * * * * * *

A.D. 1333.—Another *Subsidy Roll* is that of 1332-3, granted also for carrying on the Scotch War. The assessors, appointed as before, were sworn on the Holy Evangelists, to make a true return by Michaelmas Day of all goods within and without the houses of their several vills, and to fully tax the goods of all the Commonalty. Again there were exemptions such as saddle-horses, robes of knights and of gentlemen and their wives, vessels of gold and brass, gold buckels and silk sashes, and many other possessions of exactly the nature to demand the payment of an impost according to our ideas. But of the poor, none escaped payment except their goods were appraised at less than 10s. in places like Smethwick, or at a lower figure than 6s. gross value in boroughs like Newcastle, cities like Lichfield, or royal demesnes.

The return for Offlow Hundred commences thus—

HORBORNE ET SMETHEWYKE

	s.	d.	
De Adam de Watecrofte	v	v	qu.
Thom' Fychet	iiij	ix	qu.
Ric'o de Weley		xiij	
Will 'o Bogynge		xv	qu.
Joh'ne de Harseley		ij	ix
Joh'ne le Clerke		ij	ix
Will'o fil' Hugonis	ij	vij	ob.
Sim'oe Atte Ruffynge		xxj	
Joh'e Fremon		xxj	qu.
Henr' in le Lone		ij	j
Rad'o Gorstus		ij	iij
Ric'o de Harseley			xiij
Henr' Atte Ruddynge		xj	
Rad'o Godmon			xv
Will'o in le Byrches		vj	vj
Rob'to in le Lee		v	

The list runs on to include Honnesworth, Pyrye et Parva Barre, it being evident that Handsworth with Perry Barr and Little Barr were all in one collection this time, the whole yielding a "summa" of vj *li.* ix *s.* xj *d.*"

Several names of the former list re-appear, namely—Adam of Watecroft; William Dogging (now written Bogging, the latter spelling most probably being correct, and derived from some connection with bog-lands); John of Haustley, probably a son of the former John, as there is now a Richard of "Harseley," perhaps his brother, the two paying about the same amount as was paid by their deceased father on the same tenancy; William the son of

Hugh, who now pays 1½d. extra; John the freeman who is now paying only 21¼d.—"qu." being a contraction for "quarter of a penny"; Randolph, whose good English name of "Atte Gorstes" is now Latinised into "Gorstus"; and there are found also the former names Randolph the Goodman, William in the Birches, and Robert in the Lee, while Henry of Weoley seems to have been succeeded by his son, Richard of Weoley.

Newer names indicate an accession of population during the past six years. Among these new tenants are Thomas Fitchet, John the Clerk (perchance the learning which gave him this scholarly name had been acquired in the Abbey at Hales Owen), two tenants, Simon and Henry, at a new holding called the Ruddynge (or "ridding" of trees in a fresh clearance amidst the woodlands), and lastly "Henry in the Lone," not improbably an ancestor of the present Lones family still prominent residents in Smethwick.

* * * * * * * * * * * *

A.D. 1340.—The NONA ROLLS make a reference to Smethwick in 1341. These *Nonarum Inquisitiones* consist of the finding upon oath by the parishioners of the value of the ninth lamb, fleece, and sheep in such jurisdictions as "Ecclesia de Horbourn and Smythewyk," as this particular entry is headed; although in cities and boroughs a return of the ninth part of all goods and chattels had to be made. This was in accordance with an Act 14 Edward III., whereby a tax of one-ninth was levied for two years towards the expenditure upon the Scotch and French Wars. The record runs—

"Ricus Sterre and Wills de Smythewyk pochiani ejusdem onant p. nonis ecclie pdce de *liijs. ix*d.," which extended from the contractions of the ancient scribe may be freely rendered—

"Richard Sterre and William of Smethwick, parishioners of the same bear the burden for the *nona* (or ninth) of the aforesaid church at 54s. 9d."—the *Ecclesia* or church, of course, representing the parish. A reference to this Richard Sterre may be found in SALT, Vol. xi., p. 152.

X.—TERRITORIAL RECORDS: MANOR LANDS (1221–1263);

THE ABBEY LANDS (1229–1230).

Allusions are made in Volume IV. of THE SALT COLLECTIONS to both parcels of those Smethwick lands already referred to in Chapters VII. and VIII., namely, the Manorial lands and the Abbey lands.

In Chapter VII. it was stated that certain manorial lands in Smethwick passed from Warine fitz Gerald in 1216 to Thomas de Erdington. Evidently alluding to this same estate is a record of the Salop Assize, held Michaelmas, 1221; from which it will be noted that the case was adjourned till the January following, when the Justices had returned from their circuit.

"The King sent a writ to the Justices that the *Assize of Mordancester* [an Inquiry on the death of an ancestor, when the Sheriff viewed the land in question to recognise whether the ancestor at the time of his death was seized of it, and if defendant was the next heir] which Giles de Erdinton arraigned against Fulk de Breant and Margaret his wife, concerning land in Horeburn and Smethewic, be moved to Westminster, to be heard before them on their return from their *iter*, at a convenient day. It was, therefore, respited to the Octaves of St. Hillary."

This Giles of Erdington had considerable local territorial influence; he had just exercised the right of presentation to Aston Church.

After the lapse of over forty years another record on the Plea Rolls of Henry III., dated June, 1263, refers to this estate in these more explicit terms:—

"An Assize came to make recognition if Thomas de Erdington the father of Giles de Erdington was seized of 100s of rent and 40 acres of wood in Horeburn and Smythewyk when he died; which rent and wood the Abbot of Hales holds. The Abbot appeared by attorney and called to warranty Isabella, the sister and heir of Baldwin de Lisle. Sibilla (*sic*) was to be summoned in co. Northampton to appear on the Morrow of All Souls."

It was mentioned in Chap. VII. that the heiress of Warine fitz Gerald had married Baldwin, Earl of Devon; and that their son Baldwin was styled "de lnsula" or "de l'Isle."

This Isabella (or Sibilla), who was here to give her evidence on these Smethwick lands, was that famous Isabella, Countess of Albemarle and Devon, and *Domina* of the Isle of Wight, which she inherited as heir of the last Baldwin de l'Isle. She governed the Isle of Wight as a petty sovereign.

* * * * * * * * * * * *

In the same volume of THE SALT COLLECTIONS is also an earlier record of that case (quoted in Chap. VIII.) between the Abbot and Margaret Rivers, as it was entered at Westminster, April 29th, 1229:—

"Richard, Abbot of Hales, appeared on the fourth day against Margaret de Rivers in a plea that she should acquit him of services and customs which the capital lord claimed for the tenement which the said Abbot holds of Margaret in Horeburn and Smethewike. As Margaret did not appear she was to be attached to answer on the Sunday after Ascension Day."

This Margaret was daughter, and eventually heiress, to Henry fitz Gerald, the Bishop's tenant, A.D. 1166.

Then there follows a record of the next proceedings at the same Court of Westminster on June 17th following:—

"The Abbot of Hales appeared on the fourth day against Margaret de Rivers, to acquit him of the service and customs which the capital lord claimed for tenements which the Abbot held of her in Holeburn (Harborne) and in Smethwic. Margaret did not appear, and the Sheriff had been commanded to distrain her, but had allowed sureties to be taken for her. He was therefore commanded to distrain her by her lands and chattels, as it was formerly ordered, and to produce her at three weeks from Michaelmas."

A record of proceedings of January 20th, 1299 (? 1230) puts the same complexion on the suit as was suggested in Chapter VIII., as thus:—

"Margaret de Rivers was summoned by the Abbot of Hales to acquit him of the service which Alexander the Bishop of Coventry claimed of him for the free tenement which he holds of her in Horeburn and Smethwick, and of which Margaret is *media ie* mesne tenant) between them, and ought to acquit him. Margaret appeared by her attorney and stated she did not hold the tenement of the Bishop, and therefore could not acquit him of the service owing to the Bishop. As the Abbot did not deny this, he was *in misericordia* for a false claim; but might sue in another form if he wished."

An explanation of Margaret's successful plea was the fact Warine fitz Gerald, who was the actual holder of this Knight's-fee under the Bishop, was alive at this date, and Margaret would therefore hold of him. Harborne and Smethwick must have been a part of her marriage portion.

XI.—RISE OF THE YEOMEN AND THE LANDED GENTRY (1519–1537)

Whatever the Abbey lands may have been originally—and they were not improbably recovered from the "waste" mentioned in Domesday Book by the determined industry and enterprise of the monks—it is clear from the records contained in the preceding chapter that they were now reckoned part and parcel of the manorial estate.

As time went on, and more land was gradually brought into cultivation, the numbers of those owning or holding lands naturally, increased from year to year, or at least from reign to reign. As the sturdy yeoman and the independent freeholder thus slowly became a recognised power in English society, we find as one natural consequence an enormous amount of litigation about their landed possessions and territorial holdings.

Among the records of the reign of Henry VIII. we have two examples of those remarkable ancient legal jugglings whereby the ownership of land was transferred from one individual to the other. These "Fines," as such ponderous and antiquated proceedings were called, were of very ancient practice, and were conducted in this wise: A fictitious action was begun by the purchaser against the vendor of the estate, wherein the latter soon gave in; the case was compromised; a *fine* was paid to the Crown upon the Court giving its consent to the termination of the proceedings; and the record of all this procedure then became the purchaser's title. ["Fines and "Recoveries" were abolished 1833.]

The first case introduces the old local family of Birch, after whom Birchfields was named; and it would appear therefrom that the George Birch named was not in a position to sell more than half the estate, as his mother (re-married) being still alive, retained a life-interest in one moiety of the property. It runs thus, under date 1519:—

Between William Wyllyngton, Gentilman complainant. and George Byrch, *deforciant*, of 2 messuages, 60 acres of land, 20 acres of meadow, 100 acres of pasture, 100 acres of wood, 10 acres of moor, 20 acres of furze and heath, and 10s. rent in Smethewyke in the parish of Harborne

George acknowledged 1 messuage, 30 acres of land, 10 acres of meadow, 50 acres of pasture, 50 acres of wood, 10 acres of moor, 10 acres of furze and heath, and 5s. rent in Smethewyke, parcel of the said tenements, to be the right of William and his heirs; and further granted that the residue which Elizabeth Burton, mother of the said George, held for life, of his inheritance, may remain after her decease to the said William and his heirs; and for this grant William gave £60 sterling. [SALT XI. p. 260]

The second case stands thus, under date 28 Henry VIII.

Between Edward Warner, William Boughton, and Robert Middelmore, complainants, and Ralph Warley, and George Warley, son and heir apparent of the said Ralph. deforciants, of 2 watermills, 1 acre of meadow, and 20 acres of pasture in Horborne in Co. Stafford, and a watermill and 3 acres of meadow in Bremyntham, Hannysworth, Smethwyk, and Horborne in Co. Warwick. The deforciants acknowledged the right of complainants, for which the complainants gave them £30 [SALT XII. p. 185.]

Not only is the spelling of the names Birmingham and Handsworth very unclerkly, but there is also a remarkable vagueness in the description of the locality in question; evidently the place referred to is in the neighbourhood of the boundary brook near Slough Lane, where the three parishes of Birmingham, Handsworth, and Harborne all meet together.

* * * * * * * * * * * *

There is one other record between the date of the events of the last chapter, and those just given. But it is very vague, and somewhat uncertain as to its reference. It is an entry relating to one William Clifford, and his connection with a place named " Smythewyke," which is apparently located in Sussex. This entry is dated "Anno 10 Henry IV." (1409), and purports to record an *Inquisitio Ad Quad Damnum,* or an inquiry held by the Sheriff when any licence of alienation of lands, or the grant of any market, fair, or other privilege was petitioned for. These inquisitionS were frequently put in motion by the religious houses, such as Hales Owen Abbey; they got their peculiar name because they had to decide how far such a grant, as that prayed for, would be to the damage of the Crown or any of its subjects.

XII.—SMETHWICK LANDS PARTED BETWEEN THE PAGET FAMILY AND THE BARONS OF DUDLEY (1536-1593).

We come now to the stirring times of the suppression of the monasteries and of the Reformation which quickly followed it. The part played by Smethwick in these ecclesiastical revolutions was but a very humble one— it was mainly that its acres found new territorial overlords. Yet there is one interesting feature to note; that while the manorial rights went to the newly-important local family of Paget, the Abbey lands, the tithes, and the advowson of Harborne went to further enrich the barons of Dudley; and that during the unsettled reign of Edward VI., the first of these two families made an enemy of Protector Somerset, and the second became the victims of the Protector Northumberland.

The manorial lands of Smethwick remained in the possession of their episcopal lords for about 500 years at least—till 1546 in fact, when the change was effected after the arbitrary manner of those times.

In 1541 Henry VIII. took away from the See of Lichfield and Coventry the "Archdeaconry" of Chester, and erected it into the "Bishopric" of Chester as a separate See. In 1546 the Bishop (Richard Sampson) was compelled by the King to surrender the manor of Longdon, which was conferred upon his favourite Sir William Paget (ancestor to the present Marquis of Anglesea) and the grant was confirmed the following year, 1547, by the Dean and Chapter of Lichfield.

This piece of gross favoritism on the part of "bluff King Hal" possesses considerable local interest. Some years before this event a poor Wednesbury nailer, like another Dick Whittington, set out to seek his fortune in London. Settling in that great capital he pushed his own fortunes till he became a Sergeant at Mace to the City; and as a corporation official he managed to get his son educated in one of the public schools of the city. This son was a man of "excellent parts and great abilities"; and from being one of the Clerks of the Signet he rose to be one of the Principal Secretaries of State. It was on his death bed that Henry VIII. made this William Paget one of his executors, and a member of the Council to his successor, the young Edward VI. Being involved with Procrector Somerset he met with reverses in this reign, but was immediately restored to favour on the accession of Queen Mary. Hence it is that the confirmatory grant to William Lord Paget, K.G., is dated the first year of Mary's reign (1553). The text is no doubt a copy of Henry VIII.'s grant of the baronies of Longdon, Heywood, &c., and will be found in SALT COLLECTIONS xii., p. 194. "Smethwyke" is but one name among dozens of places conveyed to this favorite of fortune, including Burton-on-Trent, Cannock, Tipton, &c., and comprising burgages, cottages, and messuages, by the hundred; 13 water-mills, 6 fulling-mills, 2 wind-mills, 2 horse-mills, 3 iron-mills; orchards, gardens, acres of pasture, meadow and wood by the thousand, and of furze, heath, and common by the ten thousand; fisheries and free-warrens, fairs and markets; tithes of grain, sheaves, hay, wool, flax, and hemp; rents and advowsons; parks of wood and mines of coal and iron; and territorial rights innumerable, among which the manor of Smethwick was but a very insignificant item.

Manor Court Rolls, or the annual record of the transactions of the Court Baron, or of the Court Leet, used to be carefully kept on every manor. These are records of surrenders and grants of tenancy, of encroachments and enclosures, together with a certain amount of civil and criminal jurisdiction, and similar chronicles of manorial government. Those of the episcopal manor of Longdon, of which Smethwick formed part, are complete from the time of Edward I. down to almost modern days, and are preserved in the strong room of the Marquis of Anglesea at Beaudesert. From the SALT COLLECTIONS, vi., pt. 1, p. 244, it is clear that Harborne, and presumably Smethwick, had yearly to appear (representatively) at the Bishop's "view of frankpledge"—that very ancient system of police control exercised through a *pledge* of mutual responsibility for the King's *peace,* the same Court always accepting the assurances of a lord for the good conduct of every one of his landless men.

* * * * * * * * * * * *

Although the manors of Harborne and Smethwick passed into the hands of the Paget family (1547) the Dean and Chapter of Lichfield remained appropriators of the living of Harborne. The great tithes of wheat and grain were commuted for £262, and the smaller (or vicar's) tithes for £514 yearly; the appropriated glebe is 26 acres in extent, and the vicarial 25 acres.

As already noted (p. 22) the right of presentation to Harborne had been exercised by Hales Abbey; the same right was passed on to Sir John Dudley, in whom the Abbey lands became vested after the suppression of the larger monasteries in 1536.

It has been said that these lands had been promised to Edward, Lord Dudley, who was a Knight of the Garter, and a royal favorite. They would have proved a valuable addition to the Dudley barony, as was perceived by the aforesaid Sir John Dudley, who ultimately did secure them.

According to Dugdale's MONASTICON (to which interesting references are made on pp. 24 and 25 of HISTORY OF WEST BROMWICH) the Hales Owen lands produced a gross revenue of £337 10s. 6d., the net value of which was £280 13s. 2d.; as thus:—

		£	s.	d.
In Salop— Hales, manor		133	18	7
Hales, town		9	11	7
Hales, church		30	0	0
St. Kenelm, chapel		10	0	0
Others		10	16	0
		204	16	2
In Staffordshire— Horburne..		5	18	8
Smethwyke		16	0	8
Others		70	15	9
		92	15	1
In Worcestershire ..		40	9	3

Dugdale's MONASTICON thus gives, as the final return in 1539, the gross revenues of Hales Abbey as £337 10s. 6d., and the net value as £280 13s. 2d. On p. 28 of HISTORY OF WEST BROMWICH will be found the surrender of the Abbey's property, the enumeration of the vast possessions showing it to be indeed "goodly and fat" in a high degree.

At this period the barony of Dudley was held by John de Sutton, "lord of Dudley," who had succeeded his father, Edward, Baron of Dudley, K.G., in 1532. He was but a weak-minded individual, deeply entangled in the meshes of the usurer.

He is said to have been "jostled" out of his lands by a distant kinsman, this Sir John Dudley, "sometime Viscount L'Isle, Earl of Warwick, and lastly Duke of Northumberland." It is certain this latter "thirsted after Dudley Castle, the chief seat of the family," and that he managed to gain possession of it (1538) before even he was created Viscount L'Isle (1543). The dissolved Priory of Dudley he also secured in 1540. As to John de Sutton he quickly squandered all his patrimony, and became known as Lord Quondam. Yet when he died in 1553 he received a pompous funeral at St. Margaret's Westminster, accompanied by all heraldic honours. What of his estates remained went to his eldest son, Edward Lord Dudley.

Everyone familiar with history knows of the attainder and fall of John Dudley, Duke of Northumberland, on the accession of Queen Mary. All his forfeited land reverted to the Crown. The confiscated estates were then not slow in finding their way back again to the proper branch of the Dudley family.

Edward, Lord Dudley, son and successor of the spendthrift John, had been in the Scotch War in 1547; and after the surrender of Hume Castle to the English, was made Governor thereof by Protector Somerset. He found favour with the newly-crowned Queen Mary, who, by letters patent, 1554, restored to him and his heirs "all those manors of Harborne and Smethwick, with the advowson of the church of Harborne"; the Priory of Dudley, the tithes of Northfield and Sedgley; divers lands in Dudley, Cradley, and other places; all of which were in the power of the Crown by forfeiture. And later he similarly obtained the lordships of Sedgley, Himley, Willingsworth, and later still followed the parks of Dudley, Rowley, Sedgley, &c., &c. Thus the right line of the barons of Dudley was pretty fully reinstated.

Edward, Lord Dudley, was at one time (1571) suspected of participation in a plot to release Mary, Queen of Scots, from her prison at Chatsworth. It was said that Dudley Castle was especially victualled for the enterprise, but nothing was proved, and seven years later Queen Elizabeth paid a friendly visit to Dudley Castle (1578).* He died in 1586, and was also buried at Westminster.

His son, another Edward de Sutton, Lord of Dudley, held the estates; after whom came Sir Ferdinando Dudley (otherwise Sutton), K.B., in direct succession. He was another spendthrift, and rapidly consumed the family estates. The Smethwick possessions then passed into other hands.

---

* Mr. F D. Lea-Smith, of Hales Owen, still retains in his possession an extremely interesting and valuable set of horse-trappings, which were used by Edward Sutton (Baron Dudley, during the visit of Queen Elizabeth to Dudley, in 1575. The trappings consist of a large saddle-cloth, beautifully worked in gold and silver thread, on a ground of light blue velvet. The stirrups are brass, silvered and gilt, chased and engraved. The headstall is of light blue velvet, with gold and silver thread, together with rein, and crupper treated in a similar manner. To the headstall is attached the original bit which is of iron, chased and engraved, with rosettes silvered and gilt. The Barony of Dudley has been held successively by the families of Fitz Ansculph. Somery, Sutton, Ward, and Lea. The last Baron by writ was Ferdinando Dudley Lea, of Hales Owen Grange, who was summoned to Parliament in 1740 as Baron Dudley, of Dudley Castle.

XIII.—THE CORNWALLIS FAMILY (1616–1648): THE MANOR OF OLDBURY.

On the breaking up of the estates of the Dudley barony; Smethwick seems to have passed into the possession of the Cornwallis family. The main stem of this family was seated in East Anglia; but the collateral branch which appears in these records was located at Oldbury. Two members of the family became Bishops of Lichfield; namely, Frederick Cornwallis in 1750, who was translated to Canterbury in 1768; and James Cornwallis in 1781.

The local branch of this family lived at Blakeley Hall, an ancient moated house near Oldbury: here is the first record of their relationship with the manor of Smethwick.

In the reign of James I., 1616 certain depositions were taken at Walsall on September 12th, in an Exchequer suit, Cornwallis v. Thomas Wilmer,, as to the manors and lands of Dudley, Netherton, Rowley, Harborne, Smethwick, &c., to ascertain (*inter alia*) what amount of rent had been received by Thomas Wilmer (or Willmore—"the husband of my lord's half-sister Anne") since 35th Elizabeth by virtue of a commission of sequestration; and whether there had been any agreement between the said Thomas. Wilmer and Samuel Wilmer his brother, or either of them, and Edward, Lord Dudley, concerning. the said order of sequestration. The evidence is given with some fulness of detail on pp. 110–111 of SALT COLLECTIONS ix;, pt. 2.

No doubt the Cornwallis who was a party to this suit, was the local Worcestershire member of the family residing at Oldbury.

Blakeley Hall, or Blackley Hall, according to Reeves' HISTORY OF WEST BROMWICH, written. in 1836, was. "the ancient manor house of Oldbury and was surrounded by a moat"—"it was taken down 68 years. ago, and was said: to be 300 years old. The present building is near the site of the old, and is occupied by Mr. John Downing as the Farm House. March 1st, 1829, I saw the moat complete and full of water."

* * * * * * * * * * * *

This period of our Record in which it becomes involved with the records of Oldbury may serve as an opportunity for making a rapid survey of the history of the latter town; for notwithstanding the fact that Oldbury and Smethwick are located in different counties, their relationships have always been as intimate socially, as their physical contiguity would naturally warrant.

Nash's WORCESTERSHIRE gives (Vol. I.,; pp. 508—535) an exhaustive history of Hales Owen, and facing page 490 is a view of the ruins of the Abbey as they appeared when the work was published in 1781. On p. 521 we may read—

OLDBURY, a manor situate in the Shropshire part of Hales parish * * is thus described by Mr. Erdeswick * * 'Tame, the same river which gives its name to Tamworth, takes its first beginning about Oldbury * * the name of Oldbury, or Borough, an old Saxon word signifying an old place or town.' * * * In enumerating such remains of the Romans as occur within the parish of Hales. I observed that Oldbury denoted a Roman camp or station, and that a Roman road called the Portway passed very near [refer back to p. 10 of these Records]. Mr. Erdeswick is very right in saying that Old-borough points out an old place or town of account, but the same word also signifies an ancient fortified spot, where a camp or barrows still remain. No vestiges of this fort appear now at Oldbury; but a very aged inhabitant informed me that in his father's time there were apparent ruins of a town near a certain pasture called the Castle Leasow; and that a castle was said to have stood at the lower end of the said Leasow near the Well Hill. He added that a Causeway still remains in the lands of one Harold directly leading to the Castle Leasow. * * I find a general tradition that a great town anciently stood here which extended from the *present village* to the Castle Leasow lying under the Burg Hill. * * I could not discover any marks of buildings.

This does not seem to have been a manor distinct from Hales till after the dissolution of the monastery. From Henry III's reign down to Henry VIII's Oldbury occurs in Hales court-rolls as a vill or township dependent on Hales Owen; nor is it styled a 'manor' in the grant to Sir John Dudley; but being excepted in the deed of conveyance from Sir Robert Dudley to Blount and Tuckey * * and likewise excepted in their deed of sale to Sir John Lyttleton, it remained, as I conjecture, in the possession of the Dudley family—who, in all likelihood, procured a royal grant for holding a court-leet here. [The conveyance alluded to was one by *Fine* dated *4 and 5 Philip and Mary* to Thomas Blount and George Tuckeye in consideration of 190 marks paid for WARLEY WIGORN, among other places; a history of which manor occurs on pp. 522–524 of Nash.]

Nash is very vague as to the conveyance of Oldbury Manor to the Cornwallis family. He says—How it passed from the Dudleys to the Cornwallis's I am to seek; but anno 1648 Charles Cornwallis, Esq., a younger branch of the lords Cornwallis of Suffolk occurs lord of Oldbury, and as such held a Court-leet and baron here on the 29th of April that year. He died and left issue by Elizabeth his wife, the daughter of—. Calmore, Esq., two daughters.

It would appear that Oldbury was next possessed by "two joint lords of this manor"—Anthony Mingey, Esq., and William Featherstone, Esq., who had respectively married Anne and Frances, the two daughters of Charles Cornwallis. Presently, as Mingey had no issue, the whole devolved on Frances Featherstone, who left two daughters and co-heiresses, Anne, the wife of William Addington, and Elizabeth, the wife of—. Paston. No issue proceeding from the latter, Addington's two daughters next inherited Oldbury—Frances, who married Christopher Wright, of Coventry, gentleman; and Anne who married Richard Grimshaw, gentleman, joint owners of the lordship. Grimshaw left one son who died unmarried; of him Christopher Wright purchased a moiety of the manor, and became sole lord of the manor of Oldbury, although he had no child to succeed to the honour.

Oldbury Chapel appears to have been founded so late as 1529, at the expense of the principal inhabitants of the hamlet—perhaps with some of the spoils of Hales Owen Abbey. It was dedicated to St. Nicholas, and seems to have been erected on copyhold land, "for 24, Henry VIII., William Feldon, *alias* Carpenter, of Oldbury, entered into a bond with £10 penalty to Arthur Robstart, Esq., Lawrence White of Rowley, John Parke of Langley, and Edmund Darby of Oldbury, their heirs and executors; that he will not henceforth make any claim or title to the Chapel Croft, or any parcel thereof, by virtue of any copy of Court-roll touching the same; but only to hear God's service in the said Chapel, as other tenants or inhabitants of Oldbury do."

This was prior to the Reformation, and "God's service " here referred to would be according to the old rites of Romanism as practised in England.

Nash continues:—

"There being no fixed salary or endowment belonging to this chapel from its first foundation till Queen Anne's Bounty was procured; the Dissenters got possession soon after the Revolution (1688), and held it till Bishop Lloyd's time [William Lloyd, a celebrated divine, and Almoner to Queen Anne, was Bishop of St. Asaph first, then of Lichfield (1692), and was translated to Worcester, 1699] who ousted them, and notwithstanding the pretence of its standing on copyhold ground, he consecrated both the Chapel and Cemetery" [or graveyard].

By aid of Queen Anne's Bounty Fund lands to the annual value of £14 were purchased, a Mr. Thorpe was licensed to the cure on the presentation of the Vicar of Hales Owen.

The names of Parish curates since 1660 are given as—

>Thos. Wright, 28th July, 1663.
>Char. Osborn, 29th November, 1665.
>John Muckross, 30th September, 1674.
>Thos. Stinton, 28th October, 1724.
>Jos. Hipkiss, 15th January, 1728.

Reeves gives the name of the Rev. George Sproston as "the present curate" (1836): he adds that " there are in Oldbury also one Presbyterian meeting, two Methodist, one Baptist, and one Primitive Methodist. Oldbury Court House was erected in A.D. 1816."

This is as much as need be quoted with regard to Oldbury. Nash gives a history of Cradley (p. 525), and of Ludley (p. 527).

XIV.—THE PERIOD OF THE CIVIL WAR: THE FOLEY FAMILY

During the period in which the manor of Smethwick was held by the family of Cornwallis of Oldbury, the great Civil Wars broke out.

How far Smethwick was affected by the numerous stirring incidents of that memorable internecine strife can only be guessed at after taking a glance round at the active operations known to have actually transpired in its immediate vicinity.

Keeping at bay the countless traditions which always cluster around the name of Oliver Cromwell—even that relating to the leaguer of Weoley Castle; and the more romantic one, that "Blakeley Hall gave shelter to King Charles when he was being pursued by Cromwell"—the more commonly authenticated facts in the history of this locality may be briefly recapitulated.

But, first of all, before the outbreak of domestic hostilities was even contemplated, we have a record of the year 1640 relating to the war footing of Smethwick. It would appear that in this year Charles I. levied an army to suppress the Scotch Covenanters; the men mustered were partly of the old trained bands, and also consisted partly of men specially impressed for this service. A list of local names serving in this army is given on p. 113 of HISTORY OF WEST BROMWICH. On the said *Muster Roll* appears the following names, which more closely come within the scope of this history:—

	Traine.	*Presse.*
HARBOROUGHE AND SMETHICKE	Edward Hunt. John Hunt.	George Parsons. Raphe Trigge.

This *Muster Roll* also acquaints us as to the providing of the horses for carrying the ammunition; and in the "Seasdon Hundred" we note:—

MR. ROBYN'S DIVICON [division.]   li. s. d.

Tipton   2. 2 geldings baught of Henry Partridge; price 11 10 0
Rowley Regis   3. 1 gelding baught of Wm. Darby;   price   5   0 0
Wolverhampton   4. 1 gelding baught of John Dillway;   price   5   0 0

Then coming to the War, or rather to the very eve of it, in 1642, towards the close of the month of October, Charles I. passed through Smethwick on his way from Shrewsbury to Edgehill, where the first blows of the Civil War were struck.

On April 3rd, 1643, Prince Rupert attacked Birmingham while opening up a passage between Oxford and York. He made his headquarters at the Ship Inn, Camp Hill, being in command of a force of over 2,000 men. Birmingham, having declared against the King, set up a rude earthwork at Camp Hill, under the command of Captain Greaves. The Royalists prevailed, however, crossed the Rea, broke down the barricades in Digbeth, and pursued Captain Greaves to the far (or Smethwick) side of the town. Here Captain Greaves made a stand, taking up a position in Shireland Lane (now Waterloo Road), and, from the encounter, the Earl of Denbigh was carried away mortally wounded. So that the last and most deadly blows in the Battle of Birmingham were struck on Smethwick soil. The day following Prince Rupert passed on through Perry Barr, resuming his march to Lichfield.

On Monday morning, July 10th, 1643, Queen Henrietta Maria, having the preceding night slept at Caldmore, Walsall (on her return from Holland), continued her journey; passing West Bromwich, she came through Smethwick, and then on to King's Norton, her own private manor, where a lodging was provided for her reception in the ancient timber-built house adjoining the churchyard. Besides an escort of numerous cavaliers, the Queen's following included 3,000 horsemen, 30 companies of foot soldiers, a long line of baggage wagons, and a train of artillery. A camp was formed that night on the village green, King's Norton, and next morning the march was resumed till the Queen met her royal husband at Kineton, after passing one night at Shakespeare's house, New Place, Stratford.

Staffordshire busied itself intensley in the earlier stages of this great military struggle. Sir William Brereton, the renowned Parliamentary leader, complains of the "foreign forces of Shropshire, Wales, and Lancashire" flocking into Staffordshire in such numbers that he was unable to provide officers for their proper command.

The Grand Jury of Staffordshire in July, 1644, declared the county was "overtaxed beyond the rest," and that men had been so largely withdrawn that there were not sufficient left to gather in the hay and the harvest. It was in this same year that King Charles, being posted at Bewdley (just before he so suddenly marched towards Oxford, and defeated Waller at Copredy Bridge) sent 3,000 horse to relieve Dudley Castle, which was then being besieged by the Earl of Denbigh (son of the Earl previously mentioned).

"Tinker" Fox ("Tinker" was a name of contempt applied to him by his enemies—he was really a Walsall manufacturer) held Edgbaston House with a strong garrison of Parliamentarians; from which he entered Stourton Castle (1644), and a little later took prisoner Sir Thomas Littleton, of Frankley. In October of the same year, Royalists from Dudley Castle and Worcester made an attack on Edgbaston House, but without success.

On 17th June, 1645, after the defeat at Naseby, the King stayed at Bewdley; but Ticknell Palace had suffered so much at the hands of Tinker Fox that His Majesty was obliged to sleep at the Angel Inn, in Lord Street. Hartlebury Castle was then being strongly fortified, and Colonel Sandys impressed men from all around to assist in the work. In the previous month, May, the King had marched into Droitwich with his own regiment of foot and horse guards only, the rest of the army lying that night (the 11th) at Bromsgrove. His Majesty stayed at Droitwich till the Wednesday, and meanwhile Prince Rupert sat down before Hawkesley House, King's Norton, belonging to Mr. Middlemore. On this Wednesday the King came to the leaguer before Hawkesley, whereupon the garrison declined to fight when they saw him; they yielded up the house on condition they were spared the insults of the soldiers; yet the house was pillaged and then set on fire.

In 1645 (August 5th) it was complained that the Governor of Dudley Castle had lately executed one, and the Governor of Hartlebury Castle had threatened to execute another of Colonel Fox's soldiers; and reprisals were threatened.

Towards the close of 1645 a garrison was erected at Wrottesley House. Rushall Hall was taken and re-taken more than once. An indecisive skirmish was fought at Dudley, the Parliamentarians advancing to the attack from Bromwich Heath. In May, 1646, Dudley Castle quietly surrendered to the Parliament, and so far as Staffordshire is concerned, affairs quietened down a little in this locality—Worcestershire, however, as is well known, remained the scene of important operations to the very close of the Civil Wars.

* * * * * * * * * * * *

From the Cornwallis family, "Harborne and Smethwick" passed into the hands of Philip Foley, Esq.

The founder of this family was Richard Foley, of Dudley, yeoman, who, in 1616, was aged 36 years when he gave evidence as to the value of the Dudley lands (of the barony) in that lawsuit which has been previously mentioned, Cornwallis v. Thomas Wilmer. The baronial estates of Edward, Lord Dudley, were in the hands of receivers as early as 1593, under a commission of sequestration. It is interesting to note here as an illustration of a very common experience in this mundane sphere, that as the Sutton family falls, the Foleys rise. Richard Foley was the son of Richard Foley, nailer, of Dudley, where he was baptised 28th March, 1580. He died at Stourbridge, 16th July, 1657, aged 77. His father's will was proved at Worcester, 1600.

Having amassed a large fortune by his ironworks, his son, Philip, was enabled to purchase Smethwick from the Cornwallis's, and to become a territorial magnate of some consequence.

Philip Foley, Esq., of Prestwood, purchased from Wortley Whorwood, Esq., Stourton Castle and the manor of Kinver. (See HISTORY OF WEST BROMWICH, p. 57.) For the industrial eminence of the Foley family, see also pp. 47 and 54 of the same HISTORY; the romantic story of the rise of the Foleys is given in the WEDNESBURY WORKSHOPS, pp. 21 and 22.

It was this Philip Foley who sheltered the Rev. R. Hilton when, by the Act of Uniformity, he was ejected from the living of West Bromwich in 1662, and who made this Independent minister his domestic chaplain.

The other members of the Foley family (after Philip) are not concerned with the history of Smethwick. But a brief note on the family pedigree may not be out of place considering the local importance of the Foleys:—

In succession to Philip Foley we have

(1) Thomas Foley, of Whitley Court; succeeded by

(2) Thomas Foley, M.P. for Co. Worcester. created Baron Foley 1712, and died January, 1733.

    2nd son, Paul Foley, Speaker of House of Commons, 1695. another son, Philip Foley, M.P. of Prestwood, Staffordshire.

(3) Thomas Foley, 2nd Baron Foley (and son of the 1st), died 1766, when the title became extinct.

Then, immediately, Thomas Foley, of Stoke Edith, descended from Paul Foley, the Speaker, was created Baron Foley of Kidderminster in 1766, in whose family the revived title still remains.

XV.—STUART PERIOD: DESCENT OF THE MANOR TO THE HINCKLEY AND REYNOLDS FAMILIES: THE JENNINGS FAMILY: SHIRELAND HALL.

Before resuming our history of the descent of the Manor, a few odd records here lay claim to chronological precedence. They are but three in number, of the years 1653, 1662, and 1664 respectively, as followeth:—

(1) Mr. Kenward (p. 33) recounts a local example of the *marriage law* procedure under the Cromwellian Act, which made it a civil contract merely. It is the record of the marriage of Robert Povey, of Harborne, "naylor," to "Alis Grainger of ye said parish," who were declared husband and wife "at Hampstedd Hall upon ye 10 day of March, 1653, according to ye Act," before Sir John Wyrley, Knt., Justice of the Peace; and duly registered by John Millward, of Harborne—the said registrar is supposed to have lived either at Tennel Hall, or at Welsh House.

It is worthy of note, too, that in this same year (1653) Charles Cornwallis, Esq., is named among the Sheriff's list of freeholders in Smethwick.

(2) In 1662, Charles II. was granted a hearth-tax of so much money on every fire-place; as usual, in those days, the collection was farmed out to the highest bidder, and yielded his Majesty some £200,000 a year. The return of 2s. a hearth on 132 hearths in Harborne and Smethwick accounts for £13 4s. At the "better ordering and collecting" of this hearth-duty in 1663, the return for Birmingham discloses 414 hearths (including both those liable to pay and those exempt), of which number 360 were taxed, the house of the celebrated Humphrey Jennings being credited with 25. From Aston the total of 47 was made up entirely of 40 in the Hall and 7 in the Parsonage. Edgbaston paid on 37, of which 22 were in the Hall. Erdington paid on 27, and Sutton Coldfield on 67, of which two houses of the Willoughby family paid for 23. Coleshill, including 30 hearths in the house of Dame Mary Digby paid for 125 fire-places.

(3) At the *Herald's Visitation* of Staffordshire 1663-4 there were disclaimed at public assizes held at Stafford, in the August of the latter year, among numerous other pretenders to armorial distinction, the following local claimants:—

HARBORNE AND SMETHWICK	Wm. Hunt. Wm. Birch. Tho. Parker. Mr. Rowton. Tho. Milward.

The family names of Birch and Milward have been mentioned in these Records before. As to the Hunt family, we find one "William Hunt of Smethwick," who was apparently a yeoman, mentioned in a lease of the year 1605 (HISTORY OF WEST BROMWICH p. 66). The Harborne parish registers record the marriage of "Miss Jane Hunt of Smethwick" to "Benjamin Greaves, of Moseley Hall, Esq., ye 9th of July, 1691." Another member of this prominent family, recorded at Harborne, was "Beata, who died in 1714, daughter of William Hunt, of The Ruck of Stones, Smethwick, and wife of Henry Hinckley."

* * * * * * * * * * * *

From Philip Foley "Harborne and Smethwick" were purchased respectively about the year 1710 by George Birch, Esq., and Mr. Henry Hinckley.

According to Shaw's history, Thomas Birch, Esq. (son of George Birch, Esq.) possessed Harborne in 1730; and John Hinckley (son of Henry Hinckley) had Smethwick.

Shaw's STAFFORDSHIRE II., p. 125, contains the following:—

> Having already given as much of the former bistory of this manor with the above as we are able, down to a late possessor, Mr. John Hinckley, who died June 19th, 1740, æt. 47 (as appears by his monumental inscription below with others of his family there and above ported) I shall briefly observe that it is now the joint property of Mr. John Reynolds, of Shireland Hall, which he has lately rebuilt, and of Mr. John Baddely, of Albrighton, co. Salop.

This quotation naturally brings with the purview of our history an allusion to Shireland Hall, and its successive occupants, the Jennings and Reynolds families.

But first of all it may be noted that among the wills proved at Lichfield in the year 1552 was one of a certain "Robert Maslam of Shireland"— wherever that may have been. Then to continue the extract from Shaw—

> Shireland Hall, which we have before mentioned as the residence of the other lord of the manor, Mr. Reynolds, was in Plot's time (1686) the seat of one Jennins whose arms are engraved on his map, viz., Arg. three bottles Sable. These are the same as in Wolverhampton Church for Stephen Jennings (merchant tailor and Lord Mayor of London), a native of that town, who founded a free school there.

For the foundation of Wolverhampton Grammar School this same Sir Stephen (who was lord mayor in 1508) obtained two Letters Patent from Henry VIII., dated respectively 22nd September, 1512, and 12th April, 1513. In the ancient Parish Church of that town is a quaint western gallery, erected in 1610 by the Merchant Taylours' Guild. The great Jennings family of litigious fame are closely connected with the whole of this district; their estates and possessions included Aston Hall, Erdington Hall, Wednesbury Hall, Aston Furnaces, Duddeston Mill, all in this part of the country, to say nothing of that branch resident at Shireland Hall, Smethwick.

The will of Humphrey Jennings, of Erdington, dated 1689, is a very formidable document; and amongst the numerous legacies therein, is a bequest of forty shillings to his "cousin Dorothy Parkes." Whether this is the great benefactress of Smethwick or not, cannot be determined. But it is worthy of note that almost a century previous to the benefaction of Dorothy Parkes to the hamlet of Smethwick, there was another Dorothy Parkes who left a "charity" (besides presenting the silver communion plate) to Wednesbury Church, in the year 1629; and she was a daughter of Richard Greaves, of Moseley Hall (another local family to which allusion has just been made), who had married Richard Parkes, of Wednesbury.

Nothing further need be said here of the Jennings family, except that in Smethwick there are still representatives of this famous family who are claimants to the disputed estate.

To bring the history of Shireland Hall up to date, here is a quotation from a recent speech by Mr. Henry Summerton:

> Shireland Hall stood on the land east of the road now bearing that name. The farm buildings in its rear have but recently been demolished. It is within the memory of middle-aged inhabitants when the country around this house was fields and woods, luxuriating in high grass and extensive shrubs, amongst which lovers strayed and children rambled; and the primrose and violet, bluebell and anemone, and other flowers starred grove and dell. After being used as a private residence, Shireland Hall became a seminary for boys, and many eminent men received the rudiments of their education here. It afterwards became a school for girls, and is now a thing of the past, its fair site being occupied by the homes of the artisan

XVI.—THE HINCKLEYS: AND MR. JOHN BADDELEY.

As previously noted, Smethwick was purchased from Philip Foley by Henry Hinckley (1710) and had passed into the possession of his son, John Hinckley, by 1732.

In 1730 was published a topographical work, entitled MAGNA BRITANNIA ET HIBERNIA; in its article referring to Harborne we read (Vol. v., p. 19)— "From this place we are indebted to Mr. Henry Hinckley for the account of the manors, and do hereby return him our thanks, though unknown" Presently we read that "the manor of Smeethwick is the possession of John Hinckley, the son of Henry"; that "Henry Hinckley, gent., with George Birch, Esq., and Mrs. Dorothy Parkes" raised £200 to increase the living of Harborne vicarage; and further, that Henry Hinckley gave also £100 towards a charity school for "Harburne and Smeethwick, where boys and girls are taught to read and write without any charge to their parents, and learn the Church Catechism; there are seldom fewer children thus taught than fifty, and there is a good schoolmaster to teach them. Thus far Mr. Hinckley goes"—acknowledges the compiler of the book.

The testimony of a mural tablet in Harborne Church is to the following effect:—

"Under this tomb lies the body of Henry Hinckley, who departed this life December 22, 1732, *aet* 73. He was a man charitable, benevolent, and given to hospitality: A good husband, friend, and neighbour."

Of his first wife, Beata Hinckley, already mentioned as dying in 1714, it is recorded on her memorial stone that—

"She was married to Henry Hinckley, of The Beeks, in Smithwick. gent., fourth son of John Hinckley, rector of Northfield, D.D., by whom she had John, her only son, who survived her."

John Hinckley, of The Beeks, died 19 June, 1740, at the age of 47; and in the same year, 18 August, died in her 40th year, Esther, his wife, a daughter of William Booth Allestrey, of Witton Hall; they left no issue.

The only surviving representative of the family then left was Henry Hinckley, brother of John, and son of the aforesaid Henry by his second wife, Elizabeth, daughter of Robert Boyse, Esq., of Welsborne, co. Warwick.

Under date 1769, William Hutton, the historian of Birmingham, says, in his LIFE:—

"I also made two purchases of Dr. Hinckley at Smethwick. One, the Shire Ash, thirteen acres for £250. I sold the timber for £126, and let the land for thirteen guineas." (A footnote to the Second Edition, issued by Hutton's daughter in 1817, adds "This I sold June 3, 1800, for £500.") "The other, Spring Dale, eight acres, for which I gave £100. This was under a lease for ninety-nine years, twenty-four of which were to come at £3 per annum. It now lets for ten guineas." (A second footnote adds—"I sold this in May, 1803, for £400.")

(It may here be recalled that it was from the confines of Smethwick that the garrulous Hutton first caught sight of his beloved Birmingham, in 1741. As a poor wayfaring lad, seeking his fortune, he tramped into Walsall one market-day, July 14th, from Lichfield; when his feet being excessively sore, he "rubbed them with a little beef-fat begged of a Walsal butcher, and found instant relief" Finding no work there, such as he had been accustomed to upon a stockinger's frame, he passed on his way. "I wondered in my way from Walsal to Birmingham to see so many blacksmiths' shops, in many of them one, and sometimes two, ladies at work, all with smutty faces and thundering at the anvil. Struck with the novelty"—he found they were nailers, as were the majority of workers in this locality then. Then he writes, "Upon Handsworth Heath I had a view of Birmingham" and "was charmed with its beauty." But that was a hundred and fifty years ago !)

Originally the Hinckleys were a Birmingham family. The name occurs there in the taxation lists of 1327. From them, no doubt, was named that human rookery in the centre of the city, known as the "Inkleys"; a slum near John Bright Street recently demolished, and which was probably part of their burgage tenements in olden times. In later times they seem to have taken up their residence at The Beeks, Smethwick, when rural surroundings first began to be preferred to town residences, and when Smethwick was regarded as a pleasant suburb of Birmingham.

From the Hinckleys the manor passed into the possession of two owners —Mr. Reynolds, who took up his residence in Shireland Hall, and Mr. John Baddeley, a worthy of whom more anon, dividing Smethwick between them.

As to the name Beeks, where the Hinckleys resided, it is evidently derived from the Teutonic "Beck" or "Batch," signifying a *brook* or *rill;* of which there were here several in the vicinity in the era before the surface had been disturbed for manufacturing and building purposes.

Shaw says (1798) the Hinckleys sold this residence to Mr. Hanson. But Mr. Summerton, speaking of its more recent history, says—

The Beaks, in Bearwood Road, near the Bear Inn, is embowered by trees of noble growth, There are four magnificent chestnuts apparently planted at the four corners of a plot of grass, probably a bowling green at one time. This house has been severally owned or occupied by Spriggs, Smith, Astbury, &c.

* * * * * * * * * * * *

When Shaw wrote his HISTORY OF STAFFORDSHIRE in 1798, he was careful to tell us that part of the manor of Smethwick was in the possession of that ingenious optician and clockmaker, John Baddeley. As the county historian does not hesitate to devote considerable space to this worthy, the whole of Shaw's comments may be reproduced here:

Under this head of Smethwick, I am happy in the opportunity of inserting a few anecdotes of that self-taught and deserving mechanic. Those persons who are in possession of his admirable timepieces, and reflecting telescopes, will be gratified with a short account of one who has so much contributed by his labours to their convenience or amusement. Mr. John Baddely was born at Tong, in the county of Salop, September 21, 1727, and, after receiving a common school education in his native village, was put to work by his father, and followed for some years the humble calling of a blacksmith; but, being averse to *Shoeing of horses,* and feeling himself as he thought, capable of a better employment, at the age of 18 he quitted his father's business and commenced watch and clock making, an undertaking in which, by dint of superior talents, aided by great integrity. he soon established himself, and acquired the degree of reputation which he still continues to enjoy. About the year 1752 (having received some very good instructions in the principles from Mr Benjamin Talbot, the present schoolmaster of Cannock, who then lived at Newport), he first turned his attentions to optics, and constructed reflecting telescopes of uncommon excellence. In his *specula* the parabolic was preferred to the usual spherical figure, from which he conceives material advantages in point of light and distinctness are obtained. The general workmanship of his instruments is marked no less by an attention to neatness and accuracy, than to the best mechanical principles. His superiority as a clockmaker will be sufficiently told, *for some ages to come,* by the numerous domestic and turret clocks *substantially* constructed by him, in every part of the country within many miles of Albrighton, where he has long resided, Those who are desirous to appreciate his merits as an optician may be politely accommodated with the examination of reflectors of large size in the possession of Dr. Withering, of Edgbaston, and my friend, P. T. Hinckes, of Tettenhall Wood, Esq. Those upon a smaller scale, by the same artist, may be found in the hands of most persons fond of philosophical pursuits in the counties of Stafford and Salop.

XVII—THE CHAPELRY OF SMETHWICK—WHAT IS ITS STATUS AS A PARISH?

The manorial history of Smethwick has now been traced to its close. No manorial courts or customs have been in existence here within the range of living memory; nor is there any copyhold land to be found within the boundaries of the township.

But as the *manor* of Smethwick fades from view, the *parish* of Smethwick comes gradually into sight. And as there has always been some vague uncertainty as to the status of the manor, so also the legal standing of the parish calls for more than ordinary examination before any satisfactory settlement can be arrived at upon so delicate a point of civic jurisprudence.

First, then, the facts of the case must be examined.

Dorothy Parkes, of Birmingham, daughter of Thomas Parkes, by her indenture, dated May 30, 1719, gave certain lands, tenements, &c., of the yearly value of £84 15s. 0d. to the building of a chapel at Smethwick, within the parish of Harbourn; and by her last will and testament, dated Sept. 20, 1723, and by a codicil to the same, April 8, 1725, appointed a proper minister, curate, or chaplain to officiate therein, all of which was confirmed by Richard Smallbrook, bishop of Lichfield and Coventry, and allowed to be called Parkes's Chapel, 1732, when he consecrated and made it a burial place. In an old book of her accounts (says Shaw) is the following:—

"My sister Whiting's grave being raised (upon the account of water coming into it) the arch came above the floor of the chancel, so that there was a necessity of raising the chancel; which being done with the better sort of quarry, for the more decency, about the communion table, the charge, with new rails, &c., amounted to £8 13s. 4d., towards which I contributed £2 10s. I also gave a communion table, which cost £1, and a broad cloth carpet, with gold galoome, which came to £2 15s., and a damask table cloth, with a napkin, came to 7s. The Gravestone cost £2 3s. To the poor of Harbourn and Smithwick £4."

The foundation of 1732 was apparently nothing more than a "chapel of ease."

Sir R. Phillmore, in the II. volume of his ECCLESIASTICAL LAW, devotes Chapter III. to "Chapels," and in the course of it says—

Of chapels subject to a mother church some are merely chapels of ease, others chapels of ease and parochial. But *quære* if they can be both at the same time. A chapel merely of ease is that which is not allowed a font at its institution, and which is used only for the ease of the parishioners in prayers and preaching (sacraments and burials being received and performed at the mother church) and commonly where the curate is removable at the pleasure of the parochial minister * * where the minister of the mother church has the cure of them both, yet he exercises the cure there by a vicar not perpetual, but temporary, &c. * * A parochial chapel is that which has the parochial rights of christening and burying; and this differs in nothing from a church but in the want of a rectory and endowment. For the privileges of administering the Sacraments (especially that of baptism) and the office of burial, are the proper rites and jurisdiction that make it no longer a depending chapel of ease, but a separate parochial chapel. * * Till the year 1300 * * If it could be proved that any chapel had a custom for free baptism and burial, such place was adjudged to be a parochial church. * * Express care was taken at the ordination of them that there should be no allowance of font or bells. * * The Church Building Acts contain * * provisions that those which have reputed townships or districts assigned to them may, on being properly endowed, with consent of bishop, patron, and incumbent of parish, be made independent of the parish church, and their township or district may be made a parish.

THE CHAPELRY DISTRICT OF SMETHWICK 47

The Registers of Smethwick disclose this subsidiary status. At first the entries in these Registers are intermixed, as was usual in those days of official laxity; Baptisms, Marriages, and Burials being found intermingled together without any attempt at classification. But by 1743, and on November 14th of that year, appears the last entry of a marriage by banns (and in 1758 the last marriage even by license) for nearly a century; and it was not till 1840 that marriages were resumed in Smethwick Chapel under a general license to the edifice from the Bishop of the diocese. At least this is what is gathered from the official registers; although many old inhabitants have declared that the ceremony of the marriage service was performed for them in their own chapel, while the record thereof was made in the registers at Harborne Church. From this it seems that while the Vicar of Harborne could not with decency withhold the right to perform baptism and burials on the spot, he took every means to guard himself and his successors against loss of fees by throwing obstacles in the way of marriages being performed at Smethwick in preference to Harborne. The status of Smethwick as a "parochial chapel" was thus denied; and indeed no real cure of souls was formally attached to the chapelry till the year 1840 alluded to, when an Ecclesiastical district was legally assigned to it.

A chronology of the formation of Ecclesiastical districts in Smethwick runs as follows:—

1840.—Constitution of the Chapelry of Smethwick.

1842.—Notification in *London Gazette* (of October 28th) of the constitution of the Parish of North Harborne, taken out of (Smethwick really, but legally out of) Harborne proper, and carrying with it the tithes belonging thereto. This area of North Harborne is what is now known as comprising the Ecclesiastical parishes of Holy Trinity and St. Paul's, West Smethwick. The other moiety of Smethwick—and it is as near as possible half the area of the present local government district—still constituted the Chapelry district of Smethwick.

1852.—St. Matthew's Ecclesiastical district was mapped out, but not given a legal status without the tacit consent of Harborne mother parish.

1856.—In June of this year the formal boundaries of St. Matthew's parish were finally settled; but although carved out of the Chapelry of Smethwick the formal assent and acquiesence of the Vicar of Harborne had to be given and certified. Still, the patronage of the new church was vested in the Incumbent of Smethwick, as was only just and equitable, Smethwick and not Harborne having contributed towards the cost of establishing the new church and district.

1892.—St. Mary's district was formed out of "the Parish, sometime the Chapelry District of Smethwick" from the wording of which official notice it will be observed that Smethwick had at last been legally constituted a "parish" although this had occurred only a few months previous to the *Gazette* announcement from which the quotation is taken—but for this, however, the consent of Harborne was not now necessary. The official designation of the new parish stamps its origin and descent with no uncertainty—it is described as "the District Chapelry of St. Mary, Smethwick."

1893.—The parish or Ecclesiastical district of St. Michael's (Crockett's Lane) was formed with the consent of the Vicars of the Old Church, Holy Trinity*, and St. Matthew's, out of their respective parishes, and without any reference whatever to Harborne. At the present time (1896) the mother church or chapel of Smethwick has yet another daughter parish in prospect, of which St. Chad's Mission is the visible nucleus.

Till the Act of some quarter of a century ago, the incumbent of Smethwick was known as a Perpetual Curate; and the official residence was a Parsonage. In 1840 the parochial work and jurisdiction of the holder of the benefice was legally set forth, and a full claim upon the ministerial fees was then granted. Two private Acts of Parliament have been obtained for the regulation of the Smethwick benefactions, viz. :—

1815.—An Act for the more effectual administration of its charities.

1841.—An Act to enable the Trustees of the Chapelry of Smethwick to demise coal and other mines and to grant Building Leases, &c., &c. (This mining land was not within the confines of Smethwick, but just beyond its borders at Cakemore and Causeway Green on the Hales Owen side. Some 30 acres there have been sold and the proceeds very profitably invested: 8 acres or thereabouts are still held by the Trustees.)

---

* St. Stephen's mission is now forming a new Ecclesiastical district from the parish of Holy Trinity.

XVIII.—THE FOUNDING OF SMETHWICK CHAPEL, 1719.

Dorothy Parkes was the daughter of Thomas Parkes, of Smethwick, and lived a single life as she never "thought fit " to marry. She was of a highly benevolent disposition, as is abundantly evidenced by her benefactions to the Vicarage of Harborne, to the Chapelry of Smethwick, the Free Schools, and by the various Doles she set up. According to the Register of Harborne, "The Pious and Charitable Mrs. Dorothy Parkes, Foundress of ye Chappel of Smithwick, was buried January 14th, 1727"; but her body was afterwards removed from Harborne Church to the Smethwick Chapel, which she founded. A portrait of the lady, painted by a pupil of Sir Peter Lely, is still preserved in the Parsonage House.

By Indenture, 1719, she vested property in the hands of Trustees for the erection of a Chapel, School, and Parsonage House at Smethwick.

Here is a copy of the full text of the Document:—

This Indenture Tripartite made the thirtieth day of May in the fifth year of the Reign of our Sovereign Lord George by the grace of God of Great Brittain, France and Ireland King Defender of the Faith, &c., Anno Domino One Thousand Seven Hundred and nineteen Between Dorothy Parkes of Birmingham in the County of Warwick, Spinster of the first part, Charles Blackham and Isaac Spooner both of Birmingham aforesaid Ironmongers of the second part, and Sir Charles Holt of Aston juxta Birmingham in the County of Warwick, Baronet, Sir Henry Gough of Perry Hall in the County of Stafford, Knight, Charles Jennings of Gopsall in the County of Leicester, Esquire, Benjamin Greaves of Witton Hall in the Parish of Aston juxta Birmingham in the County of Warwick aforesaid, Esquire, George Birch of Harborne in the County of Stafford, Esquire, Henry Hinshlow of Harborne aforesaid Gentleman, John Hinshley Gentleman Son and Heir Apparent of the said Henry Hinshley, Edward Homer of Sutton Coldfield in the County of Warwick aforesaid Gentleman, Edward Hare of Birmingham aforesaid Gentleman, and Randall Bradburne of Birmingham aforesaid Ironmonger, of the third part, Witnesseth that for the Settling Conveying and Assuring of the Messuages, Lands, Tenements and Hereditiments herein after mentioned to and upon the Uses, Trusts and purposes herein after mentioned concerning the same declared and also for and in consideration of the sum of Five Shillings of Lawful money of Great Brittain to her the said Dorothy Parkes in hand by the said Charles Blackham and Isaac Spooner well and truly paid at or before the sealing and delivery of these presents the Recept whereof she the said Dorothy Parkes doth hereby acknowledge and thereof aquit and discharge the said Charles Blackham and Isaac Spooner, their Heirs Executors Administrators and Assigns for Deeds by these Presents and also for Deeds and other Good and Valuable consideration her the said Dorothy Parkes, "thereunto specially moveing, she the said Dorothy Parkes hath Granted Bargained Sold, Allowed, Released Confirmed and by these Presents doth Grant Bargain and Sell Allow Releas and Confirm unto them the said Charles Blackham and Isaac Spooner their Heirs and Assigns in their actual possession now being by Virtue of our Indenture bargain and sale to them thereof made bearing date the next day before the day of the date of these Presents to hold for the Term of one whole year from the day next before the day of the date of the same Indentures of Bargain and Sale and by Virtue of the Statute for transfering uses into possession all those several Messuages Cottages Farms Lands Tenements and Hereditiments with their and every of the appurtinences situate lying and being in Smethwick in the said Parish of Harborne and County of Stafford now or late in the several and respective Tenures of John Silk, Edward Fletcher, Edward Rudge, Humphrey Parkes, and Joseph Parkes and one Phillips or some or one of them, their or some or one of their under tennants or Assigns and also all those several Closes Pieces or Parcels of Land or Ground with their or every of their Appurtinences situate lying and being in Warley Wigorn in the Parish of Hales Owen in the County of Worcester now or late in the Tenure or occupation of the said Edward Fletcher his under tennants or Assigns and with more lately purchased by her the said Dorothy Parkes of and from one Mr. John Perkins and also all those several Messuages Cottages Farms Lands Tenements and Hereditiments with their and every of their Appurtinences situate lying and being in or near Titford in Worley Wigorn in the Parish of Hales Owen in the County of Worcester now or late in the Tenure or occupation of John Mucklow or of his under tennants or under tennants Assign or Assigns and which was lately purchased by her the said Dorothy Parkes of and from Elizabeth Whiteing, widow deceased late sister of the said Dorothy Parkes and also all that Messuage Cottage or Tenement and one Croft adjoining thereto with their and every of their Appurtinences situate lying or being in or near Rude End in the Parish of Hales Owen and County of Worcester aforesaid now in the Tenure or occupation of William Granger or his under tennants or under tennants Assign or Assigns and also all those three Closes Pieces or Parcels of Land with their and every of their Appurtinences lying near to the said last mentioned Messuages commonly called or known by the name of Blackleys situate and being in the Parish of Hales Owen and County of Salop now also in the Tenure or occupation of the said William Granger and all other the Messuages Cottages Farms Lands Tenements, Heriditaments whatsoever of the said Dorothy Parkes wherein she hath Estate of Freehold or Inheritance situate lying and being in the Township Parishes Places or Precincts of Smethwick Harborne Titford Worley Wigorn Rude End and Halesowen or any of them or also wherein in the Kingdom of Great Brittain—and all Meadows, Pastures Feeding Ground Leasows Commons Woods and Woods Waters Ways Fishing Barnes Stables Buildings, Houses Out Houses Yards Orchards Gardens Proffits easments commodities advantages and appurtinences whatsoever to the said Messuages Cottages Farms Closes Lands Heriditaments and Tenements or any of them belonging or appertaining and now or at any time heretofore reputed attested devised and taken as part Parcel or member thereof or any part thereof or therewith all used occupied enjoyed and the Reversion and Reversions Remainder or Remainders Rents Services Uses and Profits thereof and any part thereof and all the Estate Title Right Interest Uses Trusts Inheritance Property claim and demand whatsoever of her the said Dorothy Parkes of into or out of the said premises or any part thereof to have and to hold all and singular the said Messuages Cottages Farms Closes Lands Tenements Heriditaments premises with their and every of their Appurtinences unto them the said Charles Blackham and Isaac Spooner and their Heirs unto the several uses following (that is to say) as to for touching and concerning all those the aforesaid Lands and Tenements Parcel of the said Premises now or late in the Tenure Holding or Occupation of the said William Granger and Joseph Parkes to the only proper use and behoof of the said Dorothy Parkes her Heirs or Assigns for ever.

And as to for touching and concerning all other the said Messuages Cottages Farms Lands Tenements and Heriditaments and Premises whereof before no use is herein and hereby limited to the use of the said Dorothy Parkes or her assigns for or during the Term of her natural life without impeachment of waste and from and after the decease of her the said Dorothy Parkes then to the use and behoof of the said Sir Charles Holt, Sir Henry Gough Charles Jennings Randal Bradburne Benjamin Greaves George Birch Henry Hinckley John Hinckley Edward Homer and Edward Hare their Heirs and assigns for ever upon their several Trusts and to and for the several intents and Purposes herein after mentioned (that is to say) *IN TRUST* that they the said Sir Charles Holt, Sir Henry Gough their Heirs and Assigns shall and may have Receive and take the Rents Issues and Profits of all and singular the Messuages Lands and Premises for ever and dispose thereof in manner following In the first place that they thereout indemnify and reemburse themselves and all and every of their workmen agents and servants and every of them of and from all damages expenses costs and charges that shall or may at any time or times hereafter happen unto or befall them or any of them for or by reason of these Presents or of their execution of or acting under any of the Trusts herein after mentioned or contained then upon this further Gift and confidence that they the said Sir Charles Holt and Sir Henry Gough &c their Heirs and assigns shall in the next place yearly and every year during the natural life of Mary Halfpenny of Birmingham aforesaid Spinster now servant unto and living with the said Dorothy Parkes pay or cause to be paid unto the said *Mary Halfpenny* out of the Rents and Profits of the said Premises the yearly sum or *annuity of Twenty Pounds* without any deduction or defalcation or abatement in any manner whatsoever for or by reason of any Charges, Taxes or Impositions Parliamentry or otherwise howsoever the same to be paid her at the feast of the Annunciation of the Blessed Virgin Mary and at the feast of Saint Michael the Archangel in every year by even and equal portions the first payment thereof to be made at such of the said Feasts as shall come next after the decease of Her the said Dorothy Parkes and also in trust further that they the said Sir Charles Holt &c. their Heirs and assigns shall by with and out of the Remainder of the yearly Rents and Profits of the said premises and the moneys thereout arising and out of such other money or assistance as by the last *WILL AND TESTAMENT* of Her the said Dorothy Parkes shall be for that purpose to them given and Bequeathed commence and begin to *Build within Three Years* next after the decease of her the said Dorothy Parkes or sooner if they think fit upon some part of the said Land and Premises herein before mentioned to lie in Smethwick aforesaid in a strong decent and durable manner but not at the expense of above Eight Hundred Pounds (if it can be well done for that sum) a neat and convenient *Chappel* or Building to be used as a Chappel for and in order for the service of Almighty God therein by the Inhabitants of Smethwick aforesaid for ever and the same shall in like manner perfect erect and finish and with convenient and proper ornaments furnish (that is to say) shall provide the same with one or more Bell or *Bells* proper for the calling the Inhabitants of Smethwick aforesaid to the assembling in the same Chappel or Building for and in order to the service of Almighty God therein and also with decent fit and convenient Reading Desks Pulpit Pulpit Cloth and Cushion Bible Common Prayer Book Communion Table, Table Cloth Communion Plate Seats and other like proper and convenient necessaries and ornaments to be used in decent manner in the said Chappel or Building for and in order to such service of the Almighty God therein as aforesaid and on this further Trust and confidence that from and after such time as the said Chappel or Building shall be as aforesaid completed Built and furnished and a Minister or Divine in Holy orders to officiate therein shall be appointed fixed and settled in manner hereafter mentioned, and Mary Halfpenny shall be departed this natural life and not otherwise or before they the said Sir Charles Holt &c. their Heirs and assigns shall by with and out of the yearly Rents and Profits of the same Premises yearly and every year for ever distribute lay out and expend the annual sum of ten Pounds clear money without deduction (that is to say) the yearly sum of fifty two shillings part thereof in and for the buying of twelve pennyworth of *penny loaves of good Bread* to be distributed and given every Sunday in every year for ever unto and amongst twelve such poor Inhabitants of and in Smethwick aforesaid as shall and will in the said intended Chapel when erected and provided as aforesaid decently and reverently attend to and join in the celebration of Divine Service there both Morning and Evening of the same day the same twelve Persons to be from time to time and at all times nominated approved and appointed by the Minister or Divine in Holy Orders therein for that day officiating or any two or three other Inhabitants of and in Smethwick aforesaid who shall and will be present at such distribution immediately after the Evening Service of that day and who shall be thereunto called or nominated the same day as his assistants by the same Minister or Divine so as aforesaid on that day officiating. And also the yearly sum of Fifty-two shillings other part thereof in and for the buying of other twelve pennyworth of *penny loaves of good Bread* to be distributed or given upon every Sunday in every year for ever unto and amongst twelve such poor Inhabitants of the other part of the said *Parish of Harborne* as shall and will in the Parish Church of Harborne aforesaid decently and Reverently attend and join in the celebration of Divine Service morning and evening of the same day the same twelve Persons to be from time to time and at all times nominated and approved and appointed by the Vicar for the time being or other Priest or Deacon in the same Parish Church for that day officiating or any two or three Inhabitants of the same Parish who shall and will be present at such distribution immediately after the Evening service for that day or who shall be thereunto called or nominated the same day as his assistant by the same Vicar Priest or Deacon as aforsaid on that day officiating and the further yearly sum of Four Pounds and ten shillings other part thereof yearly and every year for ever in and for the buying of six coats or other Garments as good as the same will will purchase to be distributed and given yearly unto and amongst six honest and *Poor Women Inhabitants* of and in the said Parish of Harborne upon the Feast day of St. Thomas the Apostle in every year and which six said poor women *Three* shall be of the *village Hamlet or place of Smethwick* aforsaid and the other three shall be of the other part of the same Parish of Harborne and to be from time to time nominated and appointed by them the said Sir Charles Holt, &c., their Heirs and assigns and the yearly sum of six shillings the residue of the said yearly sum of Ten Pounds to be expended annually in *Bibles* to be given and distributed amongst such *Poor Inhabitants* of and in *Smethwick* aforesaid at the said Feast of Saint Thomas the Apostle in every year as by the Minister or Divine in holy orders fixed and settled in the said Intended Chapel for the time being shall for that purpose be nominated and appointed as in his judgment most fit to have the same and most likely to make the best use thereof. And on this further Trust if they the said Sir Charles Holt, &c., their Heirs and Assigns out of the said yearly Rents and Profits of the said Premises do and shall pay for all such *Bread and Wine* as shall be spent or used in the said intended Chapel when erected for or in administering the *Holy Sacrament* of the Lord's Supper and shall thereout pay reasonable *wages* not exceeding forty shillings yearly to a Person to be by them appointed to officiate in the said intended Chapel as or in the nature of a Clerk or *Sexton* to make responses set the Psalms ring the Bell or Bells therein and do such other like duties as are usually performed by a Parish Clerk or Sexton and shall also Fence set out enclose and maintain and keep enclosed for ever round about the said intended Chapel a most neat and convenient *Chappel* yard for the use and convenience of the said intended Chapel and otherwise for the benefit of the Minister or Chaplain settled therein and shall also from time to time and at all times hereafter for ever as oft as there shall be occasion maintain and repair and keep in good repair and order not only the said intended Chapel and Chapel yard but also all the other Buildings Walls Rails Posts, Stiles Gates Hedges Ditches Fences Mounds Ways Watercourses upon or belonging to the said messuages, Farms Tenements and Premises or any of them or any part of them thereof. Provided nevertheless that none of the said Bread or Coats shall be given to or had by any Person or Persons who shall have claimed or required any Parochial relief or Charity within the space of one whole year next before the time appointed for the giving or distributing thereof and if upon account of any accident by Fire or Tempest or other like occasion the expense of repairing the said intended Chapel Buildings and other the Premises shall become extraordinary then upon every such occasion it shall and may be lawfull to and for the said Sir Charles Holt, &c., their Heirs and assigns to cause such reparation to be made by with or out of the said yearly sum of Ten Pounds so as aforesaid Limited to the particular Charities of buying Bread Coats and Bibles and that all or any of the same particular charities or such part thereof as they shall think fit shall cease and be suspended until such repairation are duly and fully made. And upon this further Trust that from and after such time the said Chapel shall be fully Built finished fitted up and furnished as aforesaid and so from time to time and at all times thereafter as oft as any vacancy shall happen in the Curacy hereinafter designed to be provided for for ever the said Sir Charles Holt, &c., their Heirs and assigns or the greater number of them shall as soon as conveniently the same can be done by their deed or Instrument in writing under their Hands and Seals or the Hands or Seals of the greater number of them testified by three or more credible Witnesses nominate elect and appoint a certain learned and orthodox Divine or Minister in Holy Orders according to the usage of the Church of England as by law established and of the degree of Batchelor of Arts at the least and not having any Cure of Souls or other Curateship or Ecclesiastical employment of Preaching or Reading Prayers in any Church or Chapel whatsoever or then exercising the employment of a Schoolmaster or teaching, to be the Chaplain or Curate or Minister of and in the said intended Chapel therein to officiate and in devout and proper manner to do the office of Priest or Deacon by celebrating Divine Service reading the Common Prayers and Preaching the Word of God twice every Sunday in the year (that is to say) both Morning and Evening within the said Chapel and by reading the Prayers and Catechising therein on Holy days and other proper times and seasons, for his so doing and to encourage him to a diligent and faithful discharge of his duty. In Trust further that they the said Sir Charles Holt &c. their Heirs and assigns do and shall yearly and every year thenceforward and for ever pay and dispose of all the right and Residue of the clear Annual Rents and Profits of the said Messuages Farms Lands Tenements and Premises unto such Chaplain Curate or Minister so by them as aforesaid from time to time nominated and appointed to officiate in the said Chapel. But from which said Curacy or place officiating as aforesaid in the said Chapel and all Benefit and Profit to him thereby arising or intended by these Presents he shall be from time to time removed and another chosen and admitted in his room by the said Sir Charles Holt &c. their Heirs and Assigns or the greater number of them when or as often as he shall have received or taken upon himself any Cure of Souls or other Curateship or Ecclesiastical preferment whatsoever and lastly on this further trust that whensoever and as often as any one or more of them the said Sir Charles Holt &c. or their assigns from time to time for ever shall depart this natural life that then and in such case the survivors of them or the major number of them shall by Deed or Conveyance in the Law as by Council Learned shall be advised from time to time and at all times hereafter transfer convey assign and set over all and singular the said to them hereby Conveyed Messuages Lands and Premises unto two or more Proper Persons and their heirs such as they shall think fit unto the use of such Survivors and their Heirs and of such other Persons and their Heirs jointly with them as they the said Survivors or the greater number of them shall nominate and appoint. But nevertheless upon the several Trusts and to and for the several Intents and purposes thereof herein before declared limited and appointed and so as such number of Persons to be by them nominated and appointed, do not, in the whole make the number of Persons to act under the Trust and Powers limited by these presents to exceed the number of 10 and so as such Persons to be from time to time added as aforesaid to supply the places or Rooms of those deceased be of such as ever adhered to the Communion of the Church of England as by law established provided always and it is hereby declared to be the true Intent and meaning of these Presents and of all and every the said Parties hereunto that it shall and may be lawful to and for the said Dorothy Parkes at any time or times hereafter during her natural life by her Indenture in writing and under her Hand and Seal subscribed and attested by three or more credible witnesses to revoke alter change annull or determine all or any of the use or uses of all or any of the said Messuages Farms Lands Tenements and premises hereby before limited in any manner unto them the said Sir Charles Holt, &c. their Heirs and Assigns and all and every the said Trusts thereof before declared, to extinguish and make void and thereof to declare limit and appoint such new and other uses as to her the said Dorothy Parkes shall seem meet and that from henceforward the said Charles Blackham and Isaac Spooner and their Heirs and all and every other Person or Persons and their heirs seized or possessed in any manner of the said Premises or any part thereof shall be and stand seized thereof, to and for such new or other use or uses and of and for such Estate and Estates Person and Persons as by the said Dorothy Parkes shall be declared limited and appointed anything in these Presents to the contrary hereof contained in any wise notwithstanding.

In Witness whereof the said Parties first above named in these Presents have set their Hands and Seals have put the day and year first above Written.

DOROTHY PARKES.

Memorandum that the within named Dorothy Parkes first sealed and delivered the within mentioned Indenture of Bargain and Sale for one year and immediately afterwards sealed and delivered this Indenture in the presence of us who there observed Three of his Majesties' sixpenny stamps to be impressed on the margin of every respective Skin of Parchment of this Deed.

NICHOLAS HARRIS. } 27th Jany., 1727.
JOHN AVEREL JAMES. } Exh. by HENRY HINKLEY
RICHARD WOODWARD. } WM. PAYTON.

1741—6th March.

This is a true copy examined by the above attested Copy by us.

THOS. SMITH.
WILL. PAYTON.

* * * * * * * * * * * *

As the Deed of 1719 reserved a right of revocation to the Benefactress, which, however, she never felt called upon to exercise, it became desirable that confirmation of her Benefactions should be given by Dorothy Parkes in her Last Will and Testament. Here is a similarly attested copy of that document:

In the Name of God. Amen.

I DOROTHY PARKES of Birmingham in the County of Warwick Spinster, do make and ordain this my last *Will and Testament* in manner and form following (that is to say) Imprimis I give and Bequeath my Soul to Almighty God my Merciful Creator and my Body to Christian Burial at the discretion of my Executors hereinafter named yet in sure and certain hope of a joyfull Ressurection unto Eternal life through the Interest and mediation of the Ever Blessed Jesus my only Saviour and Redeemer and as to the Worldly Estate wherewith it hath pleased God to Bless me and which I have not before disposed of and settled by my *Indenture* made under my Hand and Seal bearing date the 30th May 1719 I dispose thereof as followeth (That is to say) I give and devise all my Freehold Lands and Tenements which now are or lately were in the tenure or occupation of William Granger and Joseph Parkes or either of them situate lying and being in the Parish of Hales Owen in the County of Worcester and Salop and in Smethwick in the Parish of Harborne in the County of Stafford unto my cousin William Jesson for the term of his natural life and from and after his decease then to my cousin Mary Brett her Heirs and Assigns for ever and as to my Copyhold Lands and Tenements lying and being in Langley Wallaxall in the Parish of Hales Owen and County of Salop my will and desire is that the same shall be held and enjoyed by my Cousin William Jesson and his Heirs for ever according to the custom of the manor in which they lie.

Item I give and Bequeath unto Sir Henry Gough of Perry Hall in the County of Stafford, Knight Charles Jennings of Gopsall in the County of Leicester Esqr. John Hoo of Great Barr in the Parish of Aldridge and the County of Stafford aforesaid Esqr. William Booth Allestry of Witton Hall in the Parish of Aston juxta Birmingham in the County of Warwick Esqr. Benjamin Greves late of Witton Hall aforesaid but now of Mousley in the Parish of King's Norton and County of Worcester Esqr. and Richard Greves Son and Heir apparent of the said Benjamin Greves Henry Hinckley of Harborne aforesaid Gent. John Hinckley Gent. Son and Heir apparent of the said Henry Hinckley Richard Boyse of Berkswell in the County of Warwick aforesaid Clerk Edward Homer of Sutton Coldfield in the County of Warwick aforesaid Gent. William Priest of Birmingham aforesaid Gent. and Randall Bradburne of Birmingham aforesaid Ironmonger their Executors Administrators and Assigns the sum of *Eight Hundred Pounds In Trust* nevertheless that they the said Sir Henry Gough &c. and the Survivor or Survivors of them their Executors and Administrators do and shall apply use of and interest money that shall be made from time to time thereof together with the Principle Sum of Eight Hundred Pounds for and towards the building fitting and furnishing a certain intended-to-be-erected chapel for the service of Almighty God in Smethwick aforesaid and no more if the same can be conveniently built for such sum of Eight Hundred Pounds with the increase and interest thereof in such manner as is directed and more particularly expressed in and by the aforsaid *Indenture* bearing the date the 30th day of May 1719 for that purpose made between me the said Dorothy Parkes of the first Part one Charles Blackham and one Isaac Spooner (now deceased) both of Birmingham aforesaid Ironmongers of the second Part and Sir Charles Holt (now deceased) and them the said Sir Henry Gough &c of the third part.

Item I give unto my servant *Mary Halfpenny* the sum of One Hundred Pounds in money to be paid her immediately or within three months of my decease and all my wearing Apparel to be delivered to her soon after my decease. Item I give to Catherine Grove with whom I now live Ten Pounds to buy her mourning. Item I give to the aforesaid Thomas Birch Five Guineas and to the aforesaid Henry Hinckley Five Guineas and do constitute and appoint them the said *Thomas Birch and Henry Hinckley Executors,* of this my last Will and Testament all which last mentioned Money-legacys my will is should be paid within three months next after my decease. Item I give Five Pounds to the *Poor of Birmingham.* Fifty Shillings to the *Poor of Smethwick* and Fifty Shillings more to the *Poor of the other Part of the Parish of Harborne* to be paid soon after my decease and it is my will that the aforesaid Mary Halfpenny do and shall pay distribute and dispose of certain Moneys Goods and Chattels in such manner as I shall by a Paper signed and subscribed by me left for that purpose and which shall not be brought into Court as part of a Codicil to my Will nor the Money Goods and Chattels comprised in such Paper but into the Inventry of my Personal Estate yet I desire the same may be done and performed punctually in every respect and I also desire that no one except *Mary Halfpenny* shall look into have or *Inspect the Manuscript* and collections in writing made by me or other loose Papers but that she alone may Have Keep and Dispose thereof as I shall direct and it is my will that the said Mary Haltpenny shall and may be the Executrix of this Part of my Will only and not otherwise. Item It is my will and desire that after the said intended *Chapel* shall be built my said Executors shall lay out and expend the sum Of Thirty or Forty Pounds at the most in making and erecting a *Monument* for me in the said Chapel or in Harborne Church or either of them. Item I give and Bequeath unto my Cousin Mary Brett the sum of Two Hundred Pounds to be raised and paid by my Executors out of my Personal Estate she paying Ten Pounds per annum to my said Trustees during the life of my servant Mary Halfpenny for the payment of which Ten Pounds yearly, she the said Mary Brett and her husband shall give such good Security as shall be approved of by my said Trustees and also give her what household Goods I shall leave at my decease except such as I shall direct the said Mary Halfpenny to dispose of by the above mentioned Paper I intend to sign and subscribe aforesaid.

Item I give unto them the said Sir Henry Gough, &c. their Executors Administrators and Assigns Two Hundred Pounds upon Trust that they and their Survivors or Survivor of them his Executors and Administrators do and shall lay out and employ about Forty Pounds part thereof in building a small *Charity School* if the same can be conveniently built [or that sum upon some convenient part of my Estate in Smethwick aforesaid for a Single Wooman to be from time to time chosen by my said Trustees to live in and there to teach gratis poor *Children of Smethwick* aforesaid to read, sew and knit and to learn the Church Catechism and that my Trustees will set out half an Acre of Grounds for that purpose and for a Garden and that they the said Trustees do and shall lay out the residue of the said Two Hundred Pounds in the Purchase of Lands and Tennements to be settled for the payment of five Pounds per annum for ever to such Woman for the time being as shall *teach such children* and ten shillings per Annum for Books and ten shillings for Coals to be burnt in the said School and the rest to be applied by them my said Trustees towards the *Clothing such poor Children* as are taught in the School the choice and management of which I desire may be left to the Minister of the Chapel for the time being and that he will choose such as are the greatest objects of Charity.

Item those *Divinity Books and other Books* which I have and shall leave a Catalogue at my decease I give to my Trustees in Trust and it is my will and mind that they shall settle the said Books upon the Chapel intended to be Built at Smethwick and also upon Harborne Church *for the use of the Incumbent Minister* for the time being and also for the use of succeeding Ministers of both Churches in future Generations according to an Act of Parliament for the better preservation of *Parochial libraries* in that part of Great Britain called England a copy of such Acts and Rules to be observed if my Trustees shall approve thereof and contained in a Paper Book amongst my other Books and it is my desire that the said Books devised as aforesaid shall he kept together in such place as my said Trustees shall think most proper for that purpose and that the same shall be subject to their inspection and to such Rules and orders as they shall subscribe.

Item after my Debts and Legacies and Funeral Expenses are fully paid and satisfied I give devise and bequeath all the rest and Residue overplus or surplus of all Moneys Goods, and Chattels and Personal Estates of what kind or nature whatsoever unto them the said

Sir Henry Gough, &c., their Executors Administrators and Assigns upon Trust that they will lay out the sum of about two Hundred Pounds thereof in building a *good sufficient House* upon some convenient part of my Estate near the said intended *Chapel at Smethwick* aforesaid for the *Minister* for the time being to *Inhabit and dwell in* if the same can be conveniently Built for that sum and my mind and will is that the old House wherein Milward and Rudge live in may be pulled down and the materials thereof employed towards the Building such House and it is my further will that if the overplus of my Personal Estate at my decease and also what money shall be raised out of my Estate by me given for Charitable uses by persception of the Rents and Profits thereof before the Chapel is finished shall be more than enough for what I have already proposed to be done then the overplus shall be employed and laid out in what is further necessary in and about the Chapel in *walling and fencing* the same and the Minister's House and School and in repairing the old Farm Houses and my mind and will is that if the Estate I have hereby or otherwise given for Pious and Charitable Purposes will not be sufficient to answer what I have already proposed to be done therewith and if any accidents should happen by Fire or loss of Debts or otherwise that then my said Trustees may do for the Building for so many years or such time as may be sufficient to raise money of the said Estate to supply such deficiency but if there should be sufficient at the time of my decease my desire is that they will not delay but with all expedition accomplish the several matters and things hereby and by the said Indenture directed and appointed and my mind and will further is that the Minister of the said intended Chapel for the time being shall be resident there and that *The first Person to be presented to be Minister* of such Chapel may be Mr. John Williams Curate of Saint Martin's Church Birmingham if he will accept thereof and I do hereby direct and appoint that the said John Hoo, Thomas Birch, William Booth Allestrey, Richard Greves, Richard Boyse, and William Preist shall be *added* to the Survivors of the said *Trustees* named in the said Indenture and shall from and after my decease have full powers and Authority to act with them in the execution of and management of the several Trusts herein and in the said Indenture mentioned to all intents and Purposes and in as full and ample manner as if the said John Hoo, Thomas Birch, William Booth Allestrey, Richard Greves, Richard Boyse, and William Priest had been particularly named as Trustees in the said Indenture and to the end the said intended Chapel may be duly and constantly supplied according to the true intent and meaning hereof and of the said Indenture and that the Nomination Election and Appointment of a Minister from time to time to officiate therein may for ever continue and be in their the said Sir Henry Gough, Charles Jennings, John Greves, Henry Hinckley, John Hinckley, Richard, Boyse, Edward How, Williams, Priest, and Randall Bradburne or their assigns or the major portion of them I do hereby direct and appoint and my mind and will is that the said Sir Henry Gough, &c., their Heirs and Assigns and all succeeding Trustees or the major part of them do, and shall as soon as convenient may be, after my decease make application to the Right Revd. the Lord Bishop of Litchfield and Coventry the Dean and Chapter of Litchfield and to the Vicar of Harborne for the time being in order to obtain from them some proper Instrument or *instruments in writing* giving unto them or the major part of them and their assigns and all succeeding Trustees or the major part of *them full liberty Power and Authority to erect and Build the said Intended Chapel* and to nominate elect and appoint a Minister from time to time as occasion shall require to officiate and administer the Holy Sacrament in the said Chapel and to do all other lawfull and reasonable acts and things for the more effectual execution of the several Trusts hereby and by the said Indenture in them reposed or otherwise that the said Sir Henry Gough, &c., their Heirs and assigns or the major part of them shall and may use their endeavours to procure an Act of Parliament or make use of other fit and proper means in order to obtain the ends and purposes aforsaid at such time and in such manner as they or the major part of them shall think fit and my Will is that all the costs and charges of such application endeavours and use of means shall be paid and borne by and out of the Rents and Profits of the Estate hereby and by the said Indenture given and settled for Charitable uses and I do hereby further direct and appoint and my mind and will is that if at any time or times hereafter when an *Election of Minister* is to be made or a removal intended or any other act to be done relating to the said Chapel or any other branch of the several Trusts herein and in the said indenture mentioned it shall and may happen that the Trustees then present shall or may in their *Votes* touching or concerning any such matter be equally divided that then and in such case the Senior in respect of his age for the time being of the Trustees then present shall from time to time have a casting or double vote which shall be final and decisive to all intents and purposes in all points that shall be so put to the vote and all parties concerned shall submit to and aquiesce under such determination and lastly my Will is that when any act is to be done relating to the said several Trusts of any of them all the Trustees for the time being shall have reasonable notice thereof and of the time and place of their intended meeting such notice to be given or left by the Minister of the said intended Chapel for the time being and I do hereby revoke annul and make void all and all manner of former and other Wills by and at any time or times hertofore made declaring this to be my LAST WILL AND TESTAMENT,

In witness whereof I the said Dorothy Parkes hath subscribed and set my Hand and Seal this twenty second day of   in the tenth year of our Sovereign Lord George by the Grace of God of Great Brittain, France and Ireland King defender of the Faith and in the year of our Lord one Thousand seven Hundred and twenty three.

DOROTHY PARKES.

Signed Sealed and published by the above named Dorothy Parkes upon the day of the date above written in the prescence of us whose names are now under written and also all of us subscribed our names as Witnesses in her prescence and by her direction.

TOBIAS BELLARS.
JOHN BLUNN.
THOMAS CECILL.

March, 1741.

This is a true Copy Exd. by a copy of the above Will by us

THOS. SMITH.
WM. PAYTON.

XIX.—THE FABRIC OF THE OLD CHAPEL: THE REGISTER, &c.

Smethwick Chapel is now, almost as it was a century ago, when Shaw described it—"a neat modern building," "lofty," some "60 feet by 24; and well pewed; with a gallery at the West end, thus inscribed:

> By generous contributions
> (in this and neighbouring parishes),
> This Gallery
> was erected in the year 1759.
> The annual rents of the seats to be
> applied in repairs, and
> beautifying the church, for ever."

The erection of this Gallery may be taken as indication of a growth in the population at that time; but the present inscription on it omits the final phrase, perhaps because it has been at last recognised as a hopeless task to attempt anything in the shape of "beautifying " such a building.

Yet it is a very fair specimen of a small ecclesiastical edifice in the style of the early Georgian period. It is of red brick, with stone quoins; the west end is flanked by a lofty square tower in three stages, the top stage pierced with large round-headed louvres, for a belfry containing one bell.

A diminutive coved apse, of such scanty proportions as to almost preclude anything approaching a chancel, flanks the east end; on the south-side of this there was once an east entrance which is now built up, and so affords a convenient location for the pulpit.

In the opposite angle, along the north wall, is a small modern organ by Bishop and Starr.

The commodious pews run down each side, along north and south walls, leaving between them a passage whose spaciousness is only interfered with by the Font at the near end, and a very neat brass Lectern (of the year 1870) at the farther one. The Font is elegantly designed in alabaster.

The pulpit, which was erected by subscription in 1873, is of Riga oak, carved with considerable art; and, what is far more gratifying, it is an admirable specimen of English joinery in which the fitting is so cleverly contrived that the joints are practically undiscoverable. It is hexagonal in plan, the panels separated by buttresses, and the four front angles ornamented by figures of the Evangelists.

The fenestration, like every other feature and detail of the building, is quite characteristic of the Georgian type of architecture. There are four large circular-headed windows in the south wall, four in the north wall, and one in the apsidal "chancel." The stained glass in the latter is merely a geometrical design, except that a small panel near the top contains the symbolical Holy Dove. The south window nearest to it contains much finer work (by Evans, of Smethwick), and is commemorative of the wife and children of George Hallen Smith (1865-73). In the two small circular, or " wheel-windows," at the east end, are floriated designs of no particular merit.

Coming next to the mural memorials, that of the foundress of the Chapel claims first notice.

"Against the South wall of the chancel is a neat mural marble, thus inscribed:

> Near to this place are deposited the remains of that valuable woman, MISS DOROTHY PARKES, who was born in this parish on ye 16th day of September, 1644, and departed this life at Birmingham on ye 7th day of June, 1727.

She was adorned with all the amiable virtues of the mind, and was graceful and agreeable in her person, instructive and pleasing in her conversation, and constant and diligent in the practice and exercise of all Christian duties, having spent her life in piety, devotion, and charity.

As she never thought fit to enter into a married state, and had no near relations to provide for, she long intended to dedicate great part of her worldly substance to ye publick service of Almighty God; and having, by Settlement, as well as by her last Will, given proper directions for that purpose, this Chappel, and a Charity-school (both suitably endowed), and a House for the Minister to reside in, have since her decease been built by the order of the Trustees appointed by her to put her pious designs in execution, who have also erected this monument to her memory, and to incite others to imitate the virtue and piety of so worth, a person.

The righteous shall be had in everlasting remembrance. Psalm cxii, v, 6."

Next to this, but on the east wall of the nave, is a tablet to THOMAS HANSON.

On the same wall, but on the other side of the chancel-opening is a similar one :

To the memory of THOMAS TURNER, who died the 20th of May, 1760. Aged 64

On the north wall are two: the first commemorates JOHN DYMOKE GRIFFITH, who died in 1809 at the age of 70, and his wife and eldest child. The second contains the arms of the two families mentioned upon it, and the names of (1) JONATHAN GRUNDY, died 1803, aged 59; (2) HANNAH, his wife, died 1815, aged 65; (3) HANNAH, a daughter, died 1829, aged 57; (4) JOHN, a son who died at Naples, 1801, aged 27; (5) THOMAS, who died at the age of 69; (6) ELIZABETH, wife of Thomas, died 1827, at the age of 72; (7) ELIZA, only daughter of Thomas, and only niece of Jonathan, who died 1837, at the age of 54; and (8) HENRY GOODRICH WILLETT, of The Lightwoods, and of Wigston Parva Hall, Leicestershire, who died 1857.

On the south wall are several memorial tablets; namely of—

(1) JOHN REYNOLDS, of The Coppice in this Hamlet, and of Bridgeford in the Co. of Stafford, died March, 1820, aged 84.
(2) MARY STUBBS, died 1818, aged 85; Ann, died 1821, aged 65; and Hannah, died 1828, aged 70.
(3) ANN FOX, died 1843, aged 62.
(4) MARY ANNE WOOLLEY, of Summerfield House, died February, 1839, aged 68.
[This is a small and interesting brass, of a kneeling woman.]
(5) JOHN JAMES IDDENS, of Summerfield House, died, aged 45, May, 1820.
(6) REV. EDWARD PATTESON, the second Incumbent.

The Hinckley family mentioned in ch. xvi. are also commemorated by tablets on the north wall of the chancel.

The school built by Dorothy Parkes was taken down some forty years ago, the site being utilised to enlarge the graveyard. A new and larger school was then erected on the opposite side of the churchyard.

The large lych-gate was added about six years ago.

The whole of the fabric was put into a sound state of repair in 1889 at a cost of £200. The estimated number of sittings is now an accommodation for 300 worshippers. Although Smethwick has grown so rapidly and to such dimensions, it is interesting to note that the Old Chapel is still in the midst of somewhat rural surroundings, and away from all the busier centres of population in the parish.

* * * * * * * * * * * *

The Register of Harborne dates from 1538; Yardley Register from 1539; King's Norton and Birmingham 1544; Northfield 1560; Bromsgrove 1590; West Bromwich 1608; Edgbaston 1635. That of Smethwick commences with the date "15th October, 1732."

Acts of 1597 and 1603 ordered that certified copies should be made of all Parish Registers, the transcripts to be preserved with the originals. This was done at Harborne, but the original seems to have been lost.

Copies were preserved by the Chapter authorities, generally beginning from the year 1660. These terminated in 1812 when the Registration Act of that year put an end to them. At Lichfield are preserved Transcripts for

Harborne 1660 to 1812 (1666-72 and 1689-93 missing).
Smethwick 1774 to 1812 (1795-8 missing).

The Capitular Visitations are also fully recorded at Lichfield. These were made under a Decanal arrangement for Clerical and general Parochial purposes. There were two classes of Visitations. First, there was the Triennial Visitation of the Clergy, Church-wardens, &c., at Lichfield and other centres of the diocese, when the Transcripts of the Registers were returned, Licences granted to Schoolmasters to Midwives, and in some cases to Surgeons; Wills were proved, &c. Among the records preserved at Lichfield are five returns of these Visitations dating from 1756 to 1786, and among the numerous parishes summoned will be found the names of Edgbaston, Harborne, Tipton, Smethwick, and many others. Then, secondly, there were the Twice-a-Year Visitations usually in the Spring and at Michaelmas when the chief business was the presenting of moral offenders for fornication &c., when penance was enjoined. At Lichfield are twenty seven records of such, dating from 1754 to 1782; they are divided into two heads, those of the Dean's Peculiars, and those of the Dean and Chapter's Peculiars; under the latter heading appear the names of the parishes of Cannock, Edgbaston, Farewell, Harborne, Rugeley, and Smethwick.

XX.—THE HOLDERS OF THE BENEFICE.

The creation of the living of Smethwick no doubt had some indirect influence on that of the mother parish of Harborne. The Vicar of Harborne in 1715 was Thomas Southall. It was in his time that the yearly value of the living was raised from £50 to £70 by the contributions of George Birch, Henry Hinckley, and Dorothy Parkes. The last-named then proposed the partition of Harborne by erecting the hamlet of Smethwick into an independent chapelry—full effect being given to this proposal in 1727-32 by the *Will* of 1723. It was in 1732 Thomas Green became Vicar of Harborne, and held this living for 34 years, besides being at the same time "Chief Master of Birmingham School."

The Perpetual Curacy of Smethwick, now designated a Vicarage, is returned at the net yearly value of £450, with a residence.

The first Incumbent (notwithstanding the testatrix's nominee for preferment, mentioned on p. 55) was the Rev. R. Boyce; the next was the Rev. Edward Patteson. Then came the Rev. Edward Pickering, who "farmed his own land, known as Old Chapel Farm." The Rev. Edward Dale followed, and then succeeded the Rev. Edward Addenbrooke. The present Vicar is the Rev. George Astbury, M.A.

At the east end of the Church, under the window on the outside, inclosed with rails, is an altar-tomb, thus:

> By his infant son,
> Robert Boyce,
> The first Minister of this Church,
> And son of Robert Boyce, of Wellsbourne, Esq., lies here.
>
> Fervant in prayer, and in it constant too,
> He served God as every man should do.
> To all his neighbours was both just and good,
> And did them all the services he could.
> His tender wife on all occasions prov'd
> His true affections, and how well he lov'd.
>
> He died September 8th, 1759, aged 66.
> Anne; his widow, died August 11th, 1772, aged 77.

In the grave-yard also, near the south-east corner of the chapel, is a cruciform headstone to the memory of the Rev. Edward Dale, born 1764, died 1850.

Inside the sacred edifice, and on its south wall, is a tablet thus inscribed:

> Sacred
> To the Memory
> Of the Rev. Edward Patteson, A.M.,
> Thirty-five years Minister of this Chapel,
> Who died on the 5th day of September
> In the year of Our Lord MDCCXCVI,
> And in the Sixty-fifth year
> Of his Age

Shaw (1798) alludes to the Parsonage House curing the time of the above-named Incumbent, and describes it as "a neat commodious building on the south side of the chapel-yard, and was inhabited, when I inspected this part, by the rev.—Patteson, then curate, who is since dead." The Vicarage seems to have been a residence enlarged from a small farm-house (see p. 55).

XXI.—PAROCHIAL BENEFACTIONS (HARBORNE AND SMETHWICK.)

In the early part of this century a Commission was appointed to investigate the condition of the existing or known Charities in England; and particularly of those providing for the education of the poor. A grave national scandal had arisen at that time, owing to the maladministration and open spoliation of these public properties.

A REPORT, dated January, 1823, contains on pp. 550-557 an impartial and judicial account of the state of the Harborne Charities.

1. *The Free School.*

It is under the heading of Harborne must be sought all the allusions to Smethwick; and although the Free .School was established for the benefit of both Harborne and Smethwick (see *ante p.* 46), the word Smethwick does not occur in the Report upon this particular Charity. A few condensed extracts from this Report may here be given:

> Of the origin of this school we could obtain no other information than is conveyed on a tablet in the [Harborne] church, that there is a Charity School and House at Harburne, built several years ago by subscription among the inhabitants, on a piece of land granted on lease by the late Sir Thomas Birch for 1,000 years . . . and that there are three tenements built on a piece of land given to the said school by Mr. Henry Hinckley, deceased.
>
> Two trust deeds were produced . . dated 1819, reciting that the freehold was vested in George Greaves and other surviving trustees . . it is witnessed that George Greaves conveyed to Thomas Hanson and others . . all those three messuages . . near Harborne Church, fronting the lane leading from Harborne to Tinker's Green, on trust . . to choose some person of the Church of England qualified to officiate in the said Schoolhouse as Schoolmaster, &c. . . These [school] premises have lately been rebuilt at an expense of about . £800, £350 raised by subscription. In addition to the rent above mentioned there is £125 Three per cent. Consols, standing in the names of Theodore Price and Thomas Green Simcox . . the dividends, £3 15s. per annum, are paid over to the Master.
>
> It is most probable that part of this stock arose from the donation of Henry Hinckley given by deed 1731 for bread for six children. . . . It seems probable that the Henry Hinckley . . donor of this bread money . . is the same person . . giving the land on which the houses belonging to the school charity are built. . . . Each poor family in the parish is entitled to have one child educated freely . . . all other poor children shall pay . 4d and 6d. per week each. . . The master is at liberty to take pay scholars on his own terms. There were 35 to 45 free scholars . . both sexes. They are taught reading, writing, accounts, and the Church Catechism, and are taken twice a year to the parish church to be catechised. The girls are instructed in sewing and knitting, &c., &c.

Smethwick claimed its share in the benefits of this Free School, a similar account of which may be found in THE FREE SCHOOLS AND ENDOWMENTS OF STAFFORDSHIRE *(London, Whittaker and Co.,* 1860) pp. 479-481.

2. *Elizabeth Cowper alias Piddock's Charity*

This benefactress is described as "of Smethwick"—although we have mention of Roger Cowper. of Handsworth, and of William, of King's Norton. In the reign of Elizabeth (1576) the said Elizabeth gave £40 in lands, the rent of which was to be distributed twice a year at the discretion of her sons and executors, Richard and Roger Cowper, alias Piddock. The particulars of these Trusts were found in "a copy of an Ancient Book of Charities belonging to the neighbouring parish of Handsworth." Even from this the Commissioners failed to identify the lands in question, although they were specifically described as follows: *(a)* a close called Lightwood alias Gosty Croft; *(b)* a meadow called Pig Hill Meadow; *(c)* 14 selions (a selion is a ridge between two furrows) containing 4½ acres called Green Field; (d) 5 selions of 1 acre in a field called Hinchmore—all in Harborne parish. The terms of the bequest specify the recipients as "the poor inhabitants of Harborne and Smithwick," and the distribution was appointed for St. Mark's Day, yearly. An old inhabitant testified that one of the Piddock family used to distribute 20s. a year to the poor, but that "40 or 50 years ago" (i.e previous to 1823) these lands were purchased by the parish—probably to secure the surplus rents over and above the said 20s, for the poor.

The premises formerly belonging to Piddock. and now forming part of the Parish Lands, Consist of a small farm called Green's Farm. containing 9ac 1 rood let to John Newey at £20, and a close called Pighills 1½ac, held by Mary Stevens, with other parish land, making 2ac. 3 roods at a rent of £6.

3. Parish Lands.

The origin of these is unknown, the first deed relating thereto being dated 1699. A deed of 1816 recites a decree in Chancery (John Hanson and others against Hinckley and others) settling the appointment of 8 trustees inhabitants of Harborne and 8 trustees to be inhabitants of Smithwick. The Commissioners of 1823 report upon it being "impossible to identify with particularity" the various parcels of land, although the description "unaltered since 1732," seems verbose if not explicit. This description of the situation of the Parish Lands need not be repeated here in detail: we may note, however, that there were "gardens, orchards, and hemplecks"; that some were in a "lane leading from Handsworth to a place called the Sand Pits"; that two closes and two meadows lay "adjoining to the heath called Harborne Heath"; that one tenement was known as Madge Croft, and a parcel of land as the Flagmore, &c., &c. The proceeds of this charity were to apprentice two poor children of Harborne and two of Smithwick every year on the 1st of May; and to relieve the aged poor and impotent persons of both these places. The gross acreage of the Parish Lands was over 66 acres, and the annual produce was £143 9s. On the largest tenancy, 32 acres let to John Tibbetts at £60, the Parish Workhouse had been built. There were 9 cottages in Harborne and 4 in Smithwick, inhabited rent free by poor persons. There was a parochial officer, called a Bailiff, for Harborne, who received £67 15s. of the rent, and the Bailiff for the Chapelry of Smithwick received the other portion of the £143 9s. The Overseers of each division used £5 a year for the apprenticeing, and the poor got 2s. or 3s. a week each in relief. All the properties were in good repair, and the accounts satisfactory.

4. William Cowper alias Piddock's Charity

In an indenture, dated 8th of April, 1685, and made between William Piddock, of Winson Green, In the Parish of Birmingham, of the first part; and William Piddock son and heir of the said William Maurice Piddock of Birmingham, and William his son, Roger Piddock of Handsworth, and John his son, and 12 others, of the other part; it is recited that William Cowper *alias* Piddock, theretofore of Smithwick, in the County of Stafford, by deed bearing date 20th February, 20 James I., assigned and set over to the said William Piddock, of Winson Green (by the name of William Cowper, *alias* Piddock, son of William Cowper, *alias* Piddock, of Edgbaston) and others, One Cottage and half an acre of Land to the same belonging, situate in Oldbury in the County of Salop, which he held by Copy of Court-roll, for the term of 600 years; to hold the said Cottage, Land, and the said Copy, &c., &c., for the residue of the said term of years . . upon trust . . that the profits should be distributed to Poor People being decrepid, aged, or impotent, of honest life and good conversation, not given to idleness. drunkenness, or other vices; and the said Donor appointed that 6s. 8d. should yearly be distributed among Poor Persons dwelling in the Parish of Handsworth, in the hither side of the parish toward New Inn, on Good Friday; and the remainder . . . among Poor People inhabiting the parish of Harborne and Smithwick on Good Friday and St Thomas's Day, the greater part or at least one half of the said remainder, to be given to the Poor of Smithwick, &c, &c. The premises . . in

Oldbury one of the divisions of Hales Owen parish and near Rude End are in the occupation of James Simpson. No rent has been paid for many years. Nearly 60 years ago one Jeremiah Smith was put in possession by persons acting as Trustees for the Parish, who told him if he would keep from applying for Parish Relief they would give him the house to live in. The present tenant, Simpson, married Smith's daughter . . . succeeded to the possession, paying no rent except a quit rent of 1s. to the Lord of the Manor.

Here is a typical instance of the way ancient charities, which now-a-days might prove useful if properly controlled and managed, were lost to the public. The Commissioners of 1823, however, seem to have been in time to rescue this. They found the annual value of the property to be about £10, which they report would be largely enhanced if coal were found beneath the surface. As Simpson had kept the place in good repair and had added to the Buildings, he was to hold the place in future as tenant to the Trustees, and the rent was to be divided and distributed as set forth originally.

The report of 1823 also mentions the Harborne Charities Of *Rev. W. Jephcote* and of *Mrs. Ball,* in neither of which Smethwick had any very special interest. But that benefaction in which Smethwick is more particularly concerned may here have the Commissioners' Report quoted *in extenso* in order that the 1823 status of that charity may be the more clearly apprehended. It runs—

5. Dorothy Parkes's Charities.

By indentures of lease and release, dated the 29th and 30th May, 1719, between Dorothy Parkes, of Birmingham, widow, of the first part; Charles Blackham and Isaac Spooner, of the second part; and Sir Charles Holt, baronet, and nine others, of the third part; the said Dorothy Parkes granted to the said Charles Blackham and Isaac Spooner, their heirs and assigns, divers messuages, tenements, cottages, farms, lands and hereditaments situate at Smithwick, in the parish of Harborne, in the county of Stafford, and at certain places in the parish of Hales Owen, in the county of Worcester, therein particularly mentioned and described, upon trust, as to part thereof to the use of the said Dorothy Parkes for life, with remainder to the parties of the third part, their heirs and assigns, in trust, among other things, to pay an annuity of £20 a year to Mary Halfpenny for life, and out of the remainder of the rents and profits of the premises, and out of such other monies as by the last will of the said Dorothy Parkes should be for that purpose bequeathed, to build upon some part of the lands at Smithwick, a chapel for divine service for the inhabitants of Smithwick; and when the said chapel should be built and furnished, and a minister appointed as therein mentioned, and the said Mary Halfpenny should be dead, to lay out and expend, out of the yearly rents and profits, the clear annual sum of £10 as follows: viz. 52s part thereof in buying 12 penny loaves, to be distributed every Sunday, among 12 such poor inhabitants of Smithwick as should attend divine service in the said chapel both morning and evening, to be appointed by the minister that day officiating, and two or three other inhabitants of Smithwick, who should be present at such distribution, immediately after the evening service, and who should be hereunto called by such officiating minister; 52s. other part thereof, in buying 12 other penny loaves, to be in like manner distributed every Sunday among 12 poor inhabitants of the other parts of the inhabitants of Harborne, attending at Harborne Church, to be appointed by the vicar therein that day officiating, and two or three inhabitants; £4 10s. 0d further part thereof, in buying six coats, or other garments, to be distributed, yearly, among six poor women inhabitants of the parish of Harborne, on St. Thomas's day, three to be of the hamlet of Smithwick, and three of the other part of the parish, to be nominated by the trustees; and 6s. residue of the said £10 to be expended in Bibles, to be distributed on St. Thomas's day, among such poor inhabitants of Smithwick as the minister for the time being should appoint; provided, that no such bread or coats should be given to any person who should have required any parochial relief within the space of one year next preceding. The deed contains a proviso, that on the death of any one of the trustees, the survivors should convey the premises to the use of themselves and such other persons as they should appoint, not exceeding the number of 10, on the trusts thereinbefore mentioned.

The lands possessed by the trustees, under this deed, consist of about 75 acres in Smithwick. and about 33 in Titford and Warley Wigorn, which places are in that part of the parish of Hales Owen which lies in the county of Worcester. These lands are let for rents amounting to between £200 and £300 a year. The whole of the income is received by the minister of the chapel, who applies the £10 for bread, clothes, and books, as directed by Mrs. Parkes.

One shilling a week, amounting to £2 12s. a year, is given away in penny loaves at Smithwick chapel, every Sunday after evening service, to 12 poor inhabitants of Smithwick attending at the chapel, and whom the minister selects himself. The other £2 12s. bread-money is paid over to the parish officers of the Harborne division of the parish, who make a similar distribution in the parish church to poor inhabitants, selected by themselves, and who have made previous application at the vestry after morning service.

Six gowns are provided by the minister, and given by him to three poor women of Smithwick, whom he selects, and three poor women of Harborne, who are recommended to him by the Bailiff for the Harborne division of the parish.

The 6s. given for Bibles is likewise distributed by him at his discretion.

Neither bread nor clothes are given to any who have received parochial relief within a year preceding.

The said Dorothy Parkes, by her will, dated 27th September, 1723, bequeathed to Sir Henry Gough, and twelve others (after a bequest of £800 towards the building of the said intended chapel), the further sum of £200 upon trust, to lay out about £40 in building a small charity school, if the same could be conveniently built for that sum, on some part of her estate at Smithwick, for a single woman, to be by them chosen to live in, and there to teach, gratis, poor children of Smithwick aforesaid, to read, sew and knit, and to learn the Church Catechism; and she directed her trustees to set out half an acre of land for that purpose, and for a garden, and to lay out the residue of the said £200 in the purchase of lands and tenements, to be settled for the payment of £5 per annum to such school-mistress, and 10s. per annum for books, and 10s per annum for coals to be burnt in the said school, and the rest to be applied by the trustees towards the clothing the poor children taught in the said school, the choice and management thereof to be left to the minister of the chapel for the time being, who should choose such as were the greatest objects of charity.

A school-house, consisting of a dwelling and schoolroom, was erected upon a piece of land near the chapel at Smithwick, set out by the trustees for that purpose, and for a garden, as directed by the above will. The building appears to have cost more than the £40 which Mrs Parkes appropriated for the purpose. There remains now, out of the £200 which she gave, £136, which was not laid out in land but is invested on the security of the tolls of the turnpike-road leading from Birmingham to Coventry. The interest received for this is £6 16s. a year.

A further sum of £1 13s. 9d. a year is received from the Birmingham Canal Company, as a compensation for land taken out of the school garden, for the purposes of the Canal.

This makes the income of the school £8 9s. 9d., the whole of which is paid over to a schoolmistress appointed by the trustees, and who lives in the school house rent free.

For this remuneration, she teaches from 12 to 20 poor girls of Smithwick, recommended by the trustees, to read, sew and knit, and the Church Catechism, and provides them with necessary books.

Concerning this same Charity here is a copy of a Petition allowed by the Attorney General at the instance of the Charity Commissioners, ordered to be printed by the House of Commons, 20th February, 1852:

Smethwick, Staffordshire.—Dorothy Parkes' Charity.—Petitioners: The Earl of Dartmouth; the Earl of Bradford; Wyrley Birch, of Wretham Hall, Norfolk, Esq.; Rev. Egerton Arden Bagot, of Aston, Warwickshire; Thomas Hanson, of Birmingham, Esq.; William Stratford Dugdale, of Merevale, Warwickshire, Esq.; James Taylor, of Moseley Hall, Worcestershire, Esq.; and Henry Goodrich Willett, of Lightwoods, Staffordshire, Esq.—Solicitors: Messrs. Taylor and Collison, 28, Great James Street, for the Petitioners. —16th May, 1851.

Petition allowed by the Attorney-General praying for a reference to the Master to inquire as to the propriety of a proposed purchase of land, and as to the repairs to and the pulling down of the School-house and the addition of the site thereof to the Burial-ground, and School-house being rebuilt upon another site; and as to the propriety of certain repairs to the Parsonage house, and, if proper, the repayment to the Incumbent of the sums expended thereon. The property consists of Land and Stock, the income whereof is about £320 per annum.

Griffiths' FREE SCHOOLS (1860), p. 481, says:—

The Dame's School near the Old Church at Smethwick is endowed with £8 9s. 9d. from £136 secured on the Birmingham and Coventry Turnpike tolls; as also an annuity of £33 9s. paid by the Birmingham Canal Co. for a piece of land. The number of girls varies from 12 to 20.

XXII.—THE GROWTH OF ANGLICANISM.

Since its erection 160 years ago the Old Church* has undergone no great structural alteration. Within the last half-century, however, a considerable amount of church building has been going on in Smethwick in order to keep pace with the rapidly-growing population.

Recent estimates show that for a population of 39,000, there exists church accommodation in consecrated buildings for 3,673 persons. From this, however, may be deducted 933 "appropriated" seats; while 970 places may be added for in the accommodation provided in "mission" churches. The Church Extension Society, which gets very liberal support in Smethwick, has given £750 towards Holy Trinity Church, and £220 additional towards its enlargement; £520 to St. Matthew's, and £280 towards St. Mary's, and to St. Michael's £455. Beyond this the Society contributed about £180 last year towards increasing the stipends of the assistant clergy in the parish —the total of similar contributions in the last five years amounting to £780.

The following table is instructive as showing the growth of Church work, and at the same time indicating the centres around which the working-class population of the parish gradually located itself.

In 1831 the only Church accommodation in Smethwick was provided by the Old Chapel, built in 1728, and affording accommodation for 360 people. Since then the work of the Established Church has grown as follows:—

DATE.		COST.	ACCOMMODATION.
1838	Holy Trinity	£3000	400
1855	St. Matthew's	£3000	600
1858	St. Paul's	£5000	950
1880	St. Chad's	£500	300
1881	St. Stephen's (Mission)	£500	300
1888	Holy Trinity, restored	£5600	400 (extra.)
1888	St. Mary's	£3750	420
1892	St. Michael's	£6000	600
1892	St. Paul's, restored	£1500	...
1892	St. John's (Mission)	—	120
		£28,850	4,090

(Approximate Figures.)

Holy Trinity Church.

The ecclesiastical district of Holy Trinity was formed out of Smethwick (or North Harborne, as it was called) in 1842. From its central position, it may appropriately be called the "town" church of Smethwick. The first edifice was erected at a gross outlay of £3,600 in 1838, from which year the Register dates.

In 1888 the fabric, with the exception of the tower and spire, was re-built on a much larger scale, at a further cost of £5,000 to £6,000, the work being initiated by the Vicar (the Rev. J. H. Crump) who not only gave liberally towards the cost, but upon his subsequent acceptance of the Rectory of Stoke-on-Trent he cleared off the balance of the debt before leaving Smethwick. It is in the Early English style, and consists of nave and two aisles, and a good chancel, with organ-chamber and vestry on its north side.

---

* This building does not seem to have had any dedication. It was put up at a very "low church" period. The Wake, which is held in October, is quite a modern institution, and gives no clue to the identity of a patron saint.

The south aisle has the baptistery at its west end, and a morning chapel at its eastern extremity. The entrances are on the north, and through the tower at the west end of the nave. This tower contains one bell. There are on the west wall (assuming the proper orientation of the building) memorial tablets to the local families of Adkins and Harden, and to a former curate, the Rev. W. Hammond. Painted windows (South side) commemorate William Marshall, 1876; James Reynolds, a former Parish Clerk, 1887; and (North side) Conolly and Anne O'Neill, 1893.

In a population of 9,084 souls, the structure provides seating for 883 worshippers: the Mission Church of ST. STEPHEN, however, gives accommodation for an additional 300. The Rev. C. W. Pearson is in charge of St. Stephen's Mission Church.

The living is a nominal vicarage, of the nett yearly value £250, with residence, in the gift of the Bishop of the diocese.

The first vicar was the Rev. T. G. Simcox, who came of a local family who were extensive landowners in Harborne. He was an eminent Greek scholar, and is commemorated by a brass in the church.

The second holder of the benefice was the Rev. T. Roper; he was succeeded by the Rev. J. Herbert Crump, a man of much energy and great liberality, who worked up his parish with assiduity and success. A vicarage which had been given by the first holder of the living was enlarged at his expense; a stained glass window in the east end of the church commemorates the labours of the Rev. J. Herbert Crump, R.D., who was succeeded in 1892 by the present vicar, the Rev. Thomas Ridsdel, of Queen's College, Birmingham, and St. Bees. Under the Rev. Mr. Ridsdel (who is a surrogate for the diocese) the parish is enjoying serene prosperity and a freedom from debt upon all its numerous parochial institutions.

St. Matthews Church.

St. Matthew's Church, for the period in which it was erected (1855), is by no means an indifferent piece of ecclesiastical architecture. It is of good coursed stone, with Bath stone dressings. Its west front, presented to the road, is a buttress-shaped gable, crested with double-bell gablets supported on corbels, each corbel being peculiarly differenced by a cross, forming a kind of "mask." The gablets are supported outwards by a three-staged buttress, on each side of which the west front of the nave is lighted by an early decorated window. The north and south porches are constructed of a breastwork of stone surmounted by tiled roofs carried on timber openwork. The plan of the Church consists of nave, north and south aisles, and a chancel; on the north side of the nave are the choir and clergy vestries (entered from the end of the aisle), and on the south of the nave is the organ chamber. The two porches being extremely near to the west end, allow only of a very narrow galilee, the south extremity of which serves as the baptistery. The nave has a clerestory lighted by quatre-foil windows, in sets of three over each of the five arches of its arcading, which latter is carried on four short and graceful circular columns, rising at pew-level from octagonal bases. At the south entrance is a fine new alabaster font.

In 1895 this church was further embellished by several costly memorials to the late Captain Henry Mitchell—who, by the way, was the first to suggest the collection and publication of these RECORDS OF SMETHWICK.

The Mitchell memorials consist of (1), a finely-executed stained three-light window in the chancel (by Evans, of Smethwick); illustrating the Crucifixion, presented by public subscription; (2) a richly-carved reredos, also generously given by the same public response; (3) a handsome alabaster pulpit, given by Mr. J. E. Mitchell; (4) an alabaster chancel-rail to match, with marble steps approaching to, and mosaic pavement upon, the chancel floor; the whole furnished completely by elaborate choir-stalls, clergy desks, and Communion-rail; the gift of Mr. Henry Mitchell; and (5) as a fitting supplemental gift from the family, Miss Mitchell added the alabaster font. The carving work was executed by Mr. R. Bridgman, of Lichfield, and the ecclesiastical tiles in the pavement were specially designed by Mr. J. F. Ebner, of London. The whole of the work was carried out under the direction of Messrs. Wood and Kendrick, of West Bromwich, who re-arranged and renovated much of the interior of the church at the same time.

This vicarage is set down as of the yearly value of £297 gross, with residence attached, and in the gift of the Incumbent of Smethwick. The benefice has been held by the Rev. Geo. Gilbanks (1856), the Rev. R. Ferguson (1860), the Rev. Her. Gardner (1873), and the Rev. John Wollaston, who has held it since 1880.

St. Paul's Church.

This church, erected in West Smethwick in 1858, had an ecclesiastical district assigned to it in January, 1860; the Register dates from the latter year for Marriages, and from 1850 for Baptisms. Spon Lane Schools were licensed for Baptisms in 1850.

It is a cruciform building of buff Stourbridge brick in what, by courtesy, passes for the Early English style; the nave is commodious but barn-like, and the transepts chiefly answer the purpose of an organ-chamber on the north side, and of carrying a small gallery on the south side. The organ possesses great purity of tone.

In 1891 the fabric was restored at a cost of nearly £1,000—Messrs. Chance aiding very materially. Of the original 920 seats, 320 were free: the accommodation is now reduced to 850.

The three lancet windows of the apsidal chancel contain stained glass, executed by Mr. S. Evans, of the neighbouring West Smethwick Stained Glass Works. The centre light is filled by a figure of the Saviour in the beatific attitude; erected in memory of John de Peyster Chance, 1874. On the right the window contains a similar figure of St. Paul, to whom the church is dedicated; this is commemorative of Edward Forster, 1887. The window on the left is filled by a figure of St. Peter, and was given in memory of George Downing, 1894, to whose memory a handsome stone pulpit (by Roddis) has also been erected.

The living is a nominal Vicarage of the gross yearly value of £280 or £250 nett, with a Residence; it is in the gift of five Trustees (Messrs. Chance).

The living has been held by the Rev. James P. Shepperd and the Rev. H. Stowe (1864).

The present Vicar, who has held the living since 1890, is the Rev. Thos. Wm. Wilkes, M.A., of St. John's College, Cambridge, who comes of an ancient Darlaston family. Through his successful ministry a Parish Room has become urgently necessary for the meetings of the numerous parochial institutions. Towards its erection the Church Extension Society have made a grant of £250. The Vicarage house was built as a thank-offering by the Rev. T. G. Simcox of Holy Trinity Church. The Chance family also have been great benefactors, contributing £1,000 of the £2,600 originally required to erect this church, the site for which was given by Mr. John Sylvester.

St. Chad's Church.

As the seating accommodation of the Old Chapel is but about 350, and the population of its district had in late years risen very considerably—it is now estimated at nearly 6,000 - a temporary iron church was provided in 1880 to seat an additional 300 worshippers. This Mission Church of St. Chad is now in charge of the Rev. J. Venables, and will soon give way to a permanent and larger structure. There is already a substantially erected and commodious school, although the locality is by no means so wealthy as the adjacent one of St. Mary. The initiatory work here was all performed by the Rev. H. T. Tilley, who left it to become the first Vicar of the said new church of St. Mary.

St. Mary's Church, Bearwood.

This ecclesiastical district, which apparently grew in emulation of the work in St. Chad's, was formed in 1888, in which year the church was consecrated. It serves all that outlying portion of Smethwick which almost runs into the prosperous residential suburb of Edgbaston. The building is of red brick, with Bath stone dressings, in the Early English style of architecture, designed by Mr. J. A. Chatwin of Birmingham, and erected at a cost of nearly £3,700, for the accommodation of about 420 worshippers. The organ cost £320, and was added in 1892. Much of the sanctuary furniture was given in memory of the late Mr. G. C. Adkins by members of his family. The lectern was presented by the congregation of St. Chad's, as a personal testimonial to Mr. Tilley on his leaving them to become the first Vicar of St. Mary's. The sedilia was given in memory of William Marshall, of Capethorne, Smethwick. The altar cross is a copy of an ancient monumental cross in the church at Cassington, Oxon. Of the 420 seats provided half of them are free, the pew rents producing (with offertories) £60 to £80 a year towards the minister's stipend. The living is in the gift of the Vicar of Smethwick Old Church. There is no residence attached to it. There is no endowment, but the Vicar who has been in charge from the beginning (the Rev. Henry Timothy Tilley, of Caius College, Cambridge) is none the less efficient as a parish priest on that account. On the contrary, when the work of building the new church was first undertaken, and the Chairman of the Building Committee (Mr. George C. Adkins) was attacked by an illness which became prolonged and ultimately proved fatal, the whole work and responsibility fell upon Mr. Tilley, who brought the undertaking to a successful issue. As the population has recently increased by leaps and bounds, the foresight and wisdom of providing a church in this locality are fully demonstrated. The Register dates from 1888 for Baptisms, and from 1892 for Marriages. There is no burial ground.

Church of St. Michael and All Angels.

It was in 1886 that the Bishop of the diocese marked out a district, containing an estimated population of 4,000, and consisting of portions of the three parishes of the Old Church, Holy Trinity and St. Matthew. The Rev. R. H. Cummins was appointed Curate-in-Charge and commenced work in a disused bedstead factory which was converted to the purposes of a mission church at a cost of £200. At the end of two years a congregation of 300, and a Sunday school of 200 children had been gathered together. In 1890 Mr. Cummins was succeeded by the Rev. C. E. Medhurst.

Then commenced active operations for the speedy establishment and complete equipment of a highly organised ecclesiastical district. Committees were formed, patrons were widely sought, and contributions were collected far and wide. By December of that year (1890) a site for the proposed church was purchased for £500. Plans were prepared by Mr. A. E. Street, M.A. of London, and Mr. John H. Chance becoming guarantor to the bank for an overdraft of some £3,000. building operations were begun. The foundation stone was laid June 24th, 1891, and the building was consecrated May 24th, 1892, the estimate being £4,750, with an additional £300 for so economising the site as to include a Parish-room within the building. By this time £2,122 had been collected, which by 1893 had grown to £2,473. Ultimately the expenditure upon church, schools and parsonage rose to £9,000, of which about £5,500 has so far been raised, Mr. J. H.. Chance being the largest contributor with £500. The church has taken £6,500 of the total, and the Parsonage has cost £2,000.

The style of the architecture, although at first sight unfamiliar, gradually grows upon the beholder. It is executed in red brick, and in many of its features is somewhat reminiscent of the Lombardic; not the least striking, and at the same time most admirably utilitarian in its purpose and design, is the raised platform-like chancel. Beneath this chancel, and approached by a flight of steps from the nave (as well as being accessible from the exterior) space is created—not for a crypt of ancient design, but for that more modern appendage, a useful Parish Room.

There are in all no less than 28 parochial institution organised and worked in connection with this parish, which consists almost entirely of a working-class population of about 7,650.

The living is designated a vicarage, the nett income from tithe rent being set down at £18, in the gift of the Bishop of Lichfield; the holder of this benefice is the Rev. Charles Edward Medhurst, M.A. of Hatfield Hall, Durham, who gets but about £7 of the nominal £13, and who bears the burden of the large indebtedness yet remaining on the parish establishments.

In St. Michael's district is ST. JOHN'S MISSION in Sloe Lane. The work is carried on in a disused factory which was formerly an "undenominational" mission-room.

XXIII.—THE RE-PLANTING OF ROMANISM.

On September the 4th, 1688, was opened the first Catholic Church in Birmingham since the Reformation, the consecration ceremony being performed by Buonaventure Giffard, Bishop of Madura and Apostolic Vicar. this building, dedicated to S. Mary Magdalene and S. Francis (of Assissi) stood near Dale End, and there is yet a street in that locality named "Mass-house Lane." In the following year, on November 26th, the church was pulled down by "Ye Rabble of Birmingham," and the fathers, who were of the order of S. Francis removed to Edgbaston, and took a house on the site of the present Workhouse. They did not remain long here, however, but retired to a more secluded spot at Harbourne. Here, for more than a century, they were established at a farmhouse in Pritchett's Lane near to which is another "Mass-house Lane." Hither came the few Catholics of Birmingham for the performance of their religious rites, wending their way by circuitous routes, for, it must be remembered, people were liable in those days to fine for being present at the celebration of the mass. Here, also, the fathers taught a small school, the average number of scholars being about 30. Several of these scholars continued their studies and became members of the Franciscan Order. In 1786, when toleration had become a little more established, Fr. J. Nutt who was priest in charge of the congregation and school, was emboldened to find a Mission nearer the town, and the present Church of S. Peter in Broad Street is the result of his efforts. At about the beginning of the present century the Franciscans left the "Mass-house" at Harborne, and removed to Baddesley.

Coming to Smethwick itself, the first planting of Catholicism was effected by the Oratorians under the direction of Cardinal Newman some years ago, a mission being established in High Park Road.

The work prospered, and the congregation grew, till in 1893 a new church was erected, and dedicated to St. Philip. It was built in brick and terra cotta, in the Romanesque style, from the designs of Mr. Alfred Pilkington of London. It contains one stained-glass window, of which "The Crucifixion" is the subject, executed and presented by Mr. Henry Camm, of Smethwick, in memory of Mr. and Mrs. Davis. The total cost was £4,500, of which one donor gave £1,600, while a large proportion of the remainder was collected in the offerings of the poorer members of the congregation who gave a penny a week for eleven years. To this good work they were instigated by Father Thomas Scott, who for 18 years had had charge of the Mission with its "School Chapel" He was succeeded by Father C. E. Ryder, the present parish priest.

XXIV.—THE SPREAD OF NONCONFORMITY

The three principal classes into which the Puritans, of old divided themselves were Presbyterians, Independents, and Baptists. All these denominations are represented in modern Smethwick—the Congregationalists differing but slightly from, the Independents, inasmuch as in the former each member of the community has a personal share in its affairs, while in the latter their title merely indicates that no foreign communion can be permitted to control their proceedings—although they are all of quite recent settlement here, following the tide of immigration attracted to the place by its ever-growing industries.

In taking these records of Nonconformity and Dissent, the various sects will. be given (as near as may be) the precedence due to seniority; the dates, of their respective irruptions in Smethwick being given in the head-lines.

Presbyterianism (1853).

The name *presbyteros* (Greek) signifies, "elder"; this church being governed by presbyteries or associations of ministers and ruling elders, all possessed of equal powers. Established by Calvin at Geneva in 1541, this form of ecclesiastical government was introduced into Scotland by John Knox at St. Andrew's in 1547. In 1572 the first Presbyterian church in England was registered in "the orders of Wandsworth." By 1643 (when the Westminster Assembly subscribed to the Solemn League and Covenant) the Presbyterians formed the bulk of the Puritan party. The great part taken in the religious struggles of the seventeenth century, by both Presbyterians and Independents, is a matter of history. Internal dissensions after the Revolution of 1688 led to secession in Scotland (1733), but afterwards the United Presbyterian Church resulted from an agreement consummated at Edinburgh, 1847.

The Smethwick Congregation has been in existence for over forty years. It was recognised by the Synod of the Presbyterian Church in England as a Mission or Preaching Station in 1853. In the following year the late Mr. John Henderson, of the firm of Fox, Henderson and Co., London Works, Renfrew and Smethwick, at his own expense, erected a large building for a week-day and Sabbath school for the children living in the district, and which was also to be used as a place of worship by their parents. This was known as the Cape School, and it was while occupying this edifice that those who objected to anti-Protestant views and practices, and declared adherence to the doctrine and polity of the Presbyterian Church were raised to the position of, and recognised as a regular charge or Congregation by the Synod of the Presbyterian Church in England in 1855. It was within the "bounds" of the Presbytery of Birmingham. The next year saw the congregation in the possession of their first settled minister, and their first regularly constituted local session. A brief period of steady work and progress was then enjoyed. This was suddenly interrupted by the death of Mr. Henderson in 1858, followed by the closing of the London Works and the dispersion of the majority of the workpeople. The years immediately following were times of anxiety and concern, and it was at this period that the few who remained found themselves in circumstances requiring their removal from the Cape Schools. They then planted themselves in the Six Ways district, and separating from the Presbyterian Church in England, became connected with the United Presbyterian Church of Scotland, within the bounds of the Presbytery of Lancashire. No settled ministry was enjoyed for a few years, but merely the location of preachers by the provincial Presbytery. The meeting place of the congregation at this time was the hall they had erected in Helena Street, which, with other buildings attached, form the school premises of to-day. In 1873 a movement was set on foot having for its object the building of a suitable place of worship. The site chosen was the piece of vacant ground lying between their school premises and Windmill Lane. Here they erected the building which is a conspicuous object in the thoroughfare just named. It cost, furnishings included, about £2,000, is seated for 350 adults, and was opened for public worship on Wednesday, 16th June, 1875. At this period negotiations for union were being carried on between the two sections of Presbyterians labouring in England, known respectively as the Presbyterian Church in England, and the United Presbyterian Church of Scotland. The latter denomination had a considerable number of congregations planted south of the Tweed, of which Smethwick was one. The union was agreed upon by both the Synods of England and Scotland; and it was consummated the following year (1876) the united Church taking the designation of The Presbyterian Church of England, and it consisted of 10 Presbyteries and 270 congregations, showing an income of £240,000. It is under this new name that the friends worshipping at Six Ways are now known among the denominations; and if one thing more than another distinguishes them, it is the quiet, steady, and persevering character of their labours. The congregation has never been strong, financially or numerically; and its history is marked with troubled and anxious periods, as well as with seasons of temporal prosperity and spiritual blessing. Since the Rev. Wm. Tullo, after two years' labour in connection with what, in his time, was known as the Cape Church, demitted the pastoral charge of the congregation in 1858, the following settled ministers have held office:—Rev. Wm. Dunn, the Rev. D. Patterson, ordained April, 1866; the Rev. A. M. Dalrymple, ordained June, 1868, and the Rev. David Buchanan, inducted 1886.

At the meeting of Synod held in London in April last the reports presented showed 11 Presbyteries, 301 Congregations, 69,632 Communicants, 7,452 Sabbath School Teachers, 80,969 Sabbath Scholars, 14,775 Young Men's Societies and Bible Classes; total income, £230,542 15s 10d.; Church property insured for £1,134,905.

The Congregationalists (1810).

The Jubilee of Queen Victoria in 1887 synchronised with the Jubilee of the Congregational Chapel in Smethwick. The latter event was worthily celebrated; and in one way by the publication of a pamphlet, entitled SMETHWICK CONGREGATIONAL CHURCH: ITS ORIGIN AND HISTORY. This booklet was a reproduction in print of a paper prepared and read by Mr John Thompson on Shrove Tuesday of that epoch-marking year, 1887. It was undertaken in response to the expressed wish of the Pastor and Deacons. For our present purpose of putting on permanent record all that pertains to, and is illustrative of, the religious and moral development of the community resident in Smethwick, the following copious extracts from Mr. Thompson's pamphlet will prove as interesting as they are valuable:—

> Seventy-seven years ago the Church worshipping in Carr's Lane, Birmingham—Rev John Angell James, minister—took into consideration the question of starting religious work among the thin and scattered population of the Hamlet of Smethwick, and decided to try what could be done.

DESPISED DISSENTERS!

Their first difficulty was to secure a suitable room, the quality not mattering so much as the whereabouts. The one in their judgment most eligible was situated on the Birmingham Road, near the Cape of Good Hope.

Here, on a Sunday early in May, 1810, was commenced the first Dissenting Sunday School and Preaching Station in Smethwick.

In this building Sunday School teaching and religious services were regularly carried on during a period of three years, when it became necessary to seek more ample and convenient premises, a home being found for the growing family in the house of Mr. Newland, father of our esteemed friend Mrs. Freeth, the oldest surviving member of the church. This house is still standing in the fork formed by Bearwood Hill and Bearwood Road, where whoso wills may see it. Here for ten years earnest men and women laboured vigorously, meeting with growing success as years rolled by; not, of course, without opposition, for at this time there was but one other place of worship in the village, to wit, Smethwick Old Chapel, built and endowed by an old maiden lady, Miss Dorothy Parkes, the then Incumbent being the Rev. Edward Dale, who was not pleased with Dissent or Dissenters, and who, on occasion, expressed himself in strong terms to Mr. Newland's daughter about the new invasion, enquiring in high dungeon, "Why don't you come to my church, and not go where they preach in the dark?" Whereto the lady made suitable reply: "Sir, since these friends have held service in my father's house your church has been better attended, and the people generally are more concerned about their spiritual well-being; besides which they do not worship in the dark, for the rooms are lighted with bright mould candles." "Perhaps so, perhaps so," exclaimed the clergyman, "but you'd all better come to my church. Good day."

The Lord of the Manor threatened to have Mr. Newland turned out of his house if he continued to allow *"these Dissenters"* to hold service in it. This the gentleman found was what he could not do, the house being Mr. Newland's own property.

Annoyance in other forms they had, no doubt. . . . . But spite of petulant persons, lordly squires, and wicked wags, things went forward. Smethwick grew, and Congregationalism throve, insomuch that again, in 1823, our friends had to seek a new and much larger home by reason of increasing numbers and interest. The Rev. John Angell James laid the Foundation Stone of a Chapel at the corner of Crocketts Lane on April 1st of that year. Opened early in 1824, this building was used as school and chapel for many years, and subsequently for Sunday School purposes alone.

And how was the pulpit supplied during all these years? By the deep and lasting interest of the Carr's Lane friends chiefly. Year in and year out, preachers and teachers came regularly from Birmingham to our help at Smethwick. . . . It must not be forgotten that up to this point Smethwick was very sparsely peopled. The majority of its inhabitants were of the labouring classes (as, indeed, where are they not ?) and, for the most part, very poor and not blessed with educational advantages such as fall to our lot now. . . . Once again the family house became too strait for our growing needs, and the building was enlarged by bringing the front several yards nearer the road, together with the addition of a gallery across the end opposite the pulpit. Before these alterations could be made it was necessary that many, many tons of earth should be excavated and removed. The friends were not over wealthy nor inflamed with pride.

They solved the difficulty by forming what Mr. Thompson calls "a pick and shovel brigade," laboring with their own hands till the work was done.

Other quaint incidents serve to lighten the story of Mr. Thompson's chronicle. Then he continues—

During all these early years communicants of the Church had to trudge once a month up to Carr's Lane for the Sacrament, and the Sunday School children once a year, upon Easter Tuesday, for an Address from Rev. J. Angell James.

Coming to the year 1837, it is recorded that the congregation resolved to ask the mother church for a grant of £40 per annum, in order that they might, if possible, invite a minister of their own. Upon consideration of this request the Birmingham Church cheerfully acceded to it. . . . And the stipend? £80 by the year. . . Upon the 13th April, 1837, the Rev. Owen Absalom Owen was ordained minister of the church.

The chapel was soon licensed for the solemnization of marriages. Mr. William Gosling, senior Deacon of the church to-day, and Miss Butler, a member of the church, were the first to avail themselves of the license, the second couple therein united being the young minister and Miss Jefferies, a member of the church. Timid people trembled at the temerity of marriage in a meeting-house without a church clergyman's intervention.

It was an odd habit of Mr. Owen's, for the better prevention of sleep during sermon, to ask all friends who felt drowsy to stand up, and it was a common thing for eight or ten persons to rise at different points in the chapel. . . . During many years, so long as teachers were supplied from Birmingham, one set taught (in the Sunday School) one day and and another the next Sunday. Mr. Woodman and Mr. Allen were the first superintendents. It was a curious custom at this time for all the girls, during school hours, to wear white mob caps and tippets.

Upon the retirement of Mr. Allen, Mr. John Freeth was chosen to the vacant office, and when Mr. Woodman gave up, Mr Samuel Thompson took his place. They filled their respective offices for a considerable period, and it was during their term that new school rooms were erected in rear of the chapel, and day schools, conducted upon the principles of the British and Foreign School Society, were started therein for boys and girls—Mr. Joseph Ewing and Miss Mary Trigg, of the Borough Road Training College, London, being appointed first master and mistress of the respective departments.

Mr. Owen left for Bromyard in April, 1844; in December, 1845, Mr. Wm. Shore accepted the pastorate, but died after five years' service (1850). The Rev. Thos. Arnold, of Burton-on-Trent, commenced his labours here in April, 1851.

During Mr. Arnold's ministry two important changes in the *personnel* of the Sunday School took effect. In the year 1852 Mr. John Freeth gave up the office of Superintendent of the Boys' School, and Mr. Charles Parks was chosen his successor. Two years later Mr. Samuel Thompson retired from his post at the head of the Girls' department, being succeeded by the writer. . . . For more than thirty years Mr. C. Parkes was annually chosen to the office first conferred upon him in 1852. . . . His son, Mr. Albert Parkes, was elected to succeed him.

It is now 33 years since the teachers elected the writer for the office he still holds. During that long period many changes have occurred. There are now but two teachers in the school who were in it then, viz., Mr. William Gosling and Mr. James Smith.

When Mr. Arnold left Smethwick the Church found considerable difficulty in fixing upon a suitable successor, but after a space of two years, it was decided to invite the Rev. R. A. Davies, of Birmingham, a young man who had just left the ministry of the United Methodist Free Church for that of the Congregational body, and came to us strongly recommended by the Rev. John Angell James. Mr. Davies laboured among us with faithful zeal and great success from June, 1860 to July, 1864, when he was laid aside by a severe affliction, which compelled him to retire from active work for two or three years. Subsequently, upon his partial restoration, he accepted a call from the Church at Ventnor, Isle of Wight. When Mr. Davies gave up the pastorate, the congregation, by whom he was greatly beloved, begged his acceptance of a purse containing £150, accompanied with the hearty assurance of their deepest sympathy in his affliction. Mr. Davies was succeeded in March, 1865, by the Rev. T. W. Mays, M.A., of Olney. His ministry extended over a period of twelve years. While Mr. Mays was with us the present commodious school rooms were conceived, built, and paid for. Receiving an invitation to the Church at Grantham, Mr. Mays accepted it, and left us in August, 1877. Shortly afterwards he was rendered unfit for duty by a cancerous ulcer, and this church contributed handsomely for his help. He, however, died in 1879. Gentle and inoffensive to a fault, the kindly man went to the grave in the prime of life.

On May 19th, 1878, the Rev. S. Lambrick, of Leicester, commenced his work here. He was only permitted to labour among us three years. and during the whole period he was suffering from a complication of diseases, relief from which he only found in his last resting place.

On the first Sunday in January, 1883, the Rev. Thomas Travers Sherlock, B.A., of Isleworth, commenced his ministry, and long may he continue to occupy our pulpit.

The present chapel (a blue brick edifice with massive stone quoins, standing in the High Street), was erected in 1853-4 at a cost—including ground, gas fittings, warming apparatus, organ, etc.—somewhat exceeding £3,000, the whole of which, with the exception of £650, was raised in voluntary contributions by the time the chapel was opened. . . . The London Chapel Building Society made a grant of £250 which is included in the £3,000. . . . In September, 1862, a public meeting was held in the chapel to celebrate the entire removal of the debt. Here let me insert part of the report made by myself as secretary to that meeting:—

"This Chapel and fittings cost upwards of £3,000. After the opening in 1855, there remained a debt upon the building of £650. The interest thereupon has been paid by several of the friends becoming responsible for the same upon amounts of from £50 to £100. This has prevented the annual collections from being burdened with accruing interest, and enabled us to devote the whole yield thereof to the extinction of the principal. Two years ago a movement was set on foot for the entire removal of the remaining debt of £550. . . . It is announced to-night that this chapel is entirely free from debt.

"Looking at the depressed state of trade throughout the country, it could hardly have been hoped that so heavy a sum as £550 might be cleared off in the short space of eighteen months. Most persons present will remember the recent falling in of the lecture room roof, which entailed an expenditure of £60. It was necessary to provide new gates, palisading, &c., for the front of the New Chapel, which cost upwards of £60. The Old Chapel has been made more suitable for Sunday School purposes."

So that the following summary sufficiently sets forth the state of the case:—

(1) Debt on Chapel ... ... £550.
(2) Accident to Lecture Room ... ... £60.
(3) New Gates, Palisading, etc. ... ... £60.
(4) Alteration of Old Chapel ... ... £60.
(5) Interest on debt for three years ... ... £82.

making a total of £812 raised during three years. . . . Six months after the big debt was removed a very serious accident befel the front of the Chapel. The overhanging top, being too heavy, fell with a crash. Luckily no one was hurt, but an expenditure of £217 was incurred for the necessary repairs. This further large sum was paid within a twelve-month. During this time the Sunday School was carried on in the Old Chapel which, spite of shifts and expedients, could not be rendered very efficient for its purpose, and a strong cry arose among the teachers for better accommodation, a cry which resulted in a determination to build new and more fitting premises behind the Chapel. The contract for building, fitting and furnishing the rooms, was £1,565. At the opening services, in November, 1871, it was found that the sum of £1,050 had been subscribed—leaving a deficiency of £515.

The accommodation thus provided consists of a large room, 66 feet by 34 feet, to seat 500 scholars. An infants' room below accommodates 130. There are six class rooms with an average capacity of about 20, or 700 places in all. There are separate rooms for the Superintendent and the Librarian. The old schools had 300 on the books; the new ones soon had 500 scholars. The debt was cleared off the building by one determined effort: in the space of sixty years £7,000 had thus been raised for building purposes alone.

The CONGREGATIONAL MISSION at West Smethwick was commenced by friends of the cause, in both Oldbury and Smethwick, meeting together for a number of years in Victoria Street West. In 1872 a chapel was erected in Oldbury Road at a cost of about £1,000, to accommodate 250 worshippers. At first the services were conducted by students from Spring Hill College, and by local Brethren, till in 1885 the Rev. A. A. J. Andrews became pastor. He left in 1892. In 1893 the Rev. T. Preston Yemens, who had previously been assisting the Rev. W. S. Houghton, at Edgbaston, took up the pastorate here. The Church is in a very satisfactory condition, with well-attended services, and flourishing Sunday Schools, and other Congregational institutions.

Much of the initial work was undertaken in the time of the Rev. W. W. Jubb, of Oldbury; but Oldbury has resigned all control now, and the Mission is in the hands of Smethwick Church.

The Baptists (1837)

Adherents to the principles professed by the Baptists first made their appearance among the Puritans of the reign of Henry VIII., although the first organised Baptist Church was not set up till 1607. This was established by a Mr. Smyth, in London. In 1633 a number of Baptists seceded from the Independent Church, led by John Spilsbury. In 1689 they, with forty of their bishops, assembled in London and adopted a Confession of Faith. The most illustrious of the Early Baptists was John Bunyan, born near Bedford in 1628. The Baptists regard Baptism as *the* sacrament of primary importance; they withhold it from infants; and they perform it by immersion instead of by sprinkling. As they sometimes baptised "over again" those who had been sprinkled in infancy, they got the name of Anabaptists. Their form of Church government is Congregational; in 1812 the Baptist Union was formed to promote all public objects affecting the denomination. (See Robinson's HISTORY OF BAPTISM)

Whether any of the Early Baptists were located in Smethwick is not known; though it is not at all improbable this may have been the case. The denomination seems to have been overtly introduced into Smethwick in the year 1837, when a man named William Taylor, who had removed from West Bromwich, where he was a member of the Bethel Church, set up a Preaching Room in his own house, which was situated in Hickman's Buildings, near the Crown Inn, on the Oldbury Road. Here came to preach, on Wednesday evenings, the Rev. William Stokes, of the West Bromwich Church, a man of much energy, and great organising activity. His first service was held 29th January, 1839. As the attendance steadily grew, the room became at last too small; and the emergency was met by another member of this little church (the father of Mrs. Ann Durose) offering a larger accommodation at his house, by making two bedrooms into a more commodious Meeting-room. To this room Mr. Stokes came on Sunday evenings as frequently as he could; and when he failed to appear other preachers came "on supply." Again the meeting-room space became too limited for the growing needs of the congregation; and a piece of land in Cross Street was purchased upon which was erected a chapel to seat 200 persons, opened July 12th, 1842, and which is now the Temperance Hall. A Baptistry was, of course, provided, and in this the first person to be baptised was Mr. Benjamin Halford, the ceremony being performed by the late Rev. Arthur O'Neill, of Chartist fame. Previous to the provision of this Baptistry the members of the Smethwick congregation had undergone the ceremony at West Bromwich Bethel Chapel, or at either of the Birmingham Chapels—the Circus Chapel in Bradford Street, or Graham Street Chapel. The cause in Smethwick had hitherto been maintained for five years as a branch of the West Bromwich Church; but now the nine members were dismissed therefrom, so that Smethwick Church could be formally constituted on the 12th, April, 1847. The Revs. W. Stokes, O'Neill, Phillips, Fisher, and Swan officiated on this occasion; and in the year following Smethwick Church was received into the Association.

The Rev. W. Stokes having removed to Birmingham, and the pulpit being subject to a constant change of preachers, the congregation began to decline. In August, 1849, a reorganising was attempted at the house of Mr. J. Vernon; with Mr. J. F. Lockwood as Secretary, a Committee of Management was formed, Deacons and Officers were appointed, and everything was put on a sound working basis, even to the signing of articles of faith. No pastor, however, was secured till 1851, when Mr. Rathbone took the oversight and conducted a morning service for about a year, when he died. Mr. Hossock afterwards took charge, but by 1853 the cause apparently died out, the chapel was closed, and the buildings were sold to the Temperance Society. A few of the more earnest members of the old congregation not being satisfied with this condition of affairs, appeared to the Rev. C. H. Spurgeon, before whom they laid their case so eloquently, that as a result an Evangelist was appointed to visit Smethwick and certain other weak churches; and aid in their strengthening. The man selected for the post was the Rev. C. Wilson Smith, who made his appearance in Smethwick about 1866.

At First no building of any kind could be secured for the services of Mr. Smith, so he took to open-air preaching, until at last the Patent Nut and Bolt Co. allowed the use of their large Mess-room for the holding of Sunday evening services. As a more central position was felt to be desirable a large Shed was procured in Union Street where not only Sunday services were held, but where a Sunday school was opened. At every meeting this place was crowded. As more accommodation was urgently needed, a piece of land was again bought in Cross Street, a second Baptist Chapel was erected thereon, the corner stone of which was laid by J. S. Wright, Esq., January 5th, 1869. (The Salvation Army now occupy these premises.) For a few years longer Mr. C. W. Smith laboured here with success, and then took his departure for America. After this several ministers supplied the church, and all of them acceptably. Then the Rev. G. T. Bailey, of Spurgeon's College, accepted the call to Smethwick, and his labours soon drew to the Chapel crowds which it could ill-accommodate (1876).

After such vicissitudes as these the existence of that fine classical building called Regent Street Baptist Church is evidence of the great vitality possessed by the cause in Smethwick. In September 1889 a jubilee celebration was held, at which was read an historical sketch, which was afterwards (1892) printed in the congregation's year book—No. 4 of their CHURCH MANUAL. Says the Rev. Walter H. Purchase, the compiler of this sketch, and a former pastor:—

> During Mr. Bailey's pastorate the present spacious Chapel was built, and is a fine monument to a seven years' happy and successful pastorate. In the year 1883, he received a call from the Church at Bury Road, Haslingdon, to succeed the Rev. B. B. Davis, which was accepted, The Church again being pastorless, heard several ministers with a view, and at last Mr E. C. Unmack, a student of Regent's Park College, was chosen. . . . After a very brief period the pulpit again became vacant. The result of this was the scattering of the congregation and the commencement of a rival cause, and the gloom seemed to become darkness in the home of the parent Church.
>
> After another short interval, Rev. Isaac A. Ward, of Clay Cross, was invited, and in response settled and remained about two years, and late in the year 1886, another vacancy occurred, which lasted until September 26th, 1887, and this period brings me to a point at which I would fain pass the work of recording into other hands, . . . Peace and harmony have prevailed and thank God they prevail yet, more united I believe we could not be; more zealous we may and must be if all is to be accomplished we hope and desire. A measure of prosperity has been afforded us. Sixty-three members have been added to our fellowship, and progress generally made.

Mr. Purchase adds in a Note, that between the reading of the paper in 1889, and its printing in 1892, the membership had more than doubled, great structual renovations had been effected in the chapel buildings, a new organ had been provided, and everything had prospered with the work of the church as far as they could wish. The accounts which form part of the MANUAL are full and detailed; they show the working of the various congregational institutions, and are eminently methodical and business-like. Nothing could be more straight-forward, or better presented for the satisfaction of those concerned. Beyond this, for the purposes of these Records, the following statement has been supplied, dated 11th April, 1883, of the cost of the Regent Street Church, with notes to date of other financial transactions:

	£	s.	d.
Builder's (Mr. Clulee) Contract	5300	0	0
Cost of Site	320	0	0
School and Classroom Furniture (the whole in the School-room made by the Teachers)	120	0	0
Legal Expenses	40	0	0
Amount paid to the Birmingham Building Fund due from old Chapel	143	0	0
Mortgage Expenses and Interest	200	0	0
Printing	55	0	0
Gas Fittings	32	10	4
Extras to Contractor	34	6	5
Selling Old Chapel	13	10	0
Rent of Old Chapel during building of New	7	10	0
Painting (Notice Boards, &c., and Stone-work)	7	11	0
	£6,273	7	9
Amount expended upon Renovation, Structural Alterations, and New Organ, 1891	600	0	0
Renovation of Schoolroom, 1893	17	3	0
	£6,890	10	9
Towards the Cost of New Church:—			
From Canon Street Trustees	£3000	0	0
Sale of Old Chapel (now Salvation Army Barracks)	£470	0	0

* * * * * * * * * * * *

One of the most eminent of Baptist divines, the Rev. H. S. Brown, began life as an engineer, and, not unappropriately, had some slight connection with Smethwick about the time the Baptist cause was struggling into life there. In the AUTOBIOGRAPHY OF THE REV. HUGH STOWELL BROWN *(Routledge)* occurs the following passage, descriptive of Smethwick, as it appeared about the year 1840:

I shall never forget the forlorn appearance of Birmingham in those days; the houses were very bad, but one shop in four was open in Bull Street, and the street corners were the resort of hundreds of dirty, ragged, and half-starved workmen. John Angell James was then in the height of his popularity; I went to hear him once of twice, and was not at all impressed except by the extreme plainness of the preacher. The parish of Harborne was some three miles from the centre of Birmingham; one-half of it joins the town, then called the village of Smethwick, and in Smethwick we took up our abode. Macfarlane was scarcely sober the day he went to Smethwick, but on his arrival there he made a discovery which sobered him at once. His undertaking was not exactly to make a new survey of the parish, but to correct an old map, and form one with all the alterations that had been made in the course of some twelve or fifteen years. Consequently he had taken the job at a very low rate per acre, expecting to have very little work to do, but to go over the parish with the old map and to jot down the new houses, fences, &c. The old map showed Smethwick as a place of green fields with a few farm-houses. To my master's consternation he found instead of green fields and farm-houses, a town with miles of streets, with forges, factories, and glass works, and I know not what beside. Evidently the work that was to have been done in a month would take at least four months. Macfarlane was in despair. He swore at and cursed the land agent from whom he had taken the unfortunate contract. But he had the good sense not to get drunk; he became all but a teetotaller, and continued sober all the time we were in Smethwick. He also became very penurious, and almost starved me. Drink had so damaged his stomach that he cared little for food, and could not understand the raging appetite of a strong healthy lad of fifteen, engaged all the cold and bitter day in the work of land surveying. I grew very weary both of my master and my occupation. The many engine works around me excited in me the desire to become an engineer; and as the survey approached completion I went one day to Boulton and Watts' Works, Soho, and applied for work in my capacity, but the times were so bad that I failed in my application. On the completion of the survey I bade Macfarlane farewell.

Church of the Baptist Brethren (1882)

The Church of the Baptist Brethren was commenced in April, 1882, by a few energetic workers who had just previously left the Baptist Church in Regent Street. The meetings are held in the Temperance Hall, Cross Street, which is rented for that purpose, and will seat about 400 persons. There are a number of institutions connected with the Church, viz., a Sunday School with 400 scholars, who are taught by 27 teachers; and a Pleasant Sunday Afternoon Class. The Church membership numbers 130, all of whom are expected to contribute towards the support of the work, such contributions being taken on Sunday morning at the Lord's table. No other collections are made for the work of the Church. They also support the Sunday School, the collections taken at school anniversary being devoted towards the Poor Children's Xmas Treat Fund. This fund was started some years ago, when the Church took upon itself the duty of collecting the poor children of Smethwick on Boxing Day in the Public Hall and regaling them with a good tea. The more destitute are supplied with shoes and stockings as far as funds will allow. The Church is very desirous of having a more suitable place of worship, and is making strenuous efforts to that end. This Church is very mindful of its poor members, having a fund for that purpose to which each member is supposed to subscribe a small sum weekly. Much more work would be entered upon if the Church had a place of its own which could be used on week-day evenings.

The Brethren of Bearwood Road Meeting Room (1880)

A Meeting Room was erected in the year 1880, and was the first place of worship in Bearwood. The present Meeting Room (to commemorate the silver wedding day of Mr. and Mrs. Swaine Bourne, 29th day of May, 1896), designed by G. F. Hawkes, Esq., architect, was opened on June 20th, 1896. The principles and doctrines maintained here are known as those of Brethren; Believers meet for "fellowship" and the Breaking of Bread every Lord's Day morning, and in the afternoon an efficient staff of teachers are engaged amongst the young; in the evening Gospel services are held. No public collections are ever made, save once a year for the Hospital Sunday Fund. Believers recognise baptism by immersion; and on Wednesday evenings an open meeting for the study of the Scriptures is held, with meetings for prayer every Sunday evening. The ministry of the Word on Lord's Day is known as "open ministry," and recognition is given only to those spirit taught. There is no paid ministry. Missions in other lands are contributed to from time to time.

Wesleyanism (circa 1800).

A full account of the rise and progress of local Wesleyanism in Wednesbury, West Bromwich, and Handsworth, has been given in the HISTORY OF WEST BROMWICH, pp. 84–94. The cause seems to have been introduced into Smethwick at "French Walls" very early in the present century, and not long after the founding of Nineveh Chapel. On p. 93 also appears the following:—

Spon Lane Chapel [which is within the boundaries of West Bromwich] accommodating 650 worshippers, was opened St. Barthomew's Day, 1841, when the total collection realised £195. It has cost £3,500 and is in the Smethwick Circuit, as is also Ryders Green Road Chapel.

Spon Lane Chapel was enlarged in 1878, and now accommodates 868 persons, in addition to finding Sunday School accommodation for 400 children. The earliest chapel (at French Walls) gave way in due time to one in Rabone Lane, near the corner of Bridge Street, the upper portion of whose stuccoed facade may still be seen, although the building has now been converted into shops and dwelling-houses. This, in time, was replaced by the more modern structure in New Street, which was built in 1856 at a cost of £4,892, to seat 829 persons. The commodious schools in connection with this chapel, erected at an outlay of £1,900, have been used for day school purposes till the present year, when they were transferred to the control of the School Board. The building is still used for a Wesleyan Sabbath School of 500 children. Grove Lane Chapel, built in 1864, cost £2,727, provides room for 440 worshippers, and a school for 300 children. Halford Lane Chapel, which cost £1,600, dates from 1882; it seats 382 persons. The Sunday scholars number 120. Sloe Lane Mission Chapel (1889) cost £200 to provide 120 places. Waterloo Road School-chapel was erected to seat 230 at an expenditure of £780; but a new chapel is now building for 650 persons at an outlay of £3,500. The Smethwick Circuit is in the Birmingham division.

Methodist New Connexion.

The Methodist New Connexion is represented by a vigorous Society who worship in a commodious chapel situate in Baldwin Street.

This denomination was the first off-shoot of the parent body, and has just entered upon the hundredth year of its existence. The reason of the separation was the contention of the founders of the Methodist New Connexion for equality of the laity with the ministry in matters of Church Government, and the justification of the movement has been seen in the adoption of the principle by the Mother Church.

The Society at Baldwin Street forms part of the Birmingham First Circuit. The "cause" in Smethwick originally started more than 30 years ago, and had a very humble beginning. The friends at first worshipped in a house at Brasshouse Lane; then they migrated to the old Temperance Hall. But naturally they wished for a place which they could call their own, and the building now used for a school was erected. For years, Divine service was conducted there, but the congregation grew so rapidly that it was necessary to increase the accommodation, and in the year 1885 the present structure capable of seating 430 persons was erected at a cost £1,416.

The present Circuit Ministers are the Rev. J. K. Jackson and Rev. W. Cooper, of Birmingham, but the Church is also ably served by Mr. T. Holcroft, of Handsworth, who occupies the pulpit every alternate Sunday. There is a flourishing Sunday School, an energetic Young Peoples Christian Endeavour Society, and a prosperous Pleasant Sunday Afternoon Class.

There is a debt on the whole estate of £300, and to celebrate the centenary of the Denomination, the Church has decided to make a special effort to liquidate the amount, and there is every prospect of its endeavours being realised.

Primitive Methodism

Primitive Methodism established itself in Smethwick by the holding of services in the house of the late Mr. Holloway, in Bridge Street. The first Primitive Methodist Chapel erected in Smethwick was called "The Cinder Chapel," because it was built with rough stones and cinders. It stood upon a site now occupied by the London and North Western Railway Station. This one was replaced by the second chapel, which was built in 1849 on the opposite side of Rolfe Street on land near the corner of Western Road. This chapel, like its predecessor, had a growing congregation, which led to a gallery being inserted, besides the addition of a singers' gallery and vestry. Even then it was found too small for the large congregations that assembled on special occasions, and at such times the Goods Shed of the L. & N. W. Railway was borrowed. This chapel afterwards gave place to another, which was built on the land adjoining, and was much larger than the former one, and galleried all round. The contract for it was £1,110, exclusive of the outlay of £100 for internal fittings, &c. The former chapel then became the schoolroom. This, the third Primitive Methodist Chapel, was sold to meet the requirements of the Rolfe Street Improvement Scheme. The arrangements of the sale were superintended by Mr. George Merricks, of Rolfe Street. The present chapel in Regent Street was forthwith erected. It was completed and opened in 1887. It will seat about 400 persons. In addition to the chapel, a new schoolroom was also built, together with a suite of rooms well adapted to Sunday School purposes. This chapel is one of the five places of worship comprising the Primitive Methodist "Birmingham Third Circuit," the other four places being respectively at Morville Street (Birmingham), Selly Oak, Cape, and Pope Street, Smethwick. Of these five churches the Rev. W. Forth, of Regent Street, Smethwick, is the Pastor, and in supplying their pulpits he has the constant assistance of the Primitive Methodist Lay Preachers.

The Separatists.

On the main thoroughfare, in the Oldbury Road, and at the corner of Bridge Street West, is a substantial brick chapel; or, as the preferred designation is, the "meeting hall of the Christian people called Separatists."

This sect was founded in Dublin in the year 1802 to follow the principles of Christian fellowship as it "subsisted among the first disciples of the Apostolic Churches." They connected themselves in the closest brotherhood according to the course marked out in the New Testament, but being persuaded they were not called upon to make any laws and regulations, they continued their connection with the other religious societies. This attempt to live in communion with other sects was given up in the brief space of one year, for they discovered that "the same divine rule which regulated their fellowship in the Gospel with each other forbade them to maintain any religious fellowship with others." From this view they obtained the name of Separatists.

Beside the chapel in Smethwick, they have places of worship at Dublin and at London only. That in Smethwick was founded by the late Mr. Robert Lucas Chance, who once lived at New Inn Hall, Handsworth, and subsequently at Summerfield House, Birmingham Heath. It is said he defrayed the entire cost of the erection of this Meeting Hall, which is now maintained by the generosity of his eldest son, Mr. R. L. Chance, of Edgbaston. The two gentlemen named were the only members of the firm of Chance Bros. who were associated with the Separatists. For some time meetings were held at Mr. Chance's house; and afterwards at the offices and reading room at the Spon Lane Glass Works. Service is held in the church on Sunday morning. In the afternoon the building is used for the purpose of a Bible Class, which is altogether separate from the Church.

A pamphlet containing much information as to the tenets and views of the Separatists, the writer of which is supposed to have been the late Mr. R. L. Chance, is entitled A LETTER, ADDRESSED BY ONE OF THE CHRISTIAN PEOPLE CALLED SEPARATISTS, TO AN ARDENT ADMIRER OF THE CHURCH OF ENGLAND; IN WHICH SOME OF THEIR RELIGIOUS OPINIONS ARE EXPLAINED AND VINDICATED. *(Birmingham, White and Pike, 1875.)*

The Salvation Army.

The Salvation Army unfurled its flag in Smethwick on October 21st, 1881. For some time the meetings were held in the old Theatre (a wooden structure) in Grove Lane. Subsequently the building in Cross Street, which was originally a Baptist Chapel, was taken, and it is here that the local corps carries on its work. The building contains accommodation for 400. There is a largely-attended Sunday School.

New Jerusalem Church.

The members of this Society are the custodians and students of the writings of Emanuel Swedenborg, one of whose axioms is that "all religion has relation to life and the life of religion is to do good." They hold as their fundamental doctrines—

1. That God is one in whom there is a Divine Trinity, and that he is the Lord God and Saviour Jesus Christ.
2. That a saving faith is to believe on him.
3. That evil actions ought not to be done, because they are of the devil and from the devil.
4. That good actions ought to be done because they are of God and from God.
5. That a man should do them as of himself; nevertheless under this belief that they are for the Lord operating with him and by him.

They hold, too, that certain portions of the Bible are written in a peculiar manner; that they contain an *internal spiritual sense,* which is opened to those only who are in the love of Truth; that while the letter of the Divine Word deals with past or future events the spiritual sense deals with an *eternal now.* Thus the 1st chapter of Genesis illustrates the progressive stages of regeneration. Their place of meeting is in a small house, No. 70, Bampton Road, where Divine service is conducted, and a Sunday School held. In Smethwick they are few in number, but at Handsworth they possess a very handsome building in Wretham Road. The minister is the Rev. R. R. Rodgers. In connection with the Church is an extensive library, free to visitors. In the Smethwick Free Library there are about 60 volumes of, works by Swedenborg and collateral writers, a separate catalogue of which can be obtained free from the Librarian. The first building ever erected for the Swedenborgians in England, or in any part of the world, was in Birmingham. This was the Zion Chapel of Newhall Street, opened 19th June, 1791.

Smethwick Spiritualists' Society.

This Society was formed for the purpose of promulgating the truth of Spiritualism. The first public effort was made on August 14th, 1889, at 43, Hume Street. The room, which held about 50 persons, eventually became too small to accommodate the inquirers, and on Sunday, October 7th, 1894, the Central Hall, situated at the corner of Cape Hill and Shireland Road, which was registered as a place of worship, and capable of holding 160 persons was opened. Successful meetings are held there every Sunday, very often the Hall being uncomfortably crowded. Earnest enquirers are always welcomed. There is also a Children's Progressive Lyceum connected with the Society, which is attended very regularly by the children of the members every Sunday afternoon.

XXV.—A SMETHWICKIAN SHAKESPEARE RELIC.

In tracing the history of the religious foundations in Smethwick, the fact that the place formerly boasted a parochial Library (refer back to p. 54) naturally suggested some connection between the books of this public library, and the location in which to search for a relic of Shakespeare, which, according to local tradition, took the shape of a Prayer Book, in which the immortal poet had inscribed his name.

The compiler of these RECORDS commenced the search by inserting a notice of the few known facts in the *Smethwick Telephone*; and desiring any one possessing information on the subject to communicate with the office of that paper. A response was immediately forthcoming from Mr. W. J. Moseley, of Cape Hill, in the shape of an American magazine, containing an article alluding to the subject of this inquiry—after which, the quest became very much simplified.

The following is an extract from the article in question, called "The Handwriting of Shakespeare," appearing on p. 495 of *Demorest's Monthly Magazine,* of June, 1882, published at 17, East 14th Street, New York, and which is illustrated by blocks of the six autographs mentioned:

> Not a line of Shakeapeare's manuscript is known to exist. He died in 1616, and it was not until seven years afterward that the first edition of his plays was published, from copies in the hands of his fellow-managers—Heminge and Condell. Of these manuscripts not a word remains, and the only idea we have of Shakeapeare's handwrittng is gathered from his signatures, six of which are believed to be genuine. Three of these are attached to his will, which is written on three sheets of paper, the name being on each. The will is preserved in the Prerogative Office, Doctors' Commons, London, and may be inspected by anyone for a shilling. Another autograph was found in a small volume, the first edition of Florio's translation of Montaigne which was in possession of the Rev. Edward Pattison, of Smethwick, England, and was sold in 1838 and purchased by the British Museum. The other two signatures are attached to the deed of purchase of a house in Blackfriar's, London, and to a mortgage of the same property. The former signature was bought by the Corporation of London, and is now at Guildhall; and the latter is in possession of the British Museum.

It was comparatively easy to follow up this trail; although, it will be noted, no allusion to any signature in a Prayer Book is to be found, except indeed in the one article by Dr. Furnival, to which reference will be made. And this signature is certainly a neglectable quantity, as it is deemed to be merely one of Ireland's notorious forgeries.

A pamphlet by Sir Frederick Mudden, entitled OBSERVATIONS ON AN AUTOGRAPH OF SHAKSPERE, AND THE ORTHOGRAPHY OF HIS NAME (*London, T. Rodd, 1838*), tells all that is known of the history of the copy of "The Essays of Michaell de Montaigne," translated by John Florio–London Val. Sims for Edward Blount, 1603, *fol.*—with a supposed autograph of Shakspere; which copy is now in the British Museum Library—Press-mark C. 45, K. 10.

The pamphlet, pp. 4 and 5, says—

> The precious volume which I have thus introduced to your notice is a copy of the first edition of the English translation of Montaigne's Essays by John Florio, printed in Folio, 1603, and its fortunate owner is the Reverend Edward Pattison, of East Sheen in Surrey to whom the Society (of Antiquaries) will be indebted in common with myself for any gratification they may receive from the present communication. Of its history nothing more can be stated than this, that it belonged previously to Mr. Pattison's father, the Reverend Edward Pattison, Minister of Smethwick in Staffordshire, about three miles from Birmingham, and thus contiguous to the County which gave Shakspere birth. How or when this gentleman first became possessed of it, is not known; but it is very certain that

previous to the year 1780 Mr. Pattison used to exhibit this volume to his friends as a curiosity on account of the autograph. No public notice of it, however, was at any time made; and, contented with this faint notoriety, the autograph of Shakspere continued to slumber in the hands of this gentleman and his son, until by the friendly representations of Mr. Barnwell, the present owner was induced to bring it to the British Museum for inspection.

It will be seen from this quotation that when the book was purchased by the Trustees of the British Museum in 1838, Sir F. Madden believed the autograph to be genuine. It is said he subsequently altered his opinion.

Dr. Furnivall, in an a article on "Shakspere's Signatures" in the JOURNAL OF THE SOCIETY OF ARCHIVISTS AND AUTOGRAPH COLLECTORS *(London, Elliot Stock, 1895)*, No. 1, June, 1895, simply says that it has no pedigree and need not be considered.

Halliwell-Phillipps, in his WORKS OF WILLIAM SHAKSPEARE *(London, 1853, fol.)* Vol. 1., pages 249-250, says—

A Signature in a copy of Florio's translation of Montaigne, 1603, is open to this objection; that the verbal evidence as to its existence only extends as far back as 1780, after the publication of Steevens's facsimile of the last autograph in the Will, of which it may be a copy with intentional variations.

XXVI.—THE ERA OF CANALS.

The first canal ever made in England was that of the year 1134, made by Henry I., to connect the Trent with the river Witham. After a lapse of five hundred years the New River Canal was begun in 1608. Between 1715 and 1799 no fewer than forty-five canals were undertaken in England.

An advertisement published in Birmingham, January 26th, 1767, ran thus—

> The utility of a Navigable Cut from the Wolverhampton Canal through the Coal Works to this Town having been pointed out . . . a Meeting for the further consideration of this Scheme is thought essentially necessary, &c., &c.

The meeting was held at the Swan Inn, the undertaking resolved upon, and the famous engineer Brindley was applied to. Shares were £140 each, no one being allowed to hold more than ten. (By 1782 these shares sold for £370 each)

It was again at the Swan Inn on June 4th, 1767, that Brindley produced his Plans and Estimates for the proposed canal from "the Town to the Staffordshire and Worcestershire Canal through the principal Coal Works, by two different tracks, and gave it as his opinion that the best was from near New Hall, over Birmingham Heath, to or near the following places, viz., Smethwick, Oldbury, Tipton Green, Bilston, . . with branches to different Coal Works, &c."

It was then stated the total expense would not exceed £30,000, but by July 15th, the estimate had risen to £50,000. The Bill was passed in the July of the following year, when the bells were set ringing in honour of the occasion. The work was soon commenced, and the first tribute of blood was paid on July 24th, 1769, a Saturday morning, when "a little beyond Winson Green, the earth fell suddenly in, occasioned by the heavy rains of Friday evening, and killed John Lester, one of the workmen."

Brindley's engineering followed the universal practice of that day in taking the canals at a level (or contour line) to avoid locks; a principle which is forcibly expressed in Brindley's own words, that it was safest "to keep the giant Water always on the flat of his back." This method of execution made the new water-ways somewhat tortuous, as they were planned to wind around both depressions and hills in order to avoid the cost of aqueduct or cutting. This method was soon afterwards modified to a very considerable extent.

The completion of the project in 1768-9, at the comparatively small outlay of about £70,000, had important results so far as the future development of Smethwick was concerned. Of this there can be no doubt whatever to anyone who has followed the rise and industrial progress of Smethwick, and the causes which led to this marvellous development, and the aggregation of its dense population.

At that time, however, it was a wild open region, with but a very sparse and widely scattered population. Originally, Smethwick hill was ascended by six locks, and descended by the same number to its former level again; but in 1790 these six were reduced to three, at a rectification of the original plans which had thus early to be undertaken.

The rise of water from Birmingham to Smethwick is 18 feet, which higher level is carried through West Bromwich, Oldbury, Church Lane, Tipton, and Bilston, to Wolverhampton. The canal from Ryder's Green to the old colleries at Wednesbury has a fall of 46 feet.

The then popular enterprise of canal cutting further progressed, and in November, 1770, a notice appeared in Birmingham to the following effect—

> We hear that the country is surveying from the Coventry Canal by Coleshill, Castle Bromwich, Aston, Perry, Hamstead, and West Bromwich, to the Coal Pits near Wednesbury and Bilston, and to the Lime Pits near Walsall, &c., &c.

Already this kind of enterprise had reduced the price of coals at the Birmingham wharf to fourpence-halfpenny per hundredweight; and the Canal Company resolved for the winter of 1769-70 to establish coal-yards in different parts of the town "for the better accommodating of the poor."

In this may be discovered the ostensible and direct reason for promoting artificial waterways so vigorously in this particular neighbourhood. No part of England felt the deficiency of natural waterways and good navigable rivers so much as Birmingham and the Midlands. The leading idea of the promoters was to connect Birmingham and its busy hearths and furnaces with the coal-mines of Wednesbury, then the chief source of their supply. For years the manufacturers of Birmingham had felt the inadequacy of the road traffic for their minerals, raw materials, and heavy products. "A letter from a Mechanick in the busy Town of Birmingham," "wrote in the year 1733," speaks so feelingly of the dependence of that town upon the neighbouring one of Wednesbury, that the words take this poetic guise—

> Beneath old Wedgbry's burning Banks it lies
> Where Thousands of his Slaves with glaring Eyes
> Around him wait, or near him do reside
> In Subterraneous Caverns, deep and wide;
> Where by their Chief's Command, they sap like Moles
> Supplying every Smithy Hearth with Coals.

Again, in 1769, the poet Freeth rejoices his "Birmingham Boys" with the glad tidings of cheap coal—

> For true feeling joy in each breast must be wrought
> When Coals under five-pence per hundred are bought.

—for, of course, cheap fuel to the manufacturer meant cheap coal for the poor. It was indeed a public boon when coal-barges re-placed coal-wagons (running on bad roads before macadam was known) which were scarcely more effective than the panniers across the backs of led-horses, which had preceded them.

Dr. Langford, in his CENTURY OF BIRMINGHAM LIFE, from which the foregoing rhymes have been taken, describes the rapid growth of Birmingham in the eighteenth century, and the wonders of its industrial development during that period. He quotes (Vol. I., p. 309) the following public notice:

> January 7 1782.—The Gentlemen and Tradesmen of the Town of Birmingham and its Environs, who are desirous of encouraging the Scheme now in Agitation for making a Navigable Canal from the Collieries at Wednesbury to the Lower Part of the Town of Birmingham, and from thence to Atherstone, are requested (previous to a General Meeting) to attend at the Swan Inn, in Birmingham, To-Morrow, the 8th day of January Instant, at Three o'Clock in the Afternoon, when and where the Plan of a late and improved Survey will be produced for their approbation.

The project was approved, and the work begun: On February the 4th it was announced—

> A Petition was presented in the House of Commons on Monday last for Leave to bring in a Bill to make and maintain a navigable Shaft or Canal from Wednesbury to Birmingham and from thence to join the Coventry Canal at Fazeley. Since the Subscription for carrying the same into execution was closed, Sums to a very large amount have been offered.

THE SUMMIT CUTTING (1789)

This improvement, completed in 1790, and to which allusion has previously been made, had a peculiar interest for Smethwick, to which it brought a new feature on the landscape. Here is a report of the completion of the Summit Bridge, dated 21st June, 1789 :—

That stupendous work now carrying on by the proprietors of our Navigation at the summit, near Smethwick, is at this time so far advanced that we understand the water will be let into its new course within a few days. So vast and seemingly impracticable an undertaking, has, we believe, never before been attempted in this kingdom; mountains have been raised and levelled, and a canal of a well's depth has been cut almost under the canal; in short, it is not easy to convey a just idea of what human art and labour have in this particular instance accomplished. Three hundred labourers employed in the business some in digging some in filling, and the greater part in wheeling, in succession, up the acclivity, for a mile in extent, their loaded barrows upon the stages erected for them, presents to the spectator a most pleasing, busy, and novel scene; and we sincerely hope that the spirited body who could attempt, and that the Engineers who have executed, so great and expensive an undertaking, will all derive their due advantage from its good success.

The Birmingham and Fazeley Canal was completed from Wednesbury to Broadwaters " Old Engine'" in 1786.

Of course, Birmingham, with its numerous and varied interests, was concerned in other canals than the one into Staffordshire. Therefore, when the Bill passed through Parliament, June 10th, 1791, for the making of the Birmingham and Worcester Canal, the local poet of the day once more burst forth into song in praise of the event, and in anticipation of the great advantages the newer water-way would confer. In one stanza the rhymester says—

> With pearmains and pippins 'twill gladden the throng
> Full loaded the boats to see floating along;
> And fruit that is fine, and good hops for our ale
> Like Wednesbury pit-coal, will always find sale.

—an early recognition of the clear distinction to be expected between the traffic from Worcester and that from Wednesbury.

Smethwick readers will be more concerned, however, with the former canal which passes through their own borders, maps of which may be consulted in the Birmingham Free Libraries. It is interesting to note thereon some of the old place- names in the locality.

"A Plan of the Navigable Canal from Birmingham to Aldersley, near Wolverhampton, with a Collateral Cut to the Coal Mines at Wednesbury" (1771), marks the following places along the line of route, after passing the "Cottage of Content" in Birmingham, namely—

(1). Sand-pits (R).
(2). Lodge (R).
(3). Winson Green (R).
(4). Pigmill Forge (R).
(5). Mr Robinson's (L).
(6). French-wall (L).
(7). Smithwick Hall (R).
(8). Ruck of Stones (R).
(9). Blugates (L).
(10). Holt Hall (R).
(11). Spon Lane (L) where the Collateral Cut branches to the Right.

Most of these are yet easy of identification; (4) and (5) are shown opposite to each other, as are also (9) and (10). R, of course, signifies Right side, and L, left side of Canal, proceeding from Birmingham.

A still older Map of a similar survey made in the year 1767 shows a perfectly straight underground cut from a point opposite Blue Gates, beneath Roe Buck Lane, and very nearly to Spon Lane; then, proceeding further, the following localities are marked down—

(1). Blakeley Hall (L).
(2). Mr. Taylor's Mill (R).
(3). Bromforth Lane (R).

Then the branching Cut leaving Mr. Turton's Brades far on the Left, the branch having marked on it

(4). Mr. Abney's Mill (R).
(5). Dunkirk (L).

and presently the "Cole Pits" and the "Fire Engine" at Wednesbury, the neighbourhood of Ocker Hill being shown to be then very thickly wooded.

The Birmingham Canal, passing through Smethwick, ran 22 miles, till near Wolverhampton it ran into the Staffordshire and Worcestershire Canal. It had, however, been so hastily constructed, that by the beginning of the present century it had become sadly dilapidated, in parts being little better than a ditch. Locks were bad, delays were vexatious, complaints were loud.

In 1826 the great engineer Telford was called upon to undertake the task of improving the local canals, including that through Smethwick; he cut through the hill at Smethwick, taking the canal at one level from Birmingham to Wolverhampton, while the old canal from Birmingham to Smethwick was very much straightened.

The height of this canal above sea-level is 500 feet. The storage Reservoir at Monument Lane covers an area of over 62 acres. The first boat passed through the new canal on September 28th, 1829.

Of the several fine bridges which span this newer canal, the Galton Bridge at Smethwick is the most noteworthy. It is an iron structure, with a span of 154 feet, and a total length of 264 feet; the height to the centre of the arch is 68 feet; the breadth of the roadway is 25 feet. Its weight of iron is 700 tons, and for the period in which it was erected, may be considered a fine piece of engineering work. It was opened for passenger traffic in March, 1829.

The first boat-load of coals from Wednesbury passed through Smethwick into Birmingham on November 6th, 1769. Coals which had previously been 15s. to 18s. a ton fell almost at once to 7s. 6d. If this was the immediate result to Birmingham, it is not difficult to conjecture what canal-making had in store for Smethwick. It is clear that the introduction of the canal into Smethwick was the first step towards its ultimate development.

PIGOT'S DIRECTORY, 1835, says of Smethwick that "the population of this village has greatly increased since the Birmingham Canal was cut through its northern limits; on the bank of which is a soap and red-lead factory, and also a large iron-foundry forming part of the Soho Works; and extensive iron and steel manufactories."

From the "Commercial Wharf" at Spon Lane (Samuel Southall, wharfinger) there was then formally announced a "daily conveyance by water" of goods to London, to Liverpool, and to all parts of the Kingdom.

About this time Flyboats for passengers plied between Birmingham and Wolverhampton, in competition with the omnibuses and other public conveyances. The boat-fare from Monument Lane to Wolverhampton was one shilling; it is in connection with these boats that the anecdote is told of the Frenchman who got his head damaged against the Smethwick bridge through looking out of the cabin window, and all notwithstanding the outcries of the other passengers; and who then ruefully complained "Vhen you do say 'Look out !' you do mean 'Look in!'"

XXVII.—THE SOHO INFLUENCE

The first impetus which sent Smethwick upon its high road towards industrial development was the introduction of the Canal system; as may be indubitably recognised from the local records contained in the last chapter.

The second great impulse was the establishment of Boulton and Watt's famous manufacturing concern in its immediate vicinity—in that district known as Soho, and which has been topographically described on p. 14.

Prior to 1756 the district between Nineveh and Hockley was a barren heath, the home of conies and a few beggarly squatters, until a Mr. Edward Ruston leased this land from the lord of the manor. He at once deepened the channel of the Hockley Brook, and then built a small mill by its side. This mill, in 1764, was purchased from him by Matthew Boulton (who in 1794 acquired the freehold of it) and here was fixed the site of the world-renowned Soho Works, which he laid out at a cost of £9,000. Soon after, James Watt obtained his patent in Glasgow for an improved steam engine; he came to Soho and joined Boulton in partnership (1774).

In 1774, according to SWINNEY'S BIRMINGHAM DIRECTORY, these works consisted of four squares of buildings, with workshops, &c., for more than a thousand workmen. A larger number were afterwards employed; and for long years afterwards Soho House (now a Ladies' High School), as Boulton's residence was called, was the resort of princes and philosophers, of savants and students, to a far greater extent than many of the European Courts. Soho was acknowledged as the home of the steam engine, and became the birthplace of countless inventions.

No vestige of this place is now left, the Foundry having been removed to Smethwick in 1848; the celebrated Mint was cleared out in 1850, and its walls razed to the ground in 1853.

One portion of the Works, added by Boulton, was that important establishment at some distance from the original Soho near the Great Pool, and in the Soho district of Smethwick. This was added partly to relieve the crowded workshops of the original buildings, and partly for the manufacture and finishing of heavy work, such as machinery for boring and drilling, lathes and cylinders, and especially for foundry work. In later years this place was developed and enlarged by the genius, industry, and skill of William Murdock; in 1809 solid cylinders were bored, special slide valves invented, oscillating engines perfected, models of locomotives made, gas-lighting purified, and many mechanical contrivances brought to perfection—a proud record for Smethwick, of which any place in the world might well be envious. As to the princely Boulton himself, he was a man of business, as well as a mechanician so able that it is needless to recall that his designs of presses and dies have remained unchallenged and practically unchanged down to the present day.

Under the suggestive heading, "The World of Soho," Dr. Langford gives in his CENTURY OF BIRMINGHAM LIFE (Vol. II., p.p. 145-157), a full account of all those "Captains of Industry" who made this locality so famous at the close of the last century. He quotes from Samuel Smiles' LIVES OF BOULTON AND WATT; also from the *Gazette* of August 15th, 1791, reporting the rejoicings at Soho on the coming of age of Boulton's son; and then (p. 150) we have the following extract from the same local newspaper on the opening of the new Soho Foundry at Smethwick, celebrated on Saturday, 30th January, 1796:

On Saturday last the Rearing Feast of the new Foundry, lately built by Messrs. Boulton, Watt, and Sons, at Smethwick, was given to the engine-smiths, and all the other workmen employed in the erection. Two fat sheep (the first fruits of the newly-cultivated land at Soho) were sacrificed at the Altar of Vulcan, and eaten by the Cyclops in the Great Hall of the Temple, which is 46 feet wide and 100 feet long. These two great dishes were garnished with rumps and rounds of beef, legs of veal, and gammons of bacon, with innumerable meat pies and plum-puddings, accompanied with a good band of martial music. When dinner was over, the Founder of Soho entered, and consecrated this new branch of it by sprinkling the walls with wine, and then, in the name of Vulcan, and all the Gods and Goddesses of Fire and Water, pronounced the name of it Soho Foundry, and all the people cried Amen. A Benediction was then pronounced by him upon the undertaking, and a thanksgiving offered for the protection and preservation of the lives and limbs of the workmen during the erection. These ceremonies being ended, six cannon were discharged, and the Band of Music struck up "God save the King," which was sung in full chorus by two hundred loyal subjects. After this, many toasts were given suitable to the occasion by the President of the Feast, Mr. M. Robinson Boulton, which was conducted by him with great spirit and hilarity; each toast was accompanied with three joyous huzzas and a discharge of cannon. A Ball, with tea, was given in the evening to Venus and the Graces, which ended about ten o'clock, when the concluding guns were fired, and all departed in good humour. The address of Mr. Boulton, sen., upon entering the Foundry, was conceived in the following terms:—After making an excuse to the company for not dining with them, he said—

"I could not deny myself the satisfaction of wishing you a happy and joyous day, and expressing my regard for all good, honest, and faithful workmen, whom I have always considered as classed with my best friends.

"I come now, as the Father of Soho, to consecrate this place as one of its branches; I also come to give it a name and my benediction.

"I will, therefore, proceed to purify the walls of it, by the sprinkling of wine, and in the name of Vulcan, and all the Gods and Goddesses of Fire and Water. I pronounce the name of it Soho Foundry. May that name endure for ever and ever, and let all the people say Amen, Amen.

"This Temple now having a name, I will propose that every man shall fill his pitcher and drink success to Soho Foundry."

Mr. Boulton then proceeded to give the Establishment his benediction:—

"May this Establishment," said he. "be ever prosperous, may no misfortune ever happen to it, may it give birth to many useful arts and inventions, may it prove beneficial to mankind, and yield comfort and happiness to all who may be employed in it.

"As the Smith cannot do without his Striker, so neither can the Master do without his Workmen. Let each perform his part well, and all do their duty to that state to which it has pleased God to call them, and this day will find the true rational ground of equality.

"One serious word more, and then I have done. I cannot let pass this day of festivity without observing that these large piles of building have been erected in a short time, in the most inclement season of the year, without the loss of one life, or any material accident. Therefore, let us offer up our grateful thanks to the Divine Protector of all things, without whose permission not a sparrow falleth to the ground. Let us chaunt Hallelujahs in our hearts for those blessings and with our voices, like loyal subjects, sing 'God save Great George our King!'"—which was done in full chorus, and amidst the discharge of the cannon.

Dr. Langford then alludes to Murdock, the inventor of coal-gas, and the illumination of Soho in 1802; to John Wyatt, the great mechanic; to other contemporaries and friends, such as Baskerville, Priestley, Wedgwood, and Keir, who made this locality famous in the eyes of the whole world; to the copper coinage produced at the Mint; to Francis Eginton, of Handsworth, who restored the art of painting upon glass; till, near the end, comes the record of the death of the great Father of Soho, Matthew Boulton, F.R.S., who died at his Soho residence, August 17th, 1809, at the age of 81; this was followed by death of James Watt, on August 25th, 1819, in his 83rd year. Both were buried at Handsworth. William Murdock survived till 1839, and died at Sycamore Hill, Handsworth, in his 85th year. Soho, in those days, was indeed peopled with giants.

Handsworth, in 1816, according to LEIGH'S DIRECTORY OF STAFFORDSHIRE, was an extensive and agreeable village, containing among other attractions, Hamstead House, the residence of the Birch family, lords of the manor of Handsworth. The grounds on the winding banks of the Tame were quite romantic, abounding in the foliage of full-grown trees. The factory of Boulton and Watt then employed 600 workpeople, and the huge water-wheel which supplied the works with motive power was propelled by the stream from Soho Pool.

Soho Pool had been made by the construction of an embankment in 1756-60, which impounded the waters of Hockley Brook. This pool was drained in 1866, and its site made into building land. It may be noted that there is a fall of 177 feet from the crest of Soho Hill to its foot at Hockley Bridge.

In 1816, we are told, beautiful gardens joined close up the Factory, where were made in large quantities steam-engines, buttons, buckles, watch chains, trinkets, and a diversity of useful articles, all under "Royal patronage," and which, made it in truth, "the toy shop of Europe." The coining mill, which had been erected in 1788, was then equipped with eight machines, each striking 80 pieces of money per minute.

Says that gossiping writer, E. Edwards, in his PERSONAL RECOLLECTIONS (*Birmingham, 1877*), p. 13, under date 1837:—

> Soho Park, from Hockley Bridge, for about a mile on the road to West Bromwich, was entirely walled in. The old factory built by Boulton and Watt was still in operation. I saw there at work the original engine which was put up by James Watt. It had a massive oak beam, and it seemed strange to me that it did not communicate its power direct, but was employed in pumping water from the brook that flowed hard by, to a reservoir on higher ground. From this reservoir the water, as it descended, turned a water-wheel which moved all the machinery in the place. It is not, perhaps, generally known that the same machine which was employed here in 1797 in making the old broad-rimmed copper pennies of George III. is still at work at Messrs. Heatons coining the bronze money which has superseded the clumsy coppers of our forefathers.

Notwithstanding those high hopes expressed by Boulton in his "classic" speech at the Dedication Feast, a year ago (1895) the Smethwick "Soho" had to be completely dismantled, and its contents dispersed

> Fortunately, however, there are some relics of great interest, and even of historic value. The machinery has been removed and disposed of, but the records remain. These include nearly all the books, drawings, and plans which have been preserved for nearly a century and a half; the books of letters, wages, and drawings have, happily, been preserved, and form an unrivalled mass of facts relating to the founding, development, and growth of one of the largest and most interesting departments of a great and famous industrial enterprise for more than a hundred years. Excepting the Plantin Museum, at Antwerp, where a printing office of the sixteenth century has been preserved intact, there is probably no other record so extensive as the relics of the Soho Foundry to be found anywhere. The drawings and papers include the growth and progress of all kinds of work, the history of the steam-engine, the development of gas-lighting the growth of nearly all the great industries of Soho. In many cases the details of wages, the costs of materials, estimates, &c., are preserved.

> The letters, not only of Boulton and Watt to each other, but those of Murdock, Creighton, Southern, and Buckle, the famous "Soho" men, almost innumerable letters from the most eminent scientific men of the past eighty to one hundred years, number, all told, about 15,000. All of these are full of interest, and have great historic value. Many of the minor inventions, as models, of Watt and Murdock, have been carefully preserved and endorsed; and rare engravings, the original letters patent, and daily records and incidents of scientific value have happily been saved from loss. Most of these have been unseen and unknown, and might readily have been lost but some years ago the manager (Mr. W. Henry Darlington) collected and arranged the mass of papers, drawings, and relics, and placed them in a special room, where they were overhauled and preserved—a record room which is unrivalled and which will be found to be not merely curious, but a unique summary of industrial history and of national progress.

Mr. George Tangye has generously and thoughtfully, with considerable difficulty succeeded in securing the unique collection intact. It was feared that some American millionaire might buy the whole collection, or that it might be removed elsewhere, but it is now placed safely in the Cornwall Works, and will be carefully arranged and described; and, in addition, Mr. Tangye has had a series of photographs taken of the most important parts of the once famous works.

The bibliography of Soho is very extensive. THE STORY OF SOHO, by Dr. Smiles, is almost a classic in this department of literature. A terse biographical notice of the industrial worthies connected with this locality is given by Mr. Timmins in his HISTORY OF WARWICKSHIRE, pp. 198-203. The writings of Mr. W. C. Aitken give many technical details of the processes first earned on at these famous workshops where it is said Watt even anticipated photography with his "sun pictures." All this region is classic ground in the annals of Industry—the world-renowned toyshop; "l'Hotel de l'Amitié," as Boulton called that hostelry of his at Handsworth Heath, where he was visited by the crowned heads of Europe and the notables of the world; and lastly Handsworth Old Church, that Campo Santo of the illustrious dead.

XXVIII.—A FEW INDUSTRIAL EPOCHS

To give a full record of the industrial growth of a town so purely given over to manufactures, and these so numerous and so diversified, would of itself require a volume of no mean dimensions. Nothing, therefore, will be attempted here, beyond the chronicling of those leading facts which have made the name of Smethwick so famous in the annals of industry.

Writing so early as 1798 SHAW says:

> The population of this hamlet is much increased of late years by the canal passing though it to Birmingham; on which, besides the great iron foundry belonging to Soho, Mr Whately, has a large manufactory of gun-barrels, which are forged and bored, &c., by the aid of the steam engine

The old local gun-barrel trade, now represented in the small-arms manufactures of Birmingham, had then one of its chief seats at Wednesbury, where it brought about, in due time, the invention of wrought-iron gas-tube making, at the hands of Cornelius Whitehouse.

But, for the moment, leaving the iron-trade and its many processes, we find in the fabrication and manipulation of vitrescent material another important local industry.

The Glass Trade

Glass-making has been a Staffordshire industry for a somewhat lengthened period, and during the Civil Wars was actually a monopoly here. Whether Wordsley or Tutbury, or what part of the county, is concerned in the following, cannot be decided, but here is a patent preserved among the Darwin family MSS.

> 1643, December 1st. at our Court at Oxford. Charles I., to all Sheriff~ Colonels, &c., whom it may concern: Having formerly granted to Sir Robert Mansell and his assigns the sole making of all sorts of glass in the kingdom, for which a yearly rent was to be paid, and which for sundry years past is in arrear, Sir Robert has assigned to Mr. Henry Pate the making of all broad glass, 3s. upon every case of such glass before agreed to be paid by Pate to the King, &c.

Pate's Staffordshire workmen, however, took advantage of the turmoil of the Civil War, and combined with glaziers and certain other rebels in London, to damage him, the said Pate. The royal mandate therefore straightly charged these workmen to perform their covenant with Pate; and any glass consigned to London or other places in rebellion, was to be seized and disposed of—a most remarkable attempt to coerce workmen in favour of an employer.

Coming nearer home, Leigh's DIRECTORY of 1816 says:—

> Near Soho lived Mr. F. Eginton, who had brought the art of staining glass to a higher perfection than it had ever been known before in England.

This allusion was intended to mean Francis Eginton, that genius who re-discovered the art of stained glass, and astonished the *cognocenti* by his "sun pictures" from the designs of Reynolds, West, and other great artists of the last century. These curious productions were so well executed that Wedgwood became a willing purchaser; and in many ways Eginton proved himself a valuable ally of Boulton and Watt.

(It is almost needless to interpolate that glass-making was then being pursued in the vicinity: Hawker's glasshouse in Edgbaston Street, Birmingham, dates certainly from 1785, and a few years later the same maker had a glasshouse on Birmingham Heath.)

The Handsworth establishment of Eginton was very near to the classic precincts of Soho; and among his larger productions were windows for St. George's Chapel, Windsor, and for Salisbury and Lichfield Cathedrals. Among his local works are the east window of St. Paul's, Birmingham; the east window of the south aisle of Aston Church, and some bits of his work were said also to have been placed in Wednesbury Church. One of Eginton's larger commissions was obtained from William Beckford, lord mayor of London, to place windows at Fonthill to the value of £12,000.

The *Gentleman's Magazine* in 1817 said—

> Of larger works which have been placed in ecclesiastical edifices those most noticed and approved in his day were by Francis Eginton, who established a school of glass-staining at Handsworth, near Birmingham. He died in 1805. With considerable merit of colouring there is a certain deficiency in drawing, and the carnations are not clear in several of his larger pieces. . . . . These are numerous. The most remarkable are the restored great window at Magdalene College, Oxford; one at Arundel Castle; &c. He was assisted by his son.

This son, William Raphael Eginton, appears in the Directory of 1818, as "glass painter to Queen Charlotte."

At Smethwick are now located the present-day successors of the Egintons; the place has gained a reputation from the designs and productions in stained-glass of T. W. Camm, and of Samuel Evans, whose artistic windows are known far and wide.

Then in the trade of glass-making, Smethwick boasts the possession of one of the largest concerns of its kind in the kingdom. It was in the year 1814 that the British Crown Glass Works were first established at Spon Lane by a Mr. Shut. Some ten years later Shut was succeeded by Messrs. R. L. Chance and John Hartley; and later the several members of the firm were Messrs. Robert Lucas Chance, William Chance, James Hartley, and John Hartley junr. The glass-works of Messrs. Chance, at Spon Lane, are still amongst the three largest concerns of the kind in the kingdom.

When a duty on glass was levied this firm made payments twice each quarter; and the payments made by them in November, 1835, amounted to £17,150. This duty was 2s 10½d per foot on plate-glass, and it ceased to be levied April, 1845; ordinary sheet glass then sold at about 1s. 2d. a foot, and plate-glass at 6s. per foot. A great stimulus was given to the manufacture of crown and sheet glass by the abolition of the duty.

> In the year 1832 the manufacture of Bohemian sheet glass was commenced by Mr. Robert Lucas Chance and Mr. James Hartley, but so numerous were the difficulties to be overcome that it was not completely established until the year 1838. At that time the art being new to England, foreign workmen exclusively were employed in the operation of blowing the glass, but Englishmen have been gradually initiated into the process, and the manufacturer is able to dispense in a great degree with foreign assistance. The size at first usually blown was 36in. long by 20 wide. . . A further development of the sheet glass manufacture in England was the process of grinding and polishing this glass invented by Mr James Chance. . . This glass is known by the name of patent plate.

The above extract is taken from THE BIRMINGHAM AND MIDLAND HARDWARE DISTRICT, a series of reports on the resources and industrial history of the district, edited by Mr. Sam Timmins, and published in 1866 (*London, R. Hardwicke*); *it* will be found on p. 148, in an article by Henry Chance, M.A.

[The same volume has many other interesting papers bearing directly upon the products and manufactures of Smethwick; as "Lighthouse Illumination and the Dioptric Apparatus," by James Kenward, the historian of Harborne, which is followed by another article on "Basaltic Stone Manufacture," an "abandoned" industry of Smethwick; a second paper by Henry Chance is on "The Manufacture of Alkali Acids," also intimately local; then Henry Adkins writes "On the Manufacture of Soap," and "On the Manufacture of Red Lead," both clearly descriptive of Smethwick processes.]

To resume our glance at the glass trade: The local firm of Messrs. Fox, Henderson, and Co. were the contractors for building the "Crystal Palace," when it was originally erected as the Great Exhibition of 1851; and while all the ironwork was made at their workshops in Smethwick and at Woodside, it was Messrs. Chance, also of Smethwick, who supplied the "crystal" itself from their extensive glass-works at Spon Lane. The Crystal Palace is but one monument to the vast industrial enterprise of Smethwick.

KELLY'S POST OFFICE DIRECTORY for 1850 thus describes Smethwick, as it was, about the time of the first Great Exhibition:—

Here are very extensive glass works, a brewery, also iron and steel works, and many smelting furnaces, where the iron is manufactured into a great variety of articles. There is a very extensive building at the end of Spon Lane, and contiguous to the glass and chemical works of Messrs Chance Bros., which cover a space of nearly two acres intended for Free Schools, &c., for the education of the children of both sexes of those persons who are employed at the works of the above firm, and erected at the expense of the firm. The Birmingham and Dudley canals pass by this place, the new one having been cut under the old one to the depth of 60 or 80 feet, &c.

The labouring population are many of them nailers, working in their own houses. There are some almshouses, &c.

It was in September of 1851, that the Stour Valley Station was opened in Smethwick, "swift packets" still running four times a day on the canal between Birmingham and Wolverhampton, and the Birmingham and Dudley 'buses still passed regularly along the High Street.

Tangyes Limited

Of the fame of Tangyes' engineering inventions, and their many triumphs in the application of mechanical contrivances—they are almost too numerous to mention, and their principal specialities are too well-known, such as the Hydraulic Lifting Jack, the Differential Pulley Block, the Patent Lift and and Double-acting Pump, the Direct-acting Steam Pump, the Horizontal High Pressure Engine, the Re-railing Ramp, their Screw Presses, Rock Borers, and many others—it would be here a work of supererogation to speak. For no account of the rise and growth of this great Smethwick industry could hope to vie with that most interesting and pleasantly written book, entitled ONE AND ALL: AN AUTOBIOGRAPHY OF RICHARD TANGYE, OF THE CORNWALL WORKS, BIRMINGHAM *(London, Partridge, 1889)*. It is illustrated, which adds to its local interest; and it is sold at 1s. 6d.; but the word "Smethwick" seems to occur but once in the whole of its two hundred pages, the name "Birmingham," or "Soho," being made to do duty for it everywhere except in the analytical Contents.

On p. 59 we are told how the Tangye brothers commenced to manufacture in Birmingham, and on p. 60 is a picture of their "first workshop at 4s. a week rent." The story of the foundation of their fortunes, when their hydraulic jacks launched the Great Eastern steamship for Brunel, after this famous engineer had failed in all other attempts (January, 1858), is told on p. 65; and the comment is significant—"We launched the Great Eastern, and she launched us." The next chapter is of absorbing interest to the local reader;

Weston's differential pulley-block has a history to itself, detailing the difficulties that had to be overcome to bring it to a mechanical success, and then the anxious and costly litigation which had to be borne to reap any financial benefit from this ingenious appliance. The establishment of the Cornwall Works at "Soho," is given in chapter vii. It was in the early sixties that the old Rabone Hall was swept away, the trees cut down, and the gardens drained, to provide the site for a lofty and spacious workshop. In [1871] the firm of Tangye Brothers gave their workmen, unasked, the boon of the "nine hours day"; and to Sir Richard Tangye's thoughtfulness is due the credit of instituting the "Saturday half-holiday" (p. 55) before he himself became an employer, in 1853: and he further boasts that by the economising of time, 2,000 men at the Cornwall Works can be paid their wages in less than six minutes. Of the pleasant and happy relationships between masters and workmen at this great industrial hive, it is needless here to speak; the provision of dining rooms, reading rooms, and lecture rooms, and other conveniences for the comfort of the workmen is an example of the firm's thoughtfulness and kindly feeling. Other beneficent institutions at the Cornwall Works include a Sunday School, a Library, Science Classes, a Provident Sick Society, a Works Dispensary, which is nearly self-supporting although engaging two resident surgeons and a dispenser; and lastly there was established in 1882 (by "Tangyes Limited") a scheme of profit-sharing by which foremen and the older operatives, one in twenty of the adults employed, get an interest in the business, a £50 bonus being issued to each of them bearing the same rate of interest as the dividends paid to the shareholders. This is in addition to a fund, provided by the Company, for giving £100 at death under certain conditions. But all this may be found duly set forth in that little book so happily entitled, after the good Cornish motto, ONE AND ALL.

Nuts and Bolts; Screws and Nails, &c.

The railway era introduced innumerable new trades and industries, and nowhere so many as in the Black Country. At Wednesbury, the old coach iron trade developed the patent axle for railway carriages; and the coach ironmongery trade naturally produced men capable of devising railway carriage fittings and railway plant generally. But, strange to say, in one special line, the trade forsook Wednesbury, and settled in the surrounding parishes: for this old iron-working town once produced coach-bolts and wood-screws in large quantities. But wood-screws are now almost a monopoly; in 1873, Messrs. Nettlefold and Chamberlain produced 150,000 gross weekly, or nearly seven and a quarter million gross per annum. Then, also, the old-fashioned Wednesbury artisans who had forged coach-bolts turned their attention to the making of railway bolts; but soon the system of the division of labour, and the adoption of standard gauges (founded upon that micrometrical adjustment introduced by Sir Joseph Whitworth) brought into the industrial field the modern nut and bolt manufacturer, whose improved products possess that "extreme accuracy as to diameter, parallelism of shoulder, of head, face of nut, and pitch of thread," which tended to prove how easy of accomplishment might be an universal system of screwage all over the world. And although the coach-iron trade still flourishes in Wednesbury, the making of railway bolts and spikes located itself chiefly at Smethwick and at Darlaston—at the latter town it has indeed become the staple industry in place of the decayed gun-lock trade. In Smethwick the famous Patent Nut and Bolt Company, at its Stour Valley Works (with the Cwmbran Works in South Wales) produces over 100 tons a day.

The reader in search of technical details is referred to BIRMINGHAM TRADES *(Stanford, London, 1878.)*

The firm of Nettlefold are also, by the employment of their special machinery, much in advance of others in the production of wire nails, and staples. In their nail-mill, the "Paris points," as wire nails are called, are cut from the coil of wire by the first motion of the machine as it is fed in, then headed and pointed at one operation, sizes up to one inch being turned out at the rate of 360 a minute. Spikes are made equally fast, and wire staples, three inches long, are turned out at 100 per minute. If the old-fashioned nailer, previously mentioned, who worked at his own home is not entirely superseded by improved machinery, he is by this time reduced almost to starvation prices for his work.

* * * * * * * * * * * *

The Smethwick brewing industry, the origin of which has just been mentioned on p. 95, has now attained such large proportions that any history of it would need at least a good-sized pamphlet to itself, and cannot therefore be dealt with adequately in these pages. The principal firm engaged is that of Mitchell and Co., of The Cape Brewery.

XXIX.—MINERAL RESOURCES

While, as was noted in chap. iv., there exist no exposed measures of the useful minerals, such as might have been readily workable by the earlier and less skilled inhabitants of Smethwick, there no doubt exists a vast amount of mineral wealth deep down below the surface of the parish, and at present it is only waiting for the superincumbent mass of the newer formations to be pierced by the enterprising Smethwickian miner. With the realisation of this, Smethwick may hope to be in the enjoyment of rich mineral resources when all the older portions of the great Staffordshire mining district are practically exhausted. In Bilston and Wednesbury it was once boasted that they found their coal measures "high and dry," and (in the earlier days of mining) always gettable by open-works; and when eventually pits had to be sunk, only the easiest measures were then worked, the colliers of old days contenting themselves by sententiously observing "that those who lived longest would have to fetch their coal furthest," a saying now verified by the great depth of the newer collieries of South Staffordshire, such as Sandwell.

To the west of Smethwick there are numerous evidences of the calcareous conglomerate bands of the permians having been vigorously worked in times back. There is a line of old quarries running north and south through Brandhall in Oldbury where lime-kilns once existed in plenty. But, after all, the real wealth of an English mining district is in its black rather than in its white minerals: and Smethwick is happy in the fact that the shafts of the Sandwell Colliery lie well within its borders, even though the Sandwell Estate is so entirely within the confines of West Bromwich. So intimately is Smethwick concerned in the fortunes of the Sandwell Colliery, that it may be well to recall here the somewhat romantic incidents of this venture as undertaken and carried out by the late Henry Johnson, the well-known mining expert of Dudley. Here is the account of "Sandwell Park Trial Sinking" as it was given at the time, in the *Colliery Guardian* of June 5th, 1874:—

A Thousand guineas each have been offered this week for hundred-pound shares in the Sandwell Park Company; and an announcement indicating a more brilliant success has rarely been made. Prem £940 is a figure not often seen in share lists, or rejoiced over by investors. It almost reads like a story of El Dorado, or of the benevolent eccentricity of some genie of the "Arabian Nights." Many sporting men have, no doubt, made a lucky hit at the Derby this week, and in some cases a good "tip" has led to large winning, but at Sandwell Park we see not the result of a chance speculation, or the proceeds of a wild gambling transaction, but the legitimate success of sound judgment, judicious enterprise, and dogged perseverance. Most heartily do we congratulate the shareholders in this happy undertaking, and chiefly its original promoter and principal worker, Mr. Henry Johnson, who has won both wealth and laurels. and richly deserves them. We briefly announced last week that the thick coal had been reached, and we may now add that a borehole was at once put down through it, proving it to be 6yds. 2ft. 6in. in thickness, and so far as boring could determine, it appeared to be of very fair quality. The work of sinking through it commenced on Monday, and at the time of our going to press, thirteen feet had been penetrated, and the quality was reported as exceedingly good. The depth from the surface at which the coal was struck was 418 yards. The sinking is at present a single shaft, ten feet in diameter in the clear, and four hundred and twenty-Four yards deep. It contains three lifts of pumps, fourteen inches in diameter. The pumps are carried down to a depth of two hundred and thirty-two yards, the sinkers working one hundred and ninety two yards below the water. It has occupied three years to sink, and has been carried out without a single breakage of any moment, and without a single accident to life or limb—not even so much as a broken finger. The estate belongs to the Earl of Dartmouth, and the first load of thick coal was sent to his lordship last Wednesday, and no doubt received with great pleasure. The extent of the property is 1,700 acres (on a royalty of 6d. per ton on all), in certainly as good a market as any in Europe, having canals, railways, and roads through it, lying within three miles of the town of Birmingham, and singularly free from surface buildings. As might be expected, the good news was speedily disseminated and considerable excitement was produced at West Bromwich, Handsworth, and Smethwick. The church bells were set ringing, flags were run out, and gladness prevailed throughout the district. The time for the general rejoicing of the shareholders and the local public is not yet fixed, but we understand it is to be on a scale worthy of the event and far exceeding anything that has ever been before attempted in the Black Country. A fine sample of the coal—about 4cwt.—was exhibited on 'Change at Birmingham on Thursday, and examined with considerable interest. The launching of this scheme is due to the exertions of Mr. Henry Johnson, who, single-handed, without directors, bankers, lawyers, or brokers, suggested, in a report to the public (after having made terms for a provisional lease), the desirability of testing this new region beneath the permian rocks. He put the required capital at £20,000, divided into two hundred shares of £100 each. In ten days the shares were all taken up, and then from among the intending shareholders a board of directors was formed, who at once appointed the bankers and solicitors, and elected Mr. Johnson as engineer and secretary. Without loss of time, operations were commenced, and these have been vigorously and perseveringly prosecuted until the present success has been attained. In consequence of the great depth and the increase in the price of materials and wages, there was an additional call of £10 per share, making £110 per share paid up; but now few shareholders could be found to sell much under ten times that price. All things considered, it would be difficult to find in the annals of mining the history of any enterprise carried out so successfully and brought to so happy an issue. We are glad to learn that Mr. Johnson has retained for himself a very large interest in the company, so that he will enjoy not only the glory, but much of the substantial results of his success and a good share in the golden harvest. We understand, also, that there is to be a very handsome recognition of his services and of the faithful discharge of his duties, not only by his brother shareholders, but also by the institutes connected with mining and geology, indicating their high appreciation of the skill and the daring he has displayed in carrying out an undertaking, the importance of which to the shareholders, the scientific public, and the inhabitants of the neighbourhood it is hardly possible to over-estimate.

As a memento of the local rejoicings on this occasion, but scarcely as a meritorious specimen of the ballad-maker's efforts, here is a "song expressly written for the Grand Demonstration at Sandwell, July, 1874," the only excuse for is preservation here being Smethwick's absolute poverty in ballad-lore:—

OLD KING COAL.

You've heard of "Old King Coal" no doubt, a jolly chap was he,
About two thousand years ago he thought he'd have a spree,
So he laid him down beneath the sod, some thousand feet or more,
And dared the world to find him out till eighteen-seventy-four.
      "Old King Coal," a jolly old soul,
      Long life and happiness to Old King Coal.

And, "snug as any bug in rug," the old chap had his way,
If not found out, his Sleeping bout had seen the judgment day;
But "Generals *Brooch* and *Heathen*" were in his royal train,
With "*Gubbin, Pins,* and *Herring,* to try escape were vain.
      Old King Coal, &c.

Now a dapper little Dudley lad was prowling near the spot,
At *Sandwell Park,* one night at dark, and thought he smelt a *rot*;
And with a knowing wink he said, it I am not mistaken,
My men a hole shall bore for coal: if found, t'will save my bacon.
      Old King Coal, &c.

They digged and delved and sweated, sirs, for weeks and months and years,
And digged away most manfully, in hopes, not without fears;
At last their efforts were repaid, at least so I've been told,
This Dudley Engineer declared, "twould turn out good as gold."
      Old King Coal, &c.

It proved a check tho' for a time, their pluck was brought to bay,
Yet some few stuck like blisters to it, night as well as day;
And one dry cove more thirsty than the rest, would oft declare,
"Go in and win, boys, here's your gin, I'll take my oath he's there."

    Old King Coal, &c.

And so it proved, the King got caged, and ne'er was known to wince,
And them as found him says he has behaved well ever since;
And so he will continner for to do his werry best,
To " keep the pot o'bilin," and Old Harry take the rest.

    Old King Coal, &c.

And now to finish up the work, for friends are friends indeed,
The Board declared the men upon the Bonk should have a feed.
So here we're met to-day so gay to join this festive scene,
And drink success to Sandwell Coal, and so God Save the Queen.

    Old King Coal, &c.

XXX.—LOCAL GOVERNMENT

When the hamlet of Smethwick first emerged from obscurity its earliest form of local government was by a vestry-elected Board of Surveyors of Highways.*

With the growth of its population, consequent upon the spread of its manufactures, a more representative form of local self-government was found necessary; and a Local Board of Health was established by an Order in Council (under the Public Health Act, 1848) dated the 22nd April, 1856. The first meeting of this newly-constituted body was held at the Star Inn, Smethwick, on the 16th of June of that year, when Mr. George Downing was appointed chairman.

Upon its formation the Local Board took immediate steps to have the streets and public thoroughfares lighted with gas; and it was on January 1st, 1857, that the first attempt was made at public street lighting in Smethwick, when 112 lamps were lighted under contract by the Birmingham and Staffordshire Gas Light Co. When this latter undertaking was acquired in 1875 by the Corporation of Birmingham, the Smethwick Local Board determined to avail themselves of the opportunity of taking over that portion of it which lay within the area of their own jurisdiction. The "Smethwick Local Board (Gas) Act, 1876," was accordingly obtained; and under its provisions they were enabled to purchase from Birmingham such portion of the gas undertaking as was contained within the District of the Board. Having thus acquired the distributing plant, $7\frac{1}{4}$ acres of land in Rabone Lane were purchased whereon to erect the works for gas-making. These works were formally opened by Mrs. Keen, wife of Mr. Arthur Keen, who was then Chairman of the Board, on October 1st, 1881; the cost of the whole having been about £150,000.

It was twenty years after its formation ere the governing authority housed itself and its officers in a properly-equipped public-building. The Public Offices, with a Public Hall to seat 900 persons, were erected in 1866-7 at a total cost of £6,194 16s. 8d., the original loan for which (£4,500) has been repaid.

When public spirit had at last provided a place of assembly wherein could be voiced the popular wishes of the community, the second public building was almost naturally of an educational character; at a meeting of ratepayers held in the Public Hall, on September 18th, 1876, it was resolved to adopt the Free Libraries Act. The Free Library was erected in 1879 at a

---

*Although the entire administrative County-borough of Birmingham is, for convenience, generally located in the geographical county of Warwick, that portion of it which constitutes the ancient civil parish of Harborne is really part of Staffordshire. A civil parish, or township, may be defined as a place in which a poor rate is separately levied.

The Assessment of Smethwick (whose population in 1811 comprised only 631 males and 697 females, or a total of 1,328) marks some rapid strides; as thus, in

1829	it was	£5,560.
1842	,,	16,440.
1852	,,	32,233.
1862	,,	61,278.
1872	,,	71,171.
1882	,,	103,360.

Harborne now being added to Birmingham leaves Smethwick independent—refer back to p. 47.

modest outlay of £1,810 10s. 8d., the amount of the loan raised being £1,600. Since that time a Branch Reading Room opened in Windmill Lane (1891) has cost an additional £400, of which £300 was again raised by loan.

As a sanitary authority, the Local Board addressed itself to the preservation of the public health with considerable aptitude. Land for a "tip" on which to deposit dust and other rubbish, was provided in 1879, at a cost of £500. In 1883-4 Smethwick suffered from a slight epidemic of small-pox, some 117 cases being notified. This led to the provision of an Infectious Hospital. Over eleven acres of land in Holly Lane were purchased for this purpose; and including the provision of a temporary tent hospital, the sum expended on this undertaking was £5,171 8s. 4d., the loan asked for being £4,620. As an insurance this may be considered a sound investment, for when small-pox again assumed epidemic form in 1894-5, its ready check, and entire suppression after the outbreak of only 134 cases, may be considered as eminently satisfactory for so populous a centre as Smethwick.

In 1885 a public Mortuary was provided at an outlay of nearly £300. In the following year (1886) Public Baths were erected, towards which Messrs. Tangye generously gave £1,000, the ratepayers wisely accepting the challenge by voting over £8,500 in the interests of public health and cleanliness.

Since 1888 sewers have been laid down throughout the District, and a part-ownership has also been acquired in sewers running through Handsworth, Aston, and Aston Manor to the outfall works at Saltley, at a cost of £65,150.

A United Drainage Board for Aston, Balsall Heath, Birmingham, Handsworth, Harborne, King's Norton, Northfield, Perry Barr, Saltley, and Smethwick, was formed in 1877. It was in consequence of the wholesale pollution of the Tame by the large populations dwelling upon its banks, that the Corporation of Birmingham became involved in litigation, and in turn commenced a series of actions against the local authorities on the stream above them, to compel them to cease their pollution—notably against West Bromwich, Oldbury, and Smethwick. The first two commenced operations at once, but Smethwick succeeded in obtaining an extension of time. It was in the aforenamed year (1877) that the Tame and Rea Drainage Board was instituted to provide for the drainage and sewage treatment of an area of 47,275 acres with a population amounting to 650,000. The authorities interested in this united scheme are:—*County Borough* : Birmingham. *Warwickshire:* Aston Urban, Aston Rural, Sutton Coldfield. *Staffordshire:* Smethwick, Handsworth, Perry Barr. *Worcestershire:* King's Norton.

The West Bromwich system of sewerage receives, by arrangement between the two authorities, from that part of the Smethwick district which is contiguous, the drainage of an area representing a population of some 4,400 inhabitants in Smethwick.

For its size, Smethwick has had to undertake a work of street improvement of some considerable magnitude. As well as of canals, the place possesses also a plethora of railways, and both constructed in their early eras when little or no regard was paid to the requirements of a locality, or to the possible demands of any future urban population which might grow up therein. However it may have been, there was certainly no more dangerous thoroughfare in the whole of the busy Black Country than Rolfe Street. Smethwick, during the long years that a railway level-crossing interrupted its traffic. To prevent the constant recurrence of fatal accidents there, and bring to a termination its harrowing and ever lengthening death-roll, the Rolfe Street level-crossing was at last swept away in 1889. The local authority courageously took the matter in hand, purchased the adjoining properties at a total cost (including other general expenses in connection with the solution of this long-standing difficulty) of £35,154 5s. 7d., towards which the Railway Company contributed £15,000, and further undertook the work of making the road, &c.

Although on its Worcestershire side the district of Smethwick is truly pleasant, in recent years it has become apparent that the acquisition of a public "lung" would be a highly desirable safeguard against any future congestion of the population. The precaution was taken in 1887 to secure about 35 acres of land in Bearwood Hill as a Public Park. This was purchased and laid out at a total cost of £10,300. There was no formal opening of this public pleasure ground; but a very wise step was taken in 1894, when additional land in Crocketts Lane was acquired to enlarge it, for an additional £1,000.

As early as 1885 the Allotments Act was adopted in Smethwick, and a quantity of land was purchased in Stoney Lane as a "Gravel Pit." The surplus land was utilised for the purpose of providing working men with gardening facilities.

At the commencement of 1896 a new Public Park was presented to West Smethwick by Mr. J. T. Chance. It was a noble and generous gift to this not over lovely but thickly-populated district; and altogether it cost the donor, to lay out properly for the public use, not less than £20,000. The park comprises between forty and fifty acres of land, and includes a fair-sized sheet of water large enough for boating. Mr. G. F. Chance, the son of the donor, has spent much time and trouble in laying out the land for its present purpose, and in a few years, when the newly-planted trees have grown up, it will doubtless be a very attractive place of resort. The land is well situated on a breezy site which commands some far-reaching views of the surrounding country, including Barr Beacon, the Clent-Hills, Dudley Castle heights, and other prominent points. A few chimneys are observable in the near distance in certain directions, but these will only serve to give the prospect a homely and familiar aspect to those who will mostly use the park, and will remind them that they are not far away from home. Festivities marked the public opening of this very desirable breathing-space.

As a population becomes dense, disposal of the dead presents itself as a problem for solution by the governing authorities. In Smethwick the Local Board of Health was constituted a Burial Board by an Order of Her Majesty in Council, dated 19th May, 1884. Thus empowered, a Cemetery of 20 acres was provided at the Uplands, and a Lodge and two Chapels erected thereon, and 12 acres of the land laid out at a cost of £9,696 3s. 1d. This Cemetery was opened for public interments on 12th May, 1890.

(Within the confines of Smethwick, and close to St. Paul's Church, is another large Cemetery, with two mortuary chapels. But this is under the control of the Oldbury Burial Board, and was made nearly forty years ago.)

Beyond its investiture with the powers and duties of a Burial Board, the Local Board has from time to time undergone other constitutional changes. The Board was constituted an Urban District Council by the Local Government Act of 1894: whereupon the members of the Local Board ceased to hold office, and the Urban District Councillors took office on the 31st December 1894. The first meeting of the Council was held on January 1st, 1895.

But the previous "Local Government Act (England and Wales) 1888"—that dealing with county government—had called into existence, among others, the Staffordshire County Council. To this new authority Smethwick elected its County Councillors on January 24th, 1889. There are three Councillors and one Alderman allotted to represent Smethwick at Stafford.

By an order of the County Council, dated 20th December, 1890, and made under Sec. 57 of the Local Government Act, 1888, Smethwick was divided into five wards, and the number of members on its own Urban Council was increased from 12 to 15, three members being allotted to each, ward.

XXXI.—INCORPORATION.

With material progress came, in due time, that very natural aspiration for the enjoyment of the highest form of municipal life.

It was in 1893 that the idea of incorporation was first mooted in Smethwick. No doubt the examples of West Bromwich and Wednesbury had some tendency towards directing the public mind in this channel. And, as a matter of course, when the idea took concrete form as a definite proposal, the public divided themselves into two opposing camps. Those in favor of incorporation put forth many good and cogent reasons for the course they proposed; but at the bottom of all, sentiment played the part of the chief actuating motive. And sentiment, in a case of this kind, is of itself a good thing. Public opinion is swayed by sentiment. Sentiment is often the preservative salt of public life, keeping it sound in the heat of overmuch communal activity.

On the other hand, those who opposed incorporation had equally many reasons for their antagonism; but the chief one, and the most valid, was objection to the probable costliness of this higher form of civic life. As a rule such dissentients are those ratepayers of the economical turn of mind, who object on principle to most of the expenditure from the public rates. But in the case of Smethwick there was perhaps some excuse for such objections on the part of the proprietors of large manufactories, who see in every increase of their assessments a factor which automatically raises the cost of production.

In furtherance of the scheme a Town's Meeting was held at the Public Hall on November 24th, 1893, at which the promoters carried the day, and a formal mandate was given by the ratepayers to the local authority to petition the Privy Council for a Charter of Incorporation. A petition bearing upwards of 600 signatures was forwarded to the Privy Council in July, 1894. This document so admirably summarises the record of the town's progress, that the full text of it may be very usefully quoted here. It ran:—

TO THE QUEEN'S MOST EXCELLENT MAJESTY IN COUNCIL.

THE HUMBLE PETITION OF THE UNDERSIGNED INHABITANT HOUSEHOLDERS OF THE DISTRICT OF SMETHWICK IN THE COUNTY OF STAFFORD.

SHEWETH THAT by an Act of Parliament passed in the first year of the Reign of Your Majesty, Intituled.—"An Act to amend an Act for the regulation of Municipal Corporations in England and Wales" it is amongst other things enacted that if the Inhabitant Householders of any Town or Borough in England or Wales should Petition your Majesty to grant to them a Charter of Incorporation it should be lawful for Your Majesty by any such Charter if you should think fit by the advice of your Privy Council to grant the same or extend to the Inhabitants of any such Town or Borough within the District to be set forth in such Charter all the powers and provisions of the said Act for regulating Corporations whether such Town or Borough be or be not a Corporate Town or Borough or be or be not named in either of the Schedules to the said Act PROVIDED nevertheless that notice of every such Petition and of the time when it should please Your Majesty to order the same to be taken into consideration by the Privy Council should be published in the "London Gazette" one month at least before such Petition should be considered but such publication should not need to be by Royal Proclamation.

THAT the Governing body or Authority for the District of Smethwick is a Local Board of Health constituted pursuant to and under the provisions of the Public Health Act 1848 and established by order of Her Majesty in Council on the 22nd day of April 1856.

THAT there are 8575 persons in the said District of Smethwick who are rated to the relief of the poor of the said Parish.

THAT the District of Smethwick comprises an area of 1795 acres; its population and rateable value increasing in a most remarkable manner by reason whereof Your Petitioners earnestly pray that the powers conceded under the Incorporation Acts of Parliament may be granted to them in order that efficient legislation may keep pace with the increasing needs of the District:—

THAT in 1861 the population of Smethwick was					–	–	–	13,351	
,, 1871	,,	,,	,,	,,	,,	–	–	–	17,158
,, 1881	,,	,,	,,	,,	,,	–	–	–	25,076
,, 1891	,,	,,	,,	,,	,,	–	–	–	36,170
THAT ,, 1861 their were		–	–	–	–	–	2,670 houses		
,, 1871	,,	,,	–	–	–	–	–	3,431	,,
,, 1881	,,	,,	–	–	–	–	–	5,015	,,
,, 1891	,,	,,	–	–	–	–	–	7,234	,,

THAT at the present time there are about 191 houses in course of erection nearly the whole of which are intended for Artizans' Dwellings.

THAT as a further illustration of the increase of population, the Birth Rate in 1874 was 41.1 per 1000, in 1881 was 4.29 per 1000 and in 1891 was 38.3 per 1000 and in 1892 was 35.2 per 1000.

THAT Smethwick has attained a position of great importance and is one of the principal towns in Staffordshire. It contains some of the largest and most important manufactories in the Kingdom. The Local Governing Body own the Gas Undertaking. They have also provided a Free Library, and Reading Rooms, Public Baths, Public Buildings, a Public Park, Infectious Hospital and Mortuary and they also act as a Burial Board and have acquired and laid out a Cemetery. The footpaths of a great part of the District are also paved and the Sewers are now laid in a considerable portion of the District.

THAT the density of the population is 55 per acre upon the area now built upon and if taken in connection with the unbuilt area is 19.6.

THAT the gross rateable value of the District is £137,653 7s. 6d.; the assessable value being £110,354 19s. 3d. and there are upwards of 28 miles of streets.

THAT in conclusion your petitioners are of opinion that it would be of great benefit and advantage to the District of Smethwick and to the inhabitants thereof and tend to the dignity of the Town and the Government thereof if a Charter of Incorporation were granted and Smethwick created a Municipal Borough.

THAT Your Petitioners are respectively rated to the Relief of the Poor in the said District of Smethwick in the several sums set opposite their respective names:—

> YOUR PETITIONERS therefore most humbly pray Your Majesty with all convenient speed to grant a Charter of Incorporation to the District of Smethwick within the limits to be set forth in such Charter and to extend to the Inhabitants of such District when Incorporated all the powers and privileges of the said Act and of all other Acts since passed to alter, amend or extend the same or to confer other powers upon the Borough mentioned in the Schedules to the said Act or that Your Majesty will be graciously pleased to make such further or other order in the premises as to Your Majesty may seem proper.

AND YOUR MAJESTY'S Petitioners shall ever pray, &c.

An official inquiry was held on the 10th of October, 1894. The Privy Council asked for more signatures, and a second petition bearing the signatures of about 4,000 "inhabitant householders" was forwarded in August, 1895. A second inquiry was held on the 2nd October following. The original 600 signatures were obtained under the belief that only persons directly rated to the poor could sign, but, in the second instance, a house-to-house canvas was made. In the meantime common rumour had become busy, and it was currently reported that Birmingham had opposed the scheme. Although no overt action could be proved against Birmingham, it was remembered that the city had twice successfully resisted the proposed incorporation of Aston. But in the case of Smethwick there was also a known cause of antagonism on the part of the city. When the municipal boundary of Birmingham was extended, the large contributory district of Harborne was severed from the School Board district of Smethwick, and added to "Greater Birmingham." In compensation for the loss of area and rating wealth, Birmingham was adjudged to pay the Smethwick School Board a sum of about £700 per annum in perpetuity. Birmingham, it is said, offered to withdraw their opposition to the Incorporation provided the Smethwick School Board would relinquish the £700 annuity. This, of course, the Smethwick authorities very properly refused to do, and hence it was that Birmingham attempted to block the way of its neighbour's municipal progress.

Notwithstanding all this, the Clerk to the District Council (Mr. William Shakespeare) received a request from the Privy Council Office early in 1896 to prepare a draft charter. It is proposed to divide the town into six wards, two being co-extensive with each of the three wards formed for County Council Representation in 1889. Their nomenclature will perhaps undergo an alteration, which is much to be desired; for while in this advanced age it is no longer acceptable to call wards after the saints in the calendar, it is equally inconvenient to name them after the points of the compass; for by these latter names, so much affected by the County Councils, it is scarcely possible for a native to recognise the place of his own residence without an effort of thought. Such names do not help to identification.

The Charter of Incorporation may now in all reason be expected on an early date.

XXXII.—WORK OF THE SCHOOL BOARD.

Casual references have already been made in this work to the educational institutions of Smethwick. On p. 44 may be found the records of Henry Hinckley, who gave the original endowment to the charity school, and died in 1732: on p. 54 appears Dorothy Parkes' bequest for building a charity school: on p. 61 is the text of a Government report on this particular charity, so far as the Hinckley benefaction is concerned, followed on p. 64 by a similar report on the management of the Dorothy Parkes fund, both of the year 1823: the establishment of the first British School in Smethwick, an effort of the Congregationalists about the year 1840, is chronicled on p. 74: and on p. 80 will be found mention of a Wesleyan Day School.

The establishment of the Harborne School Board followed close upon the passing of the Education Act of 1870; and its main concern became the provision of elementary education more particularly for that part of its area known as the "hamlet of Smethwick," where the population was not only thicker, but consisted so largely of a purely artisan class. The first meeting of the Board was held December 18th, 1873. In December, 1874, the first Chairman, Mr. Walter Chamberlain, was succeeded by Mr. Thomas Griffiths. For a short time in 1884-5 the Rev. A. M. Dalrymple and then Mr. A. B. Phipson presided; but in 1885 the Rev. J. Herbert Crump, M.A., R.D., became Chairman, and held the office till 1892, when the Rev. George Astbury succeeded him. The Smethwick Board now consists of eleven members, but to the Harborne School Board only four members were sent to represent Smethwick. The first four were the Rev. E. Addenbrooke, Mr. W. R. Brookes, Mr. T. Cox, and Mr. T. L. Nicklin. The offices of the Harborne School Board were of necessity located in Smethwick for greater convenience of administration.

It will be interesting to observe the order in which Board Schools have had to be erected in Smethwick.

West Smethwick was first found to be most urgently in need of school-places, and in 1874-5 the first Board Schools were erected there. Two departments only at first were provided, to accommodate 310 children; but in a few years (1878) additional accommodation was provided for 257 children, and the schools were made to consist of the usual three departments for Boys, Girls, and Infants. Further additions were made in 1883, the total accommodation being raised to 745 places, at a total cost of £8,243.

In 1875 also *Brasshouse Lane Schools* were put up for 258 scholars, in two departments; in 1878 these were doubled in accommodation, and made into three departments. Further enlargements took place in 1881 and 1892, till 1,024 scholars were provided for, the outlay altogether being £8,080.

[Harborne itself was first provided with a Board School—the only one its population needed—in 1880-1, when the High Street Schools were erected to take in the scholars which the Board had previously educated in an old British School. The site was expensive, and the total outlay of £6,860 for 500 scholars worked out at £13 14s 6d. per head.]

Corbett Street Schools, for 726 children in three departments, were opened in August, 1879. A fourth department, known as a *Junior Mixed School,* for 172 additional scholars, had to be added in two or three years. These schools have since been enlarged for a gross accommodation of 1,142, at a total outlay of £10,300.

Slough Lane Schools, consisting of Mixed and Infants' Departments for 341, were built in 1881-2; the total cost was £4,277.

Bearwood Road School was begun in 1882 with places for 70 scholars by March, 1884, the accommodation had been increased to 236. The total cost was £3,670, being about £15 11s. per school-place, a rate far above the average on account of the fact that the building was put up at two different periods. Its present accommodation is 622, and the total cost has been brought up to £6,200.

In April, 1885, *Crocketts Lane Infant School* was opened, a temporary school having previously been worked by the Board, in Hill Street, for 120 Infants.

In November of the same year a *Central School* was opened there, specially designed for the reception of advanced scholars drawn from the other Board Schools in Smethwick. A *Junior School* for 312 was added to the group in 1892, at a cost of £3,120. The Central School itself cost £7,000 for the accommodation of 686 advanced scholars. The Infant accommodation is 424: the block of schools thus takes in 1,422 children, and has cost about £13,500 altogether.

[About this time Messrs. Chance Brothers having determined to discontinue the schools carried on by them for upwards of 45 years at Spon Lane, the School Board thereupon entered into communication with Messrs. Chance, who were induced to lease the school premises for a term of years. The transfer to the Board of these premises, and some 750 scholars, took place in March, 1886.]

Although Messrs. Chance's premises helped to stay the progress of school building, on the other side of Smethwick school accommodation was now so urgently needed that *Cape Hill Schools* had to be built for no less than 889 children. This block cost £7,750, and was opened in January, 1888. Extensions necessitated by the overflow population of Birmingham coming to reside in this quarter had by 1895 brought up the accommodation to 1,312 places and the gross cost to £11,300.

The Smethwick School Board has thus erected more than the average number of schools in proportion to population, Brasshouse Lane having a separate Infants' School, and the Central both a Junior and an Infants' school. The total accommodation sanctioned by the Department for the seven groups of Smethwick schools is 6,608. The cost of the sites was £7,250 12s. 7d., and the cost of the buildings £56,006 11s. 1d. The cost of site and buildings per child was £9 11s. 5¼d. The accommodation in the whole of the schools under the Board's control is for 7,565 children. The number on the books for 1895 was 7,767, the average attendance 6,945, and the percentage 92·4. This is a remarkably high figure, and compares very favourably with that of any other School Board area in the Kingdom.

The area of jurisdiction over which the original Harborne School Board, as first constituted in 1873, held sway, was that of the whole parish of Harborne, comprising the Local Board District of Harborne and the Local Board District of Smethwick. Consistently maintaining the school supply throughout the whole period, and meeting every increase of the rapidly-growing population, by November 1891, this Board had erected in Smethwick nine blocks of schools, comprising 25 departments, while Harborne had been sufficiently provided for by the erection of one school of two departments. A set of offices for the use of the Board had also been erected in Smethwick. The school places provided up to the date mentioned was

In Harborne	540.
In Smethwick	5,965.
	6,505.

Harborne, it will be seen, was really a suburb of Birmingham, its residents being of a class who did not need much provision in the way of elementary education.

In February, 1891, the School Board received a notification that the City of Birmingham had memorialised the Local Government Board in London for an extension of its boundaries; and as one of the proposals was the absorption of the Local Board District of Harborne, this implied a serious interference with the area of the Harborne School Board. The School Board at once offered an uncompromising resistance to the Birmingham extension scheme, as bound to do, from the consideration of the following facts so ably set forth in an official document:—

The extent of the entire parish—the Education Act deals only with "parish" areas, as a rule—forming the district of Harborne School Board was made up as follows:—

Harborne	... ...	1,600 acres, with population (1891) of	8,100.
Smethwick	... ...	1,795 ,, ,, ,, ,,	36,170.
Total	...	3,395	44,270.

The value of Harborne, in relation to the public rates, was found to be one-fifth of the whole, as thus—

	Rateable Value (Per Overseers' Return, April, 1891).	Yield of a Rate at 1d. in £.
Harborne	£36,674	£126
Smethwick	£162,436	£478
	£202,110	£604

But, as has already been shewn, the educational requirements of the district had only necessitated the erection of one block of schools in Harborne, against nine blocks of Schools in Smethwick. As a consequence of this, one-thirteenth part of the whole of the Board's expenditure would go to the support of the Harborne portion of their work, and twelve-thirteenths to the support of their work in Smethwick. In other words, if the proposals of the City Council were carried out, whilst the Board would lose only one-thirteenth part of their expenditure, they would lose one-fifth part of their income, and the accruing loss would fall entirely upon the Smethwick ratepayers.

The Birmingham City Council proposed to take to the one School in Harborne with its outstanding liabilities. This would have entailed upon Smethwick a loss of no less a sum than £1,046 per year, equal to an increase in the School Board rate of 2½d. in the £ per annum.

The contention of the Board was that if Birmingham took one-fifth of the assets (or rates) they should also take an equal proportion of the liabilities in the shape of the outstanding loans payable in respect of schools in the entire parish. In support of this the Board argued that the whole rateable value of the parish was chargeable with outstanding balances, and that the Board recognised no actual difference between Harborne and Smethwick—so far as the Board were concerned they both formed one district. This, briefly stated, was the Board's position upon the charges in respect of capital account.

As to maintenance of schools account, it was also shewn that after having paid for the maintenance of its own school, and its proper proportion of the loans, Harborne had, in the past, contributed substantially towards the maintenance of the Smethwick Schools. The Board, therefore, claimed that if the Smethwick portion of the parish were to be deprived of the assistance of the richer portion (Harborne) the Birmingham authorities should make good to this Board the difference year by year in perpetuity. The Birmingham proposal to take to the liabilities in respect of the Harborne school only, represented a willingness upon their part to take to one-tenth of the Board's loans, and nothing beyond this.

This Board's claim was that Birmingham should be held responsible for one-fifth of the total loans of the parish, plus one-fifth of the cost of maintenance of the Smethwick Schools.

The representations of the Board at the official inquiry met with nothing but antagonism from the authorities in Birmingham; therefore, acting in concert with the Aston School Board, who had also certain rights to defend, Parliamentary opposition was offered to the passing of the Birmingham Bill. Before the Committees of both Houses of Parliament Harborne School Board gained the points for which they so justly contended, and clauses were inserted in the Act to give effect thereto. The document from which these proceedings are extracted closes with a dignified and an appreciative farewell of the Harborne teachers.

Thus the area of Harborne passed for ever from that joint jurisdiction with Smethwick which had existed between them for centuries—for already, as has been noted, they had long ceased to be under one local authority for municipal purposes. And after working together most amicably for eighteen years, the Harborne School Board representatives now parted from their colleagues of Smethwick who were in future to do the work alone.

Then, for reasons which appeared valid only to the official mind of the Education Department in London, the name which the local educational authority was in future to bear was "The School Board for the Extra-municipal part of the Parish of Harborne."

Such a title was as objectionable as it was cumbersome. Under the Local Government Act of 1894 the portion of Harborne parish within the city was made a separate parish under the name of Harborne, and the hamlet of Smethwick became the parish of Smethwick. No order, however, was made altering the name of the School Board. The School Board of Smethwick therefore applied that their title may be altered. A joint committee of the Staffordshire County Council and the Birmingham City Council sat at Birmingham in March, 1896, and almost immediately decided that in future the legal name should be "The Smethwick School Board" a name that had been virtually adopted after the partition of the original parish area.

It must be remembered that the population of Smethwick has more than doubled itself during the last twenty years, a large proportion coming hither to escape the overcrowding of the city of Birmingham. It has been a most difficult task to keep up with the population in school accommodation without a large increase in the rates, but the Smethwick School Board has done its work well. It is now spending upwards of £22,000 a year, and received last year from the Birmingham School Board, according to the terms of the Parliamentary clause, £556 on account of loans to be repaid, and £232 towards school maintenance, nearly £800 a year, being the amount in dispute with Birmingham City, a serious consideration for the ratepayers of Smethwick.

The demands upon the ratepayers have been amply justified by the high efficiency of the schools. The average Government grant per child, exclusive of pupil teachers last year, was £1 0s. 5½d., which may be considered very creditable indeed to all concerned. The average grant earned by School Boards throughout the country is only 19s. 1¾d. The income from the rates per scholar in Smethwick is 11s. 2½d., against 18s. 4¾d. throughout the country.

The scheme for giving Religious Instruction in the Board Schools has been of that customary colourless character which always results when the sects and denominations agree to a compromise, and make an attempt to teach religion without creed or dogma. The ratepayers' money is thus used to offend many, and to please but a few.

* * * * * * * * * * * *

The voluntary schools still working in the Board's district are:—

			Accommodation.
1. Old Church	Mixed Infants	...	199.
	(Represents Endowed Charity School).
2. St. Matthew's	Boys ...	... ...	230.
,, ,,	Girls ...	... ...	145.
,, ,,	Infants	... ...	183.
3. Holy Trinity	Boys ...	... ...	220.
,, ,,	Girls ...	... ...	200.
,, ,,	Infants	... ...	132.
4. St. Philip's (Roman Catholic) ...	Mixed Infants	...	200.

The Wesleyan Day Schools, formerly carried on in Rabone Lane, consisting of two departments for 465 scholars, have been transferred to the control of the Board since 1895.

* * * * * * * * * * * *

Beyond private adventure schools there exists no system of schools for secondary education. To attempt some supply for this deficiency, the Higher Grade School of the Board was established. The Technical School, under control of the local authority, promises to accomplish good work in the near future among the adult youth of this large industrial community.

XXXIII.—SPORTS AND PASTIMES.

No considerable head of population ever having centred themselves in the hamlet of Smethwick is perhaps the reason why there are no records here of old-time manners or quaint customs. To this fact attention has already been directed (pp. 15 and 16) as well as to the corresponding absence of Smethwick folk-lore (p. 99).

Most of the adjoining parishes and districts, however, have not failed to produce many such old-world customs which have been thought worthy of the chronicler's pen. At Handsworth, for instance, *clipping the church* was a curious practice there at Eastertide, when the school-children, with others of the adult parishioners, joined hands in a ring, and danced gleefully round and round the church, the greater fun being occasioned when any of the "link" loosed hands and sent someone flying off over the grave-mounds. The symbolic significance of this old custom might possibly be traced to the watch set by Pilate over the sepulchre of Christ.

At Deritend Chapel, it was the practice at the annual dedication feast on St. John's Day to carry bulrushes into the sacred edifice, and for the parishioners to decorate their own fire-places with the same. But this practice was all but universal in olden England. At Aston, too, there were quaint old customs of which many records exist. And so on; coming back into this county, the subject has been of sufficient interest to find matter for a small volume, entitled THE CUSTOMS, SUPERSTITIONS, AND LEGENDS OF THE COUNTY OF STAFFORD, written by C. H. Poole in 1875 *(London: Rowney and Co.)* But nothing whatever of Smethwick—no doubt owing to the absence of a parish church till such mediæval practices had long since begun to die out; and also for lack of population to indulge therein, as before surmised.

The comparative seclusion of Smethwick at one time offered it as a favourite arena wherein to bring off pugilistic encounters and other similar events of an equally illegal character. Lying as it did between Birmingham on one hand, and the populous Black Country on the other, both acknowledged centres of those sports now considered brutalising, but at that time complacently tolerated, it cannot be wondered at if its convenient position was often utilised by the various sporting fraternities of all the surrounding district. Few of these meetings are on record, simply because they were not "class" enough, being generally the "Monday fights," in which it was the common practice of the working men at one time to indulge. Before the era of Factory Acts, "Saint Monday" was always most loyally kept by the lower class of workmen in Birmingham, in Tipton, in Wednesbury, in Dudley, in Walsall, and in Wolverhampton, and indeed throughout the whole countryside round about.

In the annals of Pugilism there is just one record; it is to the effect that "on November 18th, 1833, Lane beat Ball in 21 rounds for £20 a-side at Smethwick." These combatants, however, were probably nothing more than Wednesbury or Tipton colliers bringing off a match in the customary method of those degraded times.

Going back a little further, the existence of wide stretches of waste lands and open commons had no doubt helped to make the district on the north and east sides of Smethwick somewhat notorious.

Bull baiting was another "sport" of those earlier times. The practice had been prohibited by an Order in Council as early as 1773, but it was not till 1835 that an Act was passed to put a stop to it. In 1798 a baiting was started on Snow Hill, but the Loyal Association of Birmingham Volunteers, a body which had been formed for national defence during the Napoleonic scare, turned out in the interests of law and order, and with drums beating and colours flying in right military fashion, put the bull-baiters to flight. The pursuit of them continued to Birmingham Heath, close on the confines of Smethwick, where the rebels were overtaken and soundly beaten; the Volunteers returning to town in triumph with the bull, a captive and a trophy of war at the same time.

At the junction of the four ways near where the County Council of Stafford have recently rebuilt the bridge across the Soho Brook, bull-baiting was practised as late, perhaps, as anywhere in the whole Birmingham district. The bulls were kept at the Bacchus Tavern, because it was so convenient there for crossing the Warwickshire boundary, should it be necessary to do so in defiance or evasion of the law. Gib Heath became a noted battle ground. As late as October, 1838, a great bull-baiting took place close by there in Nineveh Road—Nineveh being really a place-name significant of wicked inhabitants.

Perhaps the Loyal Volunteers felt assured of victory on the occasion just mentioned, as the whole of Birmingham Heath had been adopted by them as their practice and parade ground. Their knowledge of the Heath must have included cognisance of the evil uses to which it was put by the bull-baiting and prize-fighting fraternities. It was a welcome step in the right direction when these common-lands, which girdled all that side of Smethwick, were utilised for public purposes of quite another character. The Act for enclosing and allotting the commons and waste lands of Birmingham was passed in 1798. At the present time nearly 100 acres of the old common are covered with public buildings for such as need a "common" home in the Workhouse, the Gaol, or the Asylum—buildings which have cost nearly £400,000 of the public monies.

Handsworth common was enclosed in 1793, and the wastes and open fields of Witton, and Erdington beyond, were enclosed and divided in 1801.

* * * * * * * * * * * *

But although olden Smethwick has left no record of its former merry-makings and pastimes, the modern Smethwick have not been without a reputation in the field of sport. Probably no place of its size has so long and so consistently produced so many good cricketers as Smethwick. For twenty or thirty years this has been the case. Always more than one good club, than the titular Smethwick Cricket Club, has contrived to flourish in the place, the larger manufactories, such as the Plate Glass Works, the Railway Carriage Works, and at the present day, Mitchell's Brewery, being able to put a good cricket team in the field. Among the individual players produced by Smethwick the name of Docker takes high rank in the world of cricket.

The presence of public baths has encouraged the practice of the natatory art, and swimming, especially combined with water polo, is now popular.

Football has its numerous votaries, but no club of first-rate rank has yet had the name of Smethwick identified with it—which is somewhat strange considering the many thousands who enthusiastically follow the popular winter game as spectators and interested patrons.

XXXIV.—TOPOGRAPHICAL: PLACE-NAMES, ROADS, AND RAILWAYS.

The newer portions of the parish may be distinguished by the geometrical precision of the street building-lines, and the somewhat high-sounding titles attached to these modern highways. The few thoroughfares of olden Smethwick were generally narrow winding lanes, branching out from either side of the main turnpike road, and divided, but at very wide intervals, by those fields and grass-lands which have since been cut up into building estates. Of these ancient byeways, at least three may still be traced along well-defined lines.

The first is variously named at different sections of its length; nearer the Hales Owen side of the parish it is known as *Hales Lane*; the next portion is called *Cooper's Lane*, after the Cooper family who once resided at *The Firs* there (near the corner of *Church Lane*); striking the same line but on the opposite side of the main road is *Crocketts Lane*, perpetuating the name of a corn miller who once lived for many years at what are now the almshouses; and lastly *Rabone Lane*, a name derived from that of a Birmingham merchant who formerly resided in the adjacent Hall. These constitute the ancient road between Hales Owen and Handsworth, although modern deviations may be easily detected where the railway cuts between Crocketts Lane and Rabone Lane.

Another old road with names reminiscent of earlier times is *Holly Lane* and *Roebuck Lane;* this continues its course through West Bromwich to *Stone Cross*, where met the ancient main roads from Walsall and Wednesbury respectively.

The third is an alternative road into West Bromwich—along *Londonderry Lane, Stony Lane, Brasshouse Lane,* and *Halford Lane*. The frequent use of this word "lane" clearly points to the period when agricultural influences alone prevailed here in originating all place-names. Thus we obtain also *Watery Lane, Windmill Lane, Ruck o' Stones Lane,* (recently altered to *Lewisham Road), Spon Lane,* and *Church Lane*. Such a name as *Little Moor,* and the revived name *Uplands,* re-call the existence of open heaths and common lands in exactly the same way. As to the name *Sloe Lane,* it was originally no misnomer at all, but was actually descriptive of its natural characteristics. It is a corruption to call it *Slough Lane,* as was shown in THE MIDLAND ANTIQUARY, Vol. III., p. 34. From Reeves' HISTORY OF WEST BROMWICH, pp. 156-157, we get some doubtful derivations of local place-names, namely—

Monk Meadow, left by the Whorwood family for the support of a school [in West Bromwich] is near Mr. H. Halford's [1838] and with the barn and a few old houses belong to a charity at Coventry. This field is in three parishes, West Bromwich, Handsworth, and Smethwick.

Roebuck Lane took its name from the sign [of a public-house] at the end of the lane, kept by Francis Taylor about four-score years ago.

Spon Lane is from a family of that name, who, I suppose, lived at the premises occupied by Mr. I. Hadley about one hundred and thirty gears ago. The old people used to talk about *Spon Meadow, Spon Coppice, &c.* The original house has been taken down a hundred years.

Reeves wrote all this in 1838, and he is not accounted a very reliable authority. For another derivation of the name "Spon Lane," see HISTORY OF WEST BROMWICH by the present writer, p. 7. The Mr. H. Halford is the individual who no doubt gave his name to *Halford's Lane*, close by the site of Monk Meadow.

In 1798 *Birmingham Heath* had been enclosed, and the Commissioners then carefully laid out all the roads which in future were to be used across the common and waste lands: one ran from the Wolverhampton turnpike road through *Hockley Pool Lane* on the east of the *Warren House* to the ancient lane leading to *Winson Green;* one to Winson Green Bridge and the Dudley turnpike road; one along *Icknield Street* to *Warstone Lane, &c.;* one over the common through *Nineveh* to Handsworth; one from Nineveh over *Gibb Heath*; and several others, all fully set forth, objections to which were duly heard at the "House of Thomas Crockett, called the *New Inn,* at Handsworth." Here again is the family name of Crockett, still perpetuated in local road nomenclature.

This same year, 1798, when the baiting of a bull had been interfered with at the *Salutation Inn, Snow Hill,* an attempt was made to regularly resume it on the Heath, but this systematic revival was frustrated, although Nineveh was a favourite baiting-ground for many years afterwards. In 1815 Snow Hill was described as the greatest thoroughfare in Birmingham, "upon the Great North-West Road," along which forty Mails and Post Coaches passed daily.

Speaking of the roads hereabouts, Hawkes Smith, in his BIRMINGHAM AND VICINITY, published in 1836, says—

Dudley and its dependencies, so long connected with Birmingham, were approached either by the Oldbury Road or by the still more direct line passing a little to the right of Rowley Regis, along which are.still.discernible the traces of very ancient and deeply hollowed ways; so that the open and dreary upland now covered with the most populous part of West Bromwich lay insulated and little frequented, furrowed almost exclusively by the wheels of coal carts perpetually passing. Wolverhampton, Walsall, and Wednesbury, it is true, were busy towns. The last-named and very ancient place could almost compete with Birmingham in magnitude and wealth. Persons still living recollect to have seen in their youth the carefully-filed letters of former years, addressed by the cautious correspondent residing northward, to the friend or tradesman—

"At Birmingham, near Wednesbury."

Dealing with the natural features of the hamlet of Smethwick, with special reference to its water supply before the era of artificial waterworks, Mr. Summerton says—

An abundant supply of water for every need in those early and also much later times was obtainable from the streams which traverse its valleys, and the springs which burst through its surface. There is a very notable spring in the new Park in West Smethwick, which is the chief source of the brook on the western boundary. The undulatory surface and general character of the ground must have attracted the notice of the earliest inhabitants to its eminent fitness for cultivation. On the north and east rise high hills, then clothed with forest trees which formed a barrier to the cold and bleak north and cast winds; on the south-west extensive woods existed. which would break the violence of the prevailing west winds, thus sheltering the stock and crops.

For heights and levels refer back to page 11.

At the beginning of this century, when coaching was at its height, the place of the modern railway time-table and guide was occupied by road itineraries. These travelling guides of our grandfathers gave copious topographical items, the information relating to details of "direct and principal cross roads, inns and distances of stages, noblemen's and gentlemen's seats," with other information as to resources, products, trades, fairs, jurisdictions, and nearly everything else which the inquiring traveller might wish to learn. Here is an extract from one on the county of Stafford, published by G. A. Cooke about 1810, dealing with that main route nearest to Smethwick (the more ancient road *through* Smethwick had been abandoned; as recorded on page 14, *q.v.*):—

JOURNEY FROM SOHO TO THE WERG, THROUGH WOLVERHAMPTON

[N.B.—*The first column contains the Names of Places passed through; the figures that follow show the Distances from Place to Place, Town to Town, and Stages; and in the last Column are the names of Gentlemen's Seats and Inns. The Right and Left of the Roads are distinguished by the letters R and L.*]

	MILES		
Soho to			
New Green	1	1	
Sandwell Green	1	2	Sandwell Park, late Earl of Dartmouth, R.; near it, Sir Jervoise Clerk Jervoise, Bart.
Bromwich Heath	1	3	
A mile beyond on L. a Turnpike Road to Bilston; on R to			
WEDNESBURY	3	6	
On R. a T. R. to Walsall. Cross the Birmingham Canal.			
Bilston	3	9	
On R. a T. R. to Walsall. Cross the Birmingham Canal.			
WOLVERHAMPTON	$2\frac{3}{4}$	$11\frac{3}{4}$	Inns—*Lion, Swan*
On R. a T. R. to Stafford; or L. to Dudley.			
New Bridge	2	$13\frac{3}{4}$	
Cross the Canal.			
Tettenhall	$\frac{1}{4}$	14	F. Holyoak, Esq.m, L.
On R. a T. R. to Ivetsey Bank.			
The Werg	$1\frac{1}{2}$	$15\frac{1}{2}$	On R. $1\frac{1}{2}$ miles beyond, Wrottesley Hall, Sir John Wrottesley, Bart.

* * * * * * * * * * * *

The railway system of Smethwick is very fairly complete, except that its outlying stations, which afford communication with the different points of the compass, are not all connected to one central station.

The *Grand Junction* line, projected in 1824, and opened in 1837, left Birmingham for the north on that side more remote from Smethwick; it started from Curzon Street (now used only as a goods station) and passed away through Aston and Perry Barr, leaving West Bromwich aside at Newton Road, and cutting away between Wednesbury and Walsall at Bescot.

The first line to touch Smethwick was the *Stour Valley*, projected in 1846 and opened about five years later (see p. 95). Leaving Birmingham, it enters Staffordshire near Winson Green and Soho, and passing right through Smethwick to Spon Lane, continues through Oldbury and Albion to Dudley Port. See Dr. Langford's HISTORY OF STAFFORDSHIRE, pp. 61 and 64.

These two lines having in due time been absorbed into the great national system of the *London and North Western Railway,* a connecting link between them was made in 1886. This runs through Smethwick, joining Great Barr and Perry Barr of the former with Winson Green of the latter. The construction of this loop was mainly undertaken to relieve Birmingham New Street Station in some measure of its congested traffic; for now it is no longer necessary that the numerous heavy mineral trains from the Cannock Colliery district should run through Birmingham in order to get to the Smethwick and Soho district where the consumption of coal is necessarily very great for manufacturing purposes. The Birmingham north suburban passenger traffic is also much facilitated by this loop, which runs a circular route in and out of Birmingham.

The Great Western, opened in 1854 from Birmingham to Wolverhampton, did not enter Smethwick, but placed its Handsworth Station so close to the boundary brook, that it justified its double-barrelled name of "Handsworth and Smethwick." This company, strangely enough, never opened their goods station till five or six years ago, although it was built at the same time as the passenger station, and Smethwick had for years made great demands upon all the local railways for its goods and mineral traffic.

About thirty years ago the Stourbridge Extension line joined the London and Birkenhead section of the Great Western System with the old Oxford, Worcester, and Wolverhampton line, sometimes known as the West Midland. This connecting link leaves the former near the Handsworth and Smethwick Station, close on the boundaries of these two parishes, and running into the latter, has a convenient station known as Smethwick Junction. From this station a very short line runs to Galton Bridge, there joining it to the London and North Western Railway system, and enabling this latter Company to run coaches between their Birmingham central, New Street Station, and the Smethwick Junction Station of the Great Western Company, thus connecting the former with all trains on the Stourbridge route.

Of projected lines which would have improved the accessibility of Smethwick several have been mooted only to fall through, or to be abandoned in the earliest stages of promotion. Before the Soho loop of the L. & N. W. Railway was constructed, a proposal was made in 1879 for a line from Cannock Chase, across the Delves Common into West Bromwich; this presumably would have been continued into Oldbury or Smethwick to serve exactly the same purpose as the loop line. Another suggestion was to run round from Darlaston and Wednesbury to join the Stour Valley section near Oldbury, and so bring the heart of the Black Country into communication with Birmingham (and with Smethwick also, by virtue of this route) without sustaining the usual and inevitable loss of time at Dudley Port station. Neither of these schemes came to anything.

The Harborne line (for which the Act was obtained in 1866) was opened August 10th, 1874.

XXXV.—TOPOGRAPHICAL: OLD RESIDENCES AND FAMILY SEATS.

Says Mr. Hy. Summerton, in a recent lecture of his, on the past history of this parish—

Smethwick, in the last century, became a place of residence for the merchants and professional men of the rapidly growing town of Birmingham; in proof of which a number of mansions which flourished from 100 to 200 years ago may be mentioned.

Smethwick Hall, the present house of this name, was built about 150 years since by a Mr. Ansell, but an older structure existed at an earlier period, Smethwick Hall being mentioned by Plott in his "History of Staffordshire" written 200 years ago. The site of this older hall is not now definitely known, but from finding worked chamfered stones in the field on the east of the present hall, and the evidence that a pool existed in the lower part of the same field, it may not be unreasonable to assume that the old hall stood in this field. How it became so entirely obliterated is a matter of conjecture, but from the appearance of the stones before mentioned it is probable that the edifice was burned down, the charred evidence being still visible, particularly in stones built into the bank on the south of Stony Lane near the present hall lodge. This masonry is of a sandstone not found in the immediate neighbourhood, the nearest place being in Northfield, from whence the stone was probably brought to build the original hall. The Ansells, who built the present hall, desired to plant an avenue of trees from the hall to Cape Hill, and by the permission of landowners *en route* accomplished their desire, excepting in two short distances near their residence. viz., on the ground where the Spout House garden is, and on the opposite side of the road from Londonderry Lane and Hales Lane. This land belonged to a Mr. Chesshire, and he positively refused to allow the trees to be planted on his ground. Tablets in memory of the Ansell family are to be seen in the Old Chapel now. The present pool was made by the Canal Company to collect the flood waters, which they conveyed to their reservoir near the Old Chapel (now done away with) by a very meandering conduit through the heart of our modern Smethwick.

A strange botanical specimen once grew in the grounds of this ancient mansion, a description of which is given by Dr. Plot, as mentioned by Mr. Summerton. Says that quaint and garrulous county historian, writing in 1686 (p. 207):

Much rather should I think the Yellow Yew near Smethwick Hall to be an undescribed tree, which has some branches with all the leaves of a bright yellow colour; this I thought at first might proceed from some disease, or that those branches might have been wounded, but upon examination I found them all sound. Nay, so far was this part of the tree from weakness, that it had berrys on it, when the green part had none, and yet it differing from other yew trees only in colour, and not in any of the essentials. I can neither afford to pronounce it a distinct species, nor allow it for an undescribed plant, the difference seeming but accidental, though perhaps hard enough to be accounted for.

Smethwick Hall, now the residence of Mr. H. Lincoln Tangye, is still in admirable order.

The Lightwoods is about 750 feet above sea-level; this is comparatively very high, for the Council House in Birmingham stands at 463 feet, the Selly Oak Tree at 487 feet, and the highest point in the West Bromwich tableland (Thynne Street) reaching but 569 feet. Wednesbury Old Church on the other side of the Tame rises only to 537 feet. Mr. Summerton calls The Lightwoods "a fine old mansion situated at the extreme south-west of the hamlet. Within its precincts are some very fine trees. It was built in 1791 by Madame Grundy." From this lady, whose arms are on her memorial tablet in the Old Chapel (see p. 58), the house passed to the Willett family (p. 64), and has since been acquired by the Adkins family. As a place-name, "Lightwoods *alias* Gorsty Croft" has been mentioned on page 61.

The Elms, at the junction of Bearwood Hill and Waterloo Road, was formerly known as Blood Hall, owned and occupied for many years by Lawyer Spurrier, of whom there are many sensational tales related. But similar traditions of betrayal and blood money are told in many parts of the country.

In Cape Hill, on the opposite side to *Kelvin Grove*, was the residence of one Reynolds, whose gardens were of the Italian style, and noted for their beauty. It was afterwards used as a Reformatory. At Kelvin Grove lived the celebrated Dr. Dunn.

Grove House, still standing in Grove Lane, now used as offices by the Screw Company, was formerly the residence of the Moillietts, Birmingham bankers.

The Firs, in Cooper's Lane, was owned by a Mr. Cooper, who kept there a pack of harriers. Just beyond the borders of Smethwick, at Sloe Lane, stood a mansion occupied by the Stuarts, members of the Royal Family. The place was once noted for its cedar trees.

Rabone Hall, till over 30 years ago, stood where Tangyes' works now flourish. It was inhabited by Birmingham merchants named Rabone, who sold it to Gillott, the pen maker, and by him to the Tangyes. *Soho Cottage*, with its pretty garden, has given place to Soho Goods Station.

The Woodlands, situate in the street of that name, was for many years the residence of the Unetts, who at one time owned the greater part of Smethwick;

Many of these names are retained in the present street nomenclature, and serve as memorials of the wealthy families and their mansions of a past day and generation.

But going outside Smethwick into the older portions of Harborne parish some very striking names are met with.

Mr. Kenward, in his HISTORY OF HARBORNE (p. 45), says there is an unfathomable mystery about the name of Mock Beggar Farm. This name may seem a strange piece of nomenclature, but it is not unique. There is, for instance, a Mock Beggar Hall on the high road between Bloxwich and Shareshill, built about a century ago by Col. Hilton, who, it is said, "was determined to show the British workman how he should live." So he put up this large building, standing well back from and high above the road, and forming a conspicuous object from afar. It is divided into flats, &c., for the residence of a number of labourers. The common tale is, that beggars and vagrants discerning the building from afar, imagine it to be no less than a gentleman's mansion, and duly set their footsteps towards it in the expectancy of alms; and that their disappointment on finding it occupied by the poorest of the labouring class has gained it the widely known appellation of Mock Beggar Hall.

Warley Hall (according to Shaw) "was likewise purchased from Mr. Russell by Mr. Galton, of Birmingham, who has there (1798) made great improvements." In THE AGREEABLE HISTORIAN OR COMPLEAT ENGLISH TRAVELLER, published in 1746, is contained a map of Staffordshire. On this map, which is by "Samuel Simpson, Gent.," may be found not only "Smethick" and "Harborn," but "Warley Hall" is also marked, which may be taken as indicative of its being a place of some importance. *Warley Abbey*, "on a site of grange of Hales Owen Abbey," the residence of Sir Hugh Gilzean Reid, is pictorially illustrated and fully described on p. 223 of HISTORIC WORCESTERSHIRE.

Ravenhurst, or the "raven's wood," at Harborne, is a place-name applied to not a few country houses. There is evidently a second Ravenhurst near Birmingham, for in Dugdale's WARWICKSHIRE (1656) may be found a view of that city "from Ravenhurst, neere London Road, in the south-east part of the Towne." Mr. Kenward (p. 43) says "The two dwellings called *Ravenhurst* are finely placed country houses with much of the ancient character about the gardens and outbuildings. The name is evidently older than the dwellings. Fancy would like to connect it with the Danes, but it means more probably 'the wooded haunt of the ravens.'"

XXXVI—BIBLIOGRAPHICAL: EMINENT PERSONS, FAMILIES, AND NAMES OF NOTE.

As a starting-point in the bibliography of Smethwick, it may be mentioned that the name of this place has also been used as a personal name; but whether adopted after the early fashion of taking the name of one's birthplace as a surname, cannot be determined. Anyway, one *Smethwicke* was the printer and publisher of one of the earliest editions of HAMLET; and again in 1630 a 12mo. edition of MICHAEL DRAYTON bears the imprint of "Will. Stansby for *Iohn Smetwick.*"

The name "*John Stevenes of Smethewyk*" *is* perhaps one of the earliest examples of that of a family attached to the soil here. The name occurs in a lawsuit of 14 Richard II. (1391) quoted in SALT COLLECTIONS XV., p. 31.

Another local family of note were the *Lanes,* mentioned in a Survey of Birmingham, 1553; a note on them in THE MIDLAND ANTIQUARY IV., p. 143, runs:—

> Although three members of the *Lane family* were tenants of the manor of [Birmingham] at the date of this Survey, namely, William, Henry, and Thomas, there is little doubt they were all members of a family of Handsworth and Smethwick, yeomen and millers, and sons of John Lane, of Smethwick. By a deed of 28th November, 1546 (I Edward VI.), in the possession of Mr. Tertius Hadley, "Thomas Lane, of Houndesworth, yeoman, son and heir of John Lane, of Smethwicke, released to Henry Lane, of Wytton, a cottage or tenement and garden within the Borough of Byrmingham, in the Welch End, between the tenement of William Lane on the north, and the tenement of William Colmore on the south, and between the High Street (*Altu Vicu*) of Byrmyngham on the west, and the land of William Lane on the east." This family was of some local importance, holding scythe and other mills, and also a part of Bustleholme Mill. The Lanes of Birmingham, Witton, and Erdington, of whom numerous records exist, all proceeded from this stock. Among the tenants of the Gild was William Lane in a house near the "Peacock," near Dale End. William Lane left a small dole to Handsworth Church.

The middle of the last century produced, among numerous other "Uneducated Poets," a poetaster at "Rowley, near Smethwick." This was one *James Woodhouse,* a shoemaker. His writings (1764) are said to have won the commendation of Wordsworth, and a portrait of the Rowley shoemaker poet, at the age of 81, is in the possession of Mr. Sam. Timmins. Dr. Langford, for the purpose of his CENTURY OF BIRMINGHAM LIFE, had the use of his MS. poems from a relative of the poet, Mr. John Woodhouse, of West Bromwich.

It is worth remembering that Harborne is justly celebrated for its connection with *David Cox.* This eminent painter was born in Birmingham (1783), and after a life rich in the number of its local associations, died, and was buried at Harborne, 1859. Timmins HISTORY OF WARWICKSHIRE, p. 139, says—

> As an etcher, by the soft-ground process, he won great fame by his fine folio of drawing lessons in all stages. under the title of "A Treatise on Landscape Painting and Effect in Water Colour," in 1814. . . . The fame of David Cox, as one of the greatest water colour artists of his day, is world-wide, and the Art Gallery of Birmingham contains a large number of his less known but highly valued landscapes in oil.

In 1874 a memorial window to David Cox was placed in Harborne Church. The avenues to the church are preserved in some of his pictorial work.

Speaking of Harborne in regard to its association with names of note, Mr. Kenward, p. 54 of his HISTORY, says—

> Let it not be forgotten that Harborne was the cherished home of a David Cox, and an Elihu Burritt, who, if not natives, were attached to it by many a tie of sympathy and love. We all know the house in the Greenfield Road in which David Cox worked and died. Twenty-five years have elapsed [since 1885] since he was laid in the leafy churchyard in whose avenues he delighted to wander, but his fame abides and grows with the century.

When, over a quarter of a century ago, the American Consul in Birmingham was no less than the aforementioned learned *Elihu Burritt*, a most interesting and gossipy book was written by him, entitled WALKS IN THE BLACK COUNTRY AND ITS GREEN BORDERLAND. Notwithstanding that it is practically of an official character, being a Consular report for the Department of State at Washington, it is most enjoyable reading, and is of more than ordinary interest as the expression of the views of a stranger upon the Black Country district and its surroundings.

The localities brought under review include Dudley, The Brades, Willenhall, Halesowen, Oldbury, West Bromwich, Wednesbury, Tipton, Walsall, and many other places, Smethwick not omitted, among what the genial American calls "one great cloud of industrial communities." Of Smethwick itself he wrote thus (in 1868) on p. 318 of his work:

Smethwick is one of these centres of population and industry, and is the seat of several large establishments, including the London Works of the Patent Nut and Bolt Company, Patent File Company, and several other extensive manufactories. Soho, a centre of mechanical genius and enterprise which once put forth such an influence over the world under Boulton and Watt, has lost its pre-eminence since their day. Still, important works are carried on in the parish, of which those established by the late George Frederick Muntz, M.P., for the manufacture of Metal Sheathing, are the most noted and extensive.

Then the writer goes on to deal with Oldbury, the celebrated Brades Works, the Bromford Works of Messrs. Dawes, and the chemical works of Messrs. Chance at Oldbury. Strangely enough, a full and glowing description of Messrs. Chance's Glass Works is given in quite another part of the book, on pp. 258-269.

It has already been mentioned (p. 95) that the Crystal Palace was built by the Smethwick firm of *Fox, Henderson, and Co.* Of the senior partner in this firm mention is made in THE LIFE AND ADVENTURES OF GEORGE AUGUSTUS SALA *(Cassell and Co., 1896)*, where that genial autobiographer under date, May, 1851, speaking of Alexis Soyer's famous restaurant, says he there met many noted men of the day:

Conspicuous among these acquaintances was the well-known civil engineer, Mr. (afterwards Sir) *Charles Fox*, who, with his partner, Mr. Henderson, had taken the Contract for building Paxton's great Palace of Glass. He gave me a card of admission to the Exhibition building many weeks before it was open to the public. The card bore the magic words, "Pass Everywhere," and I was consequently enabled to inspect all the details of the works in progress, and to strengthen thereby the passionate love for technical knowledge which has always been predominant in me.

[It was this Sir Charles Fox who, in Liverpool some sixty years ago, taught Mr. Richard Williams mechanical drawing. When the latter came as a young mechanician to take part in managing the Patent Shaft Works at Wednesbury in the year 1844, there came also from Liverpool another young mechanic of the name of Astbury, who made his name almost as conspicuous in the industrial annals of Smethwick, as did Mr. Richard Williams in those of Wednesbury. Alderman Williams speaks highly of Sir Charles Fox, and equally so of his Scotch partner, *Mr. Henderson,* a wonderful man of business who had the faculty of dissecting his thoughts so completely that he could dictate four different letters to four separate clerks at the same time, and know where he had left off with each letter, even to the capital letter or point of punctuation. A useful accomplishment, certainly, when the art of shorthand was not practised as it now is in commercial houses.]

The *Galton family* were once a well-known firm of gun, sword, and bayonet makers in Steelhouse Lane, opposite the Upper Priory, Birmingham. Their works were close by in Weaman Street, but their mills for grinding and polishing blades and barrels were at Duddeston, and Duddeston Hall was the country-house of the Galtons. Lady Selborne, in her DIARY, states that in 1765 she had the strange experience of visiting an arms factory kept by a member of the peace-loving Society of Friends. But it was not till 1796 that the remonstrances of the Quakers induced the senior partner to abandon this trade. The Galton family held the freehold of Warley for over a century-and-a-half; the Warley Galtons were originally Quakers, but after the Oxford movement they joined the Catholic Church. The most famous of the family was Mary Anne Galton, afterwards *Mrs. Schimmelpenninck* (1773-1856), the daughter of Samuel Galton, F.R.S. Her husband was a Dutch merchant of Bristol, and she afterwards became a Moravian, although in early life a Quakeress surrounded by the most cultivated society of the sect. Among her writings are "Theory of the Classification of Beauty and Deformity" (1815) and "Gothic and Grecian Architecture" (1820). Galton Bridge in Smethwick derives its name from this family, whose local influence was very considerable.

The mention of this family naturally suggests another local name, of eminence in the world of culture, flourishing about the same period. This is the name of *William Withering, M.D., F.R.S., F.L.S.* (1741-1799), who lived at Edgbaston Hall. Born near Ercall, Salop, his first professional work in Stafford gave him as a vast field of study the banks of Trent, the North Stafford hills, and the untrodden recesses of Cannock Chase. Like the Galtons, he was a friend of Boulton, Watt, Priestley, Smeaton, Keir, Murdock, Darwin, and others who formed the famous Lunar Society, so-called because its meetings were held so as to enable the members to have a moonlight ride home after dinner at each other's houses—all round Birmingham—where philosophical questions were discussed. Among his works is "British Plants" (1776). His "Digitalis" was printed in Birmingham in 1785. In Botany his name is preserved in "Witheringia," given to certain of American plants; and a similar honour is accorded him in Metallurgy, the name "Witherite" being given to the native carbonate of barytes which he first discovered.

Mr. Kenward quotes from A WALK THROUGH SMETHWICK, by Charles Hicks, 1850 (see HARBORNE AND ITS SURROUNDINGS, footnote p. 53):

Bless your heart, sir, I can remember when there were scarcely a dozen houses within a mile of where you now stand—(and we were supposed to be standing in the centre of modern Smethwick)—there was a homestead here and a cottage there, and generally the place wore a rural aspect; nothing met you but green fields, and cornfields and arable land, and meadow land, quiet roads and narrow lanes, whistling ploughmen and bonny dairy maids.

Surely a reprint of this description of Smethwick, as it was half a century ago, would be very welcome now.

By way of conclusion we quote what may fairly be regarded as the world's estimate of a modern Smethwickian, who shone in the world of dramatic literature with some amount of brilliance. This was the late Henry Pettitt, who was born in Smethwick in 1848, and died a year or two ago. He was the son of a local civil engineer, and the *Daily Telegraph* gave the following obituary notice of him:

When he was only thirteen years of age he was thrown on his own resources, owing to his father having lost all his money in perfecting a patent in cotton machinery at Manchester, which, if it had succeeded, would have effected a revolution in cotton-spinning. The elder Pettitt going abroad, his son was taken from the Rev. William Smirdon's school, and left to struggle for himself. One day be called upon the manager of Sadler's Wells Theatre, determined to try his fortune at acting. He was engaged, and made his first appearance in a small Irish part in a pantomime called "The Rose of Blarney, or Danny-manoranyotherman." But he got so excited over his part as to hit a "super" on the head with such force that he nearly broke it. For this display of energy he was discharged. After this, Henry Pettitt endured many and strange vicissitudes. He soon began to devote his spare time to writing for the various boys' periodicals then being published; and numerous short stories and poems written by him appeared in the *Boys' Miscellany* and other papers, for which, however, he never obtained any remuneration but once, and that was when a microscope was offered for the best Christmas Story, and he won the prize. It was a proud moment when he and another lad of about the same age (now a well-known and successful artist) left the publisher's office with a microscope, which, however, was not long to remain in his possession. Pettitt's taste was not scientific, but theatrical; and he and his chum promptly pawned the literary prize for ten shillings, and, after a sumptuous repast of chops and tea at the Adelaide Gallery, went to the Strand Theatre, and spent the balance in ginger-beer and cakes on the road home. Soon after this Pettitt obtained a junior clerkship in Pickford's head offices in the City; but as he spent most of his employer's time in writing songs, essays, and love-letters for his fellow-clerks while they did his work for him, his promotion was not rapid. He remained, however, for two years; but one afternoon the head of the Department, happening to return suddenly, found young Pettitt giving a burlesque lecture on the advantage *of* higher wages and less work, and the result was a private interview. "Mr. Pettitt, I believe you are a very clever lad," said the head of the department. Pettitt was silent, he was anxious to know what was coming next. "You are exceedingly well informed, for your age, on all literary, poetical, and historical subjects, and have, I am told, considerable literary capacity, besides being a very ready debater and speaker," Pettitt blushed, shifted his feet uneasily, and remained silent. "But, unfortunately for Messrs. Pickford and Company, and perhaps for yourself, these are not the qualifications necessary for the down-carriage department, and if you can obtain some more congenial employment before my monthly report goes down to.the principals I should advise you to do it. You see," he added in a friendly manner, "it will be of such advantage to you to say you resigned." During his stay at Pickford's Pettitt and a few congenial spirits had organised, for the purpose of mutual improvement, a club called the "Cicero", of which somewhat ambitiously named coterie he was secretary, and afterwards president. Among the invited guests one evening was one of the classical masters of the North London Collegiate School at Camden Town, who, having heard Pettitt read an essay and afterwards defend his views in the debate that followed, conceived a friendship for him, and most kindly offered to assist him in his studies. This generous offer was at once accepted by Pettitt, and his obligations to his new found friend were considerably increased when he was introduced to the Rev. Doctor Williams, head master of North London Collegiate School, and obtained the post of junior English master in the classical department of the College. As there were 500 boys in the School, and twenty-four masters, the majority of whom were University graduates, Pettitt soon found that his new post was no sinecure; and the next two years were occupied with work and the hard study inseparable from a schoolmaster's life. He, however, became a great favourite, not only with Dr. Williams, who made him the secretary of the College and took great interest in his subsequent advancement, but with the pupils, to whom (like Oliver Grossmith) he was very fond of telling stories, and giving the one touch of romance to history, geography, and other subjects that made them interesting and attractive to boys. During six years' stay at the college he wrote numerous short stories, sketches, and songs, and he was strongly advised by the late Andrew Halliday and George Honey to write for the stage. He sold his first piece, "Golden Fruit," to Mr. Morris Abrahams, of the Pavilion Theatre, for the not very extravagant sum of five pounds. A short time previous to this he had been introduced by Mr. T. Mead to a young friend of his, Paul Merrit, who had just had his first comedy-drama accepted by Mr. George Conquest of the Grecian Theatre. The two young men entered into collaboration, and their first joint work, "British Born," was produced at the Grecian Theatre, and achieved a great success. This was the beginning of an association that has brought singular good fortune to both authors, and the foundation of a personal friendship that has been lasting and sincere. Henry Pettitt then gave up the appointment at the College, and travelled with the Grecian play; and for two years he was associated with travelling dramatic, operatic, and equestrian companies, thus forming a thoroughly practical knowledge of the stage. Returning to London, he became the treasurer of the Grecian Theatre, and, entering into collaboration with Mr. George Conquest, he produced a series of powerful melodramas.

With the possession of such a Shakespearian relic as that described in Chapter XXV,, and the breeding of such a dramatic author as Henry Pettitt, the erection of a new Theatre in Smethwick cannot be deemed an uncalled for undertaking. At the least, the dramatic "records of Smethwick" are something out of the common, and the town is surely not unworthy of a Thespian Temple.

INDEX

Addenbroke	60, 108
Adkins	66, 68, 95, 119
Advowson	22, 33
Aid	19
Alcester	8, 9
Aldridge	7, 53
Almshouse	115
Arden	8, 12
Assessment	101, 106, 110
Assize Roll	24
Astbury	45, 60, 108
Aston	2, 13, 26, 28, 41, 42, 49, 53, 64, 86, 102, 106, 117
Baddeley	42, 45
Bailey	77
Balsall Heath	102
Barr	7, 10, 26, 53, 103, 117
Baths	102, 106
Beeks	44, 45
Bear, Bearwood	45, 103, 109, 119
Bilston	24, 85, 98, 117
Birch, Birchfield	25, 26, 30, 41, 42, 44, 49, 50, 54, 55, 61, 64
Blackham	49, 50, 52, 54, 63
Blakeley	13, 35, 38, 87
Blue Gates	87
Bordesley	12
Borough	4, 105-107
Booth	54, 55
Boulton	14, 89-92, 122, 123
Boyse	44, 53, 55, 60
Bradburne	50, 53
Brades	88
Bradley	24
Brewood	17
Broadwaters	87
Bromford, Bromforth	87
Bromhale	20
Bromsgrove	39, 44
Buchanan	72
Burritt	121, 122
Camm	70, 94
Campbell	38
Canals	3, 7, 64, 85-88, 89, 116
Cannock	12, 18, 32, 59, 117, 123
Cape Hill	13, 71, 72, 73, 83, 97, 109, 119
Causeway Green	48
Cemetery	103, 106
Chance	67, 69, 81, 82, 94, 95, 103, 109, 122
Chapel	3, 5, 36, 46-69
Commons (see "Heaths")	12, 50
Conolly	66
Cooper	115, 120
Coppice	58
Cornwallis	35, 36, 38, 40, 41
Courts	16, 33, 36, 37
Coventry	12, 17, 22, 29, 36
Cowper	61, 62
Cox	121

Cradley	18, 34, 37
Crockett	109, 115, 116
Crump	65, 66, 108
Cummins	67, 68
Customs	113
Dale	60, 73
Danes	7, 9, 10, 120
Daneshaft	10
Darleston	67, 96, 118
Delves	10, 117
Docker	114
Downing	67
Druids	7
Duddeston	42, 123
Dudley	12, 13, 18, 23, 32, 33, 34, 39, 40, 98, 99, 103, 113, 117
Dunn	120
Durose	76
Edgbaston	8, 13, 22, 26, 39, 59, 62, 123
Eginton	93, 94
Erdeswick	18, 35
Erdington	19, 21, 28, 41, 42, 114
Essington	15
Ethelfleda	10, 23
Etymology	6, 10, 12, 18, 35, 45
Evans	67, 94
Eyton	16
Ferguson	67
Foley	38-44
Forests	12, 13, 17
Forster	67
Fox, Henderson, and Co.	122, 71, 95
Frankley	39
Frankpledge	33
Free Schools	49, 58, 60, 61, 64, 108
French Walls	3, 79, 80, 87
Gaia	22
Galton	89, 118, 120, 123
Gardner	67
Gerold	19, 20, 21, 28, 29
Gib Heath	11, 114, 116
Gifford	70
Gilbanks	67
Glebe	33
Gosling	73
Gough	13, 49, 50, 53, 54, 55
Greaves	38, 41, 42, 50, 53, 55, 61
Griffiths	58, 64, 108
Grundy	119
Hales Owen	12, 14, 18-23, 27, 28, 31, 33-35, 37, 48, 50, 53, 63, 120
Halford	76, 115
Halfpenny	50, 54, 63
Hammond	66
Hamstead	13, 41, 86, 91
Handsworth	2, 6, 8-11, 26, 30, 31, 45, 61, 62, 80, 89, 91, 92, 94, 102, 113, 118, 121

INDEX

Hanson	45, 58, 61, 62, 64
Hare	49, 50
Harden	66
Hartley	94
Hearth Tax	41
Heaths	6, 11, 14, 40, 45, 89, 93, 113, 116
Hilton	15, 40
Hinckley	41, 42, 44, 45, 49, 50, 53, 54, 55, 58, 61, 62, 108
Hockley	8, 13, 89, 91, 116
Holt	49, 50, 54, 63, 87
Holy Trinity	47, 48, 65, 66, 112
Hoo	53, 55
Hopkins	13
Hospital	102, 106
Hunt	38, 41
Hundreds	24, 26
Icknield	7, 8, 116
Iddens	58
Inkleys	45
Inquisitio Ad Quod Damnum	31
Iron Trade	40
Jennings	11, 41, 42, 49, 50, 53
Jesson	53
Johnson	98, 99
Jus primæ noctis	15
Keen	101
Keir	90, 123
King's Norton	7, 39, 59, 102
King's Standing	8
Kirby's Quest	20, 21
Knight's Fee	19, 20, 22, 29
Liber Niger	19
Library	54, 82, 83, 96, 101, 102, 106
Lichfield	12, 16, 17, 22, 23, 26, 35, 38, 44, 46, 59, 95
Lightwoods	58, 61, 64, 119
L'Isle	28, 34
Littley de	24, 37
Lones	27
London Works	71
Longdon	15-17, 18, 21, 32
Manor	4, 15, 41, 46, 73
Margaret de Redvers	19
Margaret de Rivers	22, 28
Markets, Fairs	16, 32
Marshall	66
Medhurst	68
Mercia	8, 18
Metchley	7, 8, 9, 11
Middlemore	39
Millward	41
Minerals	5, 7, 10, 63, 98-100, 118
Mint	89
Mitchell	66, 67, 97, 114
Moat, Moatfield	13, 35
Mock Beggar Hall	120
Moilliett	120
Monk Meadow	115
Mordancestor	28
Moseley	41, 64, 83
Muntz	3, 122
Murdock	89, 90, 123
Muster Roll	38
Nailmaking	40, 41, 96, 97
Nettlefold	96, 97
Newey	62
New Inns	13, 62, 117
Newland	73
Nineveh	79, 89, 114, 116
Nonarum	27
Northfield	59, 102, 119
Oakeswell	13
Ocker Hill	87
Offlow	26
Ogilby	13
Oldbury	8, 13, 14, 35-37, 62, 63, 75, 85, 98, 102, 103, 116, 117, 122
Oldford	8
O'Neill	66-76
Overseer	62, 110
Parish	2, 14, 46, 101, 106, 110
Parish Lands	62, 114
Parish Relief	63
Parker	41
Parkes	42, 44, 46, 49, 56-58, 63, 64, 73, 108
Patent Nut and Bolt	77, 96
Pattison	58, 60, 83, 84
Payton	53, 56
Perry Barr	13, 26, 49, 53, 86, 102
Pettitt	123, 124
Pickering	60
Piddock	61, 62
Population	101, 102, 106, 110, 113
Portway	35
Purchase	77
Pype	24
Queen Anne's Bounty	36, 37
Quia Emptores	15
Rabone	96, 101, 115, 120
Railways	4, 14, 81, 95, 103, 114, 117, 120
Ralph	20, 21, 22
Registers	47
Reynolds	42, 45, 58, 66, 120
Ridding	27
Ridsdel	66
Roads	7, 8 12-14, 35, 36, 64, 97, 115
Rood End	63
Roper	66
Rowley	2, 10, 11, 18, 34, 35, 38, 116
Rowton	41
Ruck of Stones	41, 87, 115
Ryder	70, 79

Salt, Saltways	9, 12
Saltley	102
Salvation Army	77, 78, 82
Sandwell	12, 23, 98-100, 117
Scutage	19
Sedgley	34
Selly Oak	8, 14, 81, 119
Sewerage	102, 106
Shepperd	67
Sherlock	74
Shire Ash	44
Shireland	13, 42, 43, 45
Simcox	61, 66, 68
Sloe Lane	109, 115, 120
Smith	45, 77
Someri	18, 23, 34
Soho	14, 89, 91-94, 96, 114, 117
Spon Lane	66, 79-81, 87, 88, 94, 109, 115
Spooner	49-52, 54, 63
Spriggs	45
St. Chad's	48, 65, 68
St. John's	68
St. Mary's	47, 48, 65, 68
St. Matthew's	47, 48, 65, 66, 112
St. Michael's	48, 65, 68
St. Paul's	47, 65, 67, 103
St. Stephen's	48, 65, 68
Stone Cross	115
Stowe	67
Subsidy Roll	25, 26
Summerfield	58, 81
Summerton	45, 116, 119
Summit	5, 87
Sutton	6-8, 34, 41, 102
Sylvester	68
Tame	8, 35, 91, 102, 119
Tamworth	17, 18, 35
Tangye	92, 95, 96, 102, 119, 120
Taylor	76, 88
Taxatio Ecclesiastica p. Nich.	24
Taxes, &c.	25, 39, 41, 110, 111
Temperance	79, 80
Tennel House	41
Tettenhall	12, 117
Thimble Mill	5
Thompson	72-74
Tirley	68
Timmins	92, 94
Tinker's Green	61
Tipton	16, 21, 32, 38, 85, 113
Tielry	15
Train Bands	38
Unett	120
Uplands	103, 115
Valor Ecclesiasticus	24
Vernon	76
Visitation (Heralds')	41
Volunteers	114
Wake	65
Walsall	14, 18, 35, 44, 86, 113
Warine	19, 20, 28
Warley	7, 13, 30, 36, 49, 120, 123
Watt	3, 89-92, 122, 123
Wednesbury	3, 9, 10, 12-15, 18, 21, 23, 32, 40, 42, 79, 85, 86, 93, 94, 96, 98, 105, 113, 116-119, 122
Welsh House	41
Weoley	13, 23, 25, 27, 38
West Bromwich	6, 7, 10, 13, 14, 23, 24, 39, 40, 59, 76, 79, 85, 86, 91, 102, 105, 116, 117, 119, 121
Whiting	46, 49
Wilkes	67
Willingsworth	11, 13, 34
Willet	58, 64
Williams, R.	122
Wilmer	40
Winson Green	62, 85, 87, 114, 116, 117
Withering	123
Witton	44
Woden	9
Wolfere	9
Wollaston	67
Wolverhampton	9, 12, 14, 38, 39, 85, 88, 113, 116-118
Woodhouse	121
Wood and Kendrick	67
Woolley	58
Worcester	12, 39, 40, 87, 118
Wordsley	93
Workhouse	62, 114
Wyrley	13, 41
Yardley	59
Yellow Yew	119
Yemens	75